# Good Old Dog

# Good Old Dog

Expert Advice for Keeping Your Aging Dog
Happy, Healthy, and Comfortable

By the Faculty of the Cummings School
of Veterinary Medicine at Tufts University

*Edited by Nicholas Dodman, BVMS*
*With Lawrence Lindner, MA*

HOUGHTON MIFFLIN HARCOURT
*Boston   New York   2010*

For information about permission to reproduce selections from this book, write to Permissions, Houghton Mifflin Harcourt Publishing Company, 215 Park Avenue South, New York, New York 10003.

www.hmhbooks.com

*Library of Congress Cataloging-in-Publication Data*
Good old dog : expert advice for keeping your aging dog happy, healthy, and comfortable / by the faculty of the Cummings School of Veterinary Medicine at Tufts University ; edited by Nicholas Dodman, with Lawrence Lindner.
    p.  cm.
    Includes index.
    ISBN 978-0-547-23282-9
    1. Dogs. 2. Dogs—Aging. 3. Dogs—Health. 4. Veterinary geriatrics. I. Dodman, Nicholas H. II. Lindner, Lawrence. III. Cummings School of Veterinary Medicine.
    SF427.G66 2010
    636.7'089897—dc22   2010026066

Book design by Lisa Diercks
The text of this book is set in Celeste.

Printed in the United States of America
DOC 10 9 8 7 6 5 4 3 2 1

Illustration credits appear on page 249.

While this book is based on extensive scientific research and contains instructions and safety precautions based on that research and on clinical experience, it is not intended to replace the services of a veterinarian. An essential element of taking responsibility for your pet's health is having scheduled checkups and, when it's deemed necessary, emergency visits with your veterinarian. The authors, Tufts University, and the publisher disclaim any responsibility for any adverse effects resulting directly or indirectly from information contained in this book.

# Contents

# A Note to the Reader

WE TRY HARD in *Good Old Dog* never to refer to a dog as an "it." Your canine companion is not an "it," but rather a "he" or "she." Which pronoun to use, however? The exclusive use of either one leaves out half the canine population. And constant use of "he or she"/"him or her" language construction makes reading cumbersome. To get around the problem, we alternated. In the odd-numbered chapters, dogs are referred to with female pronouns; in the even-numbered chapters, with male pronouns.

We did the same for veterinarians, referring to them with female pronouns in the chapters with odd numbers and with male pronouns in those with even numbers.

# Preface

THE VERY IDEA of a dog's "old age" is relatively new. It wasn't too many generations ago that dogs were still viewed largely as utilitarian workers, nonsentient creatures bred to keep a flock of sheep in line or spot prey. The notion of a dog having a comfortable, happy old age would never even have been considered.

Now, dogs are full-fledged members of the household, with a strong reciprocity of feeling between pet and owner—so much so that research has shown that having a dog in the home reduces blood pressure and, thereby, the risk for heart disease. Dog owners even report improved psychological well-being, largely attributable to reduced feelings of loneliness and isolation, as well as a reduction in stress. We know; most of us number among them.

Surely, many of those positive associations come from the relationships people develop with their pals as the years pass. There's something more serene, *wiser,* about an older dog, even one who still has plenty of energy. A dog you've had for more than just a handful of years can simply understand you better, accommodate your moods better.

Of course, too, there's extra closeness with a dog you've known for a long time. How could the bond *not* strengthen after one's four-legged friend has turned seven, ten, twelve years old? After all, the better part of a decade or more has been spent nurturing the relationship—helping the dog grow from a "baby" who needed to be taught the rhythms of your home to a mature soul who can easily read your mood and provide comfort, protection, or simply good company whenever it is needed.

Perhaps you and your older dog have watched children go off to college together, grieved a loss, relocated, or dealt with a career change. Surely, you've taken walks by each other's side, watched favorite TV shows, greeted each other enthusiastically after a long day apart, and been a reassuring presence to each other at bedtime.

During checkups and other visits, we see the closeness in the way people interact with their more senior companions. There's a comfort level, a *something* that can be taken for granted, that isn't yet present between people and their younger dogs.

Bring into the mix that a pet is so innocent, so unquestionably devoted and accepting, and it's not at all surprising that even the toughest among us might blink back tears at the thought of a faithful companion getting on in years. Such emotion doesn't make us softies or weirdos; it makes us human. It's simply an indication that we're able to respond to all the depth of feeling a companion dog is able to elicit.

No wonder it has become important for people to increase not only a dog's life span but also their pet's health span, changing what it means to be geriatric.

By the numbers, "geriatric" signifies the point at which 75 percent of one's anticipated lifespan has gone by. The good news—what this book is about—is that passing that milestone no longer means "over the hill." Sophisticated advances in veterinary medical technology help dogs remain healthier for much longer even as they reach significantly older ages, thereby compressing the amount of time a dog will be infirm or uncomfortable before reaching the end of life. Thus, just as silver-haired men and women in their seventies and eighties now go traveling and white-water rafting and lead active, fulfilling lives—something that was once largely unthinkable—twelve-, fourteen-, and sixteen-year-old dogs can now continue to enjoy their usual romps and shenanigans with the help of modern veterinary medicine.

Fifteen years ago, if you told someone you were taking your

dog to the radiology department of an animal hospital for a CT scan or perhaps even an MRI, that person would likely have looked at you as if you were crazy. Today, neither procedure is considered rare or experimental. In fact, CT scans for dogs have actually become a lot faster, a good thing because it means they require less anesthesia to keep a dog still during the procedure.

Just a few decades ago, if a dog had a cataract, particularly in a locale away from an urban center, the dog went blind. Today, your pet can undergo ophthalmologic surgery to remove the cataract and save his sight.

Only twenty years ago, many people did not take care of a dog's teeth. By age ten, the teeth would be caked in tartar, and the bacteria that caused infections in the dog's mouth could travel through her bloodstream to bodily organs and potentially shorten her lifespan. Today, dogs are privy to routine dental care. And, since the 1990s, even procedures such as root canals have become more commonplace in order to save a tooth and help keep a canine friend healthy overall. Furthermore, a dog with heart failure can be kept alive with drugs that weren't on the market only a couple of years ago. Veterinary researchers are even looking into surgery to replace leaky canine heart valves — a concept that hadn't yet made it to the drawing board when your dog was a pup. No wonder some dogs are now reaching their late teens with verve when it used to be that a dog's reaching sixteen or seventeen was a feat in itself.

Many of these advances are due to a boom in veterinary specialization, with increasing numbers of vets whose focus is strictly on such fields as internal medicine, cardiology, neurology, dentistry, and ophthalmology. Veterinary medical care has in fact been following on the heels of breakthroughs in human medicine, much more so than in the 1970s and '80s, and is comparable in many ways. Some specialties — for example, canine orthopedics — are as sophisticated as human orthopedics. In other words, dogs are often in as good a position as humans to be treated for skeletal problems causing pain and immobility, meaning that a dog with, say, severe arthritis no longer has to be euthanized for lack of a better solution.

All of which goes to say that whenever your dog enters old age, the good life can largely continue with the help now available.

We here at Tufts University's Cummings School of Veterinary Medicine are in the best position to know. Not only do we conduct some of the most cutting-edge research on geriatric dog care, we also have a yearly caseload of about eight thousand old dogs at our clinic, which allows us to see firsthand the latest research put into practice and for our specialists to make tweaks and other adjustments where necessary.

In the following pages, we pass along this information to you. No other book on taking care of older dogs contains the accumulated knowledge and experience of an entire group of board-certified veterinary specialists whose entire aim is to further the good years of pets' lives.

We have not underestimated your part in the endeavor. You are the most important partner on your old pal's healthcare team — always the most critical player when it comes to the decision making, and sometimes you may even be called into action as a skilled veterinary healthcare worker in the process. Consider that owners are on the front lines in administering insulin to dogs with diabetes, giving injections of fluid to dogs with kidney disease who would otherwise become dangerously dehydrated, dispensing special medicines to treat a host of other conditions, and the list goes on.

Your role in preventive medicine — what people commonly call wellness care — is crucial, too. Keeping your older pal trim, watching for particular changes on your dog's body or in your pet's behavior that should prompt a call to the veterinarian, making sure to feed the most well-balanced diet possible — you'll see that all of these and more make serious contributions to pushing back age-related illness and infirmity and sometimes even avoiding them altogether. That is, extending both the quantity and quality of your dog's life is to no small degree dependent on your own commitment as you partner with your veterinarian on behalf of your friend's well-being.

Your good old dog has already been in your reliable, loving hands for a number of years. Read on to learn how you can best keep tending to your faithful companion as she or he returns the favor with unalloyed adoration and, by your keeping on top of all the best in cutting-edge healthcare options, all the mirth and good times to which the two of you have grown accustomed.

Good Old Dog

# 1 "Old" Is Not a Disease

I HAD MET Bucky four times over the previous eight months. He wasn't the kind of dog who bounded around the waiting room, but this gigantic, obese ten-year-old was a happy goober, always glad for a belly rub or an affectionate stroke on the side of his face whenever he came to the clinic. He still had plenty of good-natured slobber in him; it was always a treat to see him.

His owners were referred to us from his primary care veterinarian. I could see from their address that each visit meant a forty-mile drive down the turnpike, then ten more miles past the office parks, until the road gave way to cows grazing on the hills where we let out the larger animals that we take care of.

They brought in Bucky, a velvety chocolate Lab, because he had a condition that makes it difficult to breathe — laryngeal paralysis, which occurs in older dogs. He needed an operation to correct the problem, but his owners kept resisting because they were afraid for their old dog to undergo surgery. They felt it was too much to put him through.

A lot of owners fear surgery for their dogs, particularly their older ones, in part because they project their experience, or that of a relative, onto their animal. But while dogs do contend with postsurgical pain, they tend to deal with operations very differently than people do and heal faster, putting them back on their feet and into their normal routine much sooner. That's true even for dogs of ten or older.

I explained this to Bucky's family at our first meeting, but still, they were skittish about the surgery and asked whether there was any alternative. Because Bucky was so overweight, I explained that slimming him down would at least buy some time by helping to keep the problem from progressing rapidly. Relieved, they went home determined to curb Bucky's calories and also have him burn off some pounds with increased activity.

But a couple of months went by, and when Bucky showed up at our clinic again, his breathing was more labored. He had not lost an ounce.

This happened two more times. Finally, Bucky came in barely able to breathe. He was so unable to take in air that he had to be anesthetized so a tube could be put down his throat to help with respiration. We thought that might give him the boost he needed, but every time we woke him up to see if he could breathe on his own, his tongue turned blue from lack of oxygen.

Sending him home and waiting for the next crisis was no longer an option. This *was* the ultimate crisis: he couldn't breathe on his own.

With misgivings, the owners gave permission for the procedure. Bucky came through with flying colors, as most dogs do, and went home within two days, breathing normally and comfortably.

About six months later, a chocolate Lab came in with a laceration in his paw that needed to be tended to professionally. The dog had been running along the beach and cut himself on some rocks. He was happy and calm, albeit dripping some blood from his foot pad.

It took only a moment to realize the dog was Bucky — not Bucky as I had first met him more than a year earlier, but Bucky the way his owners remembered him from before his laryngeal paralysis ever developed: exuberant, charged up, and happy to run around — as well as a little thinner because he became more active with the improvement in his breathing. The old boy lived a couple more years after that, with a wonderful quality of life unhindered by significant health problems.

— *Scott Shaw, DVM, Assistant Professor, Department of Clinical Sciences/Emergency Critical Care*

BRANDY SUDDENLY collapsed at home one morning while chewing on some rawhide. The family rushed her to the emergency room. They had no idea what was going on. She was eleven, but she had seemed perfectly fine until then. She was so sweet — a little curly-haired dachshund.

It turned out she had advanced heart disease that hadn't been picked up. But that morning, a valve malfunction in her heart apparently caused the pressure there to go high enough that she actually tore the wall of her left atrium. So much blood spilled into the sac around her heart that it just looked like a huge round basketball on an X-ray.

It was a bad sign — advanced heart failure. Her prognosis was only six to eight more months of life.

The family was panicked. They didn't see this coming. They had first brought Brandy home as a young puppy when the wife was pregnant with their first child, and the tiny thing would cuddle on the woman's stomach, even though a kick from the baby was enough to send her tumbling. Now the family numbered four — the children were ten and nine.

Scared as they all were, they sprang into action. They kept Brandy on the necessary exercise restriction. They enrolled her in a clinical trial at Tufts to test a new drug meant to treat heart failure — never knowing whether Brandy would get the drug or the placebo. They kept her from being startled, even telling people not to ring the doorbell, because the excitement would cause Brandy to faint. They taught the kids to administer extra Lasix to Brandy if they found her short of breath. They even allowed us to put her on Viagra, a potent pulmonary vasodilator that would open the vessels in her lungs, although it was prohibitively expensive.

The parents would come in with spreadsheets listing all the medicines Brandy was on, her dosages, and how often she was supposed to take them. And, beyond all probability, they rigged an oxygen cage for her at home from the wife's late father's oxygen concentrator — he had had emphysema — which we tested at the hospital to make sure it worked. That cut down on hospital stays, which cut down on costs. They were the most amazing people, and Brandy would always continue to run around like a loopy bandit, even though her heart by that point literally took up her entire chest.

My office isn't in the small-animal hospital itself. It's in the red barn on the other side of the road. I don't know how many times I ran across the way to see Brandy for various emergencies. When she finally died in the emergency room one night at age thirteen, twenty-two months after her first visit, we all had a good cry, including the husband, a six-foot-four lug of a man who was not prone to displays of raw emotion. It was cathartic. Though shaking with tears, the family had done everything they could to give Brandy almost two good years she wouldn't have had without them.

— *Suzanne Cunningham, DVM, Cardiology Assistant Professor, Diplomate of the American College of Veterinary Internal Medicine (Cardiology)*

OWNERS OF OLD DOGS often come in understandably frightened. They hear terms like "heart failure" or "laryngeal paralysis" and assume all is lost. Or maybe it's simpler. Their dog has lost bladder control to the point that expensive rugs in the house have been ruined and the owners are at their wits' end. Or a dog's joints are so stiff she can't make her way into the car, and they assume they will soon need to make an awful decision. Maybe nothing in particular is wrong, but the very idea of a dog's drawing near to the full span of life expectancy often fills owners with dread. Indeed, of the four million dogs relinquished to shelters every year in the United States, almost a million are given up because they're "too old."

But old age is not a disease. It's a stage of life.

Yes, the older a dog, the more vigilance is needed to combat various illnesses, and the more challenging the medical treatments. But, as they say, with age, what is lost on the swings is gained on the merry-go-round. An older dog may be more physically vulnerable, to be sure, but at the same time she may be more serene and easier to get along with—qualities that come with ripening, if you will.

Bucky and Brandy, for instance, still had a lot of life in them, but without the challenges of a puppy's incautious exuberance and curiosity—licking up antifreeze and other toxins, running into the road after a squirrel, jumping on everyone who walks into the house.

*A twelve-year-old Border collie takes a momentary break from chasing a ball in the park.*

In other words, a dog's later years simply comprise one of a number of life phases with its own pluses and minuses, and are not to be dreaded but embraced.

Therein lies much of the pleasure we derive from our work—helping people enjoy their dog's old age rather than spend it in worry and despair.

## JUST WHAT IS "OLD," ANYWAY?

The baseball legend Leroy "Satchel" Paige once asked, "How old would you be if you didn't know how old you was?"

It was a rhetorical question, posed to make the point that age isn't just a number. It's also very much a state of mind, as well as a state of physical health. There are eighty-year-olds who seem more like sixty-year-olds, and people in their sixties who come across like octogenarians.

So it goes with dogs. We've cared for a thirteen-year-old poodle who had so much energy and joie de vivre you'd swear she was five. By the same token, we've taken care of five-year-old dogs hobbled by arthritis, diabetes, and other conditions typically associated with old age. That is, chronological age is fixed, but "old" age can be hard to pin down.

That's part of the reason that estimating a dog's age by employing the popular 7:1 ratio—assigning seven human years for every actual year a dog has lived—has its limitations. Because the passage of time plays out differently for different dogs and different people, it's not possible for there to be a fixed correlation. But there's also another issue.

The 7:1 ratio doesn't even apply across the board as a general estimate. That's a reasonable guide for mid-sized breeds and mutts—those dogs weighing somewhere between twenty and fifty pounds. But large dogs, such as Labrador retrievers, collies, and Saint Bernards, age more quickly, and small dogs, like Scottish terriers, Chihuahuas, and pugs, age more slowly. For instance, an eight-year-old dog who weighs fewer than twenty

*When the Great Pyrenees, left, reaches age seven, she will be geriatric. At the same age, the Shih Tzu at right will still be in the prime of his life.*

pounds tends to be around forty-eight in people years — squarely in middle age, with only six people years assigned for every actual year lived. An eight-year-old dog who weighs more than ninety pounds, on the other hand, is more likely to be roughly sixty-four in people years — closer to old than middle aged, with a ratio of 8:1 — eight people years for every year lived.

That's why the bigger the dog, the shorter, *on average,* her lifespan will be. Almost 40 percent of dogs weighing fewer than twenty pounds live ten years or longer (sometimes as long as twenty years), while only 13 percent of giant breeds like Great Danes and Newfoundlands live at least ten years.

We say *on average* because, again, aging and lifespan don't play out according to a precise formula. There are small dogs whose lives are cut short by unexpected disease and large dogs who beat the odds and live closer to twenty years than ten or fifteen. It's like weather; meteorologists talk about the average temperature and average amount of rainfall for the month, but you would be hard-pressed to find an actual "average" day.

Given that "age" and lifespan are a bit tricky to pin down, when does a dog pass from middle-aged adulthood to her geriatric years? The question presents some of the same problems

## Your Dog's Age in People Years

It is impossible to translate exactly the age of a dog into a human age. Use the numbers in this chart as estimates.

| Actual Age (in Years) | "Age" If Under 20 lbs | "Age" If 20–50 lbs | "Age" If 51–90 lbs | "Age" If Greater Than 90 lbs |
|---|---|---|---|---|
| 6 | 40 | 42 | 45 | 49 |
| 8 | 48 | 51 | 55 | 64 |
| 10 | 56 | 60 | 66 | 78 |
| 12 | 64 | 69 | 77 | 93 |
| 14 | 72 | 78 | 88 | 108 |
| 16 | 80 | 87 | 99 | 123 |
| 18 | 88 | 96 | 109 | |
| 20 | 96 | | | |

| Age at Which a Dog Needs Increased Veterinary Monitoring |
| :--- |
| Follow these guidelines as a rule of thumb:<br><br>Fewer than 20 pounds: 11 to 12 years<br>20 to 50 pounds: 10 years<br>51 to 90 pounds: 9 years<br>Greater than 90 pounds: 7 years |

that calculating a dog's age does, because old age is not a fixed threshold that all dogs of a certain size cross at the same time.

That said, we have established cutoff points for when a dog should be considered geriatric, or old, depending on her size. This is necessary because after a certain point, veterinarians need to monitor a dog's health a little differently than they would a younger dog, as you'll see in subsequent chapters. Nutrition needs change as well.

Don't get too hung up on the exact numbers. If your dog is young for her age and the vet starts checking her more thoroughly for various conditions common in old age before it is truly necessary, she will not be any worse off for the extra care. And if your dog is somewhat old for her age, a vet who has been taking care of her for a while should be able to ascertain any changes from her baseline health and treat her accordingly. You'll start to notice, too. Dogs, like people, often begin to slow down a little as they make their way into old age.

The longest-lived dog is said to be an Australian cattle dog who died at the super-ripe old age of twenty-nine. But that was reported in the 1930s, and there is no proof. And since Australian cattle dogs are medium-sized, weighing about thirty to thirty-five pounds, we have our doubts. The oldest dog we have on record at our clinic, where more than 100,000 dogs have been seen, is a twenty-one-year-old Chihuahua named Trudy.

## WHAT HEALTHY AGING LOOKS LIKE

There's no getting around the fact that certain diseases are much more common in older dogs. For instance, three in five dogs eventually die of cancer, kidney disease, or heart disease (the subjects of Chapters 5, 6, and 7, which will explain how to successfully manage these illnesses, often for long periods). A number of conditions that are not immediately life-threatening

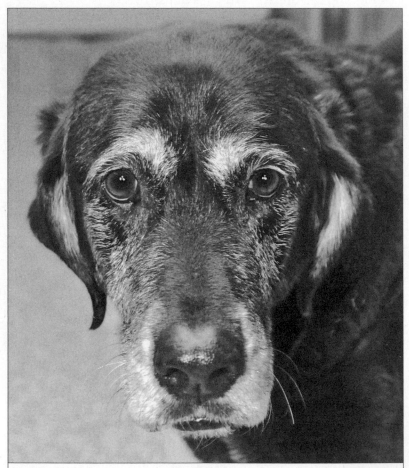

*Older dogs often go gray around the muzzle. We think it adds character — no Clairol needed.*

but are chronic and require ongoing medical therapy also strike older dogs more commonly. These include diabetes, Cushing's syndrome, and several others (covered in Chapter 3). Furthermore, every body system is more likely to fail in an older dog than in a younger one.

But there's no such thing as a dog (or a person, for that matter) dying of old age or "natural causes." A severely diseased organ is always involved.

That said, there are changes a dog goes through that have nothing to do with disease processes but, rather, are simply normal physiologic shifts. To help you distinguish aging from illness, here is a rundown of those natural, expected modifications that occur as a dog enters and passes through her geriatric years. You'll see that many of them are similar to changes that people undergo, but which do not grip them with fear of imminent death or disability. They simply require a little more attention on the part of those caring for canine loved ones, along with an appreciation that the dog may very well need your sensitivity with regard to exercise intensity, severe weather conditions, and so forth.

**Graying hair.** The graying of humans' hair is most noticeable on top of the head. A dog's hairs, just like a person's, also start to turn gray in her later years, but the graying normally occurs right on the face, particularly around the muzzle. Nothing to worry about. Your pet won't even try to pluck them. (Some breeds, including golden retrievers, can go gray very early.)

**Slower metabolism.** Just like older people, older dogs burn fewer calories than they did in their younger years. Some of the decrease results from slower cell turnover and slower movement of bodily substances within and between cells—a decrease in activity on the biological level. And some results from the fact that dogs, like people, develop a higher fat-to-muscle ratio as they age; fat burns calories more slowly than muscle.

But most of the decrease in metabolic rate comes simply from dogs tending to become less physically active in old age. The less active they are, the more their muscle cells go unused and therefore atrophy and die off, increasing their fat-to-muscle ratio even more. Also, their heart, lungs, and the rest of their cardiovascular network become less revved, so those body systems need fewer calories to sustain themselves.

A slower metabolism, concomitant with a loss of muscle and a relative increase in fat, is not a catastrophe; metabolic decline happens. But a dog, like a person, will remain stronger and fitter — slower to become infirm — if she can hold on to muscle and retard the slowing of metabolic rate as she advances through the aging process. The silver lining here: slowed physical activity often comes from conditions like obesity or arthritis, which are more treatable than ever. Once these conditions are dealt with and the dog becomes more active again, she can build up more muscle and enjoy a renewed rise in metabolic rate, keeping her younger longer.

**Difficulty adapting to hot and cold temperatures.** Chicago is stuck in a deep freeze for two weeks. Houston swelters for days on end, with temperatures topping 100 degrees. In which group of people do news reporters broadcast deaths from hypothermia or heat stroke, or at least emergency visits to the hospital? The elderly.

Older dogs are also less physiologically tolerant of very hot or very cold weather. A geriatric dog left outside for a long time on a humid summer day with the sun beating down is more likely to become dehydrated and fall ill. That same dog will also have a harder time staying warm enough in frigid weather. Her body can adjust to the cold only so much.

Is it normal? Yes. Is it comfortable? No. Can it sometimes cause unnecessary illness or worse? Most definitely. It's important to keep in mind that (1) we don't all live in a San Diego–like climate, and (2) our dogs age a lot faster than we do. Thus, just because your dog was able to jog with you in 85-degree weather when you were thirty-two and she was two doesn't mean she'll be able to when you're thirty-nine and she's nine. That's seven years for you, but half a lifetime for her. Go easy.

Similarly, take simple steps to ensure your dog's comfort when it's very cold or very hot. Put her in a fuzzy dog bed with a blanket over her when it's cold out and you've lowered the thermostat to 60 degrees to conserve oil. (It's especially important because your dog is close to the floor, and hot air rises toward the ceiling, while cold air in the room sinks.) You may even want to get her a heating pad—some are made especially for dog beds nowadays.

In hot weather, make sure your pal has plenty of water available and is near a source of coolness or at least shade. And if you fly her from one place to another once or twice a year, consider buying a climate-controlled pet carrier that can heat or cool. (See Resources in the back of the book.) One of the most stressful places for the canine body in terms of extreme heat and cold might be an airport. The belly of the plane may be temperature-controlled, but not the tarmac in frigid or blazing hot weather.

**Decreased Immunity.** One of the most common questions people ask veterinarians as their dog gets older is whether she still needs her vaccinations. In fact, a lot of people with dogs skip the vaccinations in later years, figuring that their pet has already been vaccinated against various illnesses a number of times and has not gotten sick to that point, so why put the animal through more shots? It's a grave mistake. Older dogs need their shots even more than when they were young and middle-aged. The immune system, like other body systems, slows down in old age, making a dog more susceptible not only to diseases such as cancer but also to infections. She simply cannot mount a sufficient immune response to illnesses she might have been able to ward off in her younger days.

Consider the following scenario, which we have seen more

than once. An older dog is not kept up to date with her vaccines, but her people continue to let her romp where as-yet-unvaccinated puppies roam, or they introduce a still-unvaccinated puppy into the household. The older dog ends up with parvo virus, which attacks the gastrointestinal tract and immune system and causes severe vomiting and diarrhea. It can also cause a secondary bacterial infection that spreads from the GI tract to the rest of the body, sometimes resulting in death.

It's precisely because of unanticipated exposure to vaccine-preventable viruses that an older dog's vaccination schedule *must* be maintained. Her age is not a signal to slack off but, rather, all the more reason to make sure she gets her regular shots. Modern medicine can really be useful to counteract a normal, age-related decline, and it should be fully taken advantage of.

**Decrease in heart and lung function.** Aging dogs do not get coronary artery disease, and they don't get heart attacks, as people do. Rather, as a dog ages, she does not respond as efficiently to physiologic stress—an increase in heart rate resulting from exercise, for example. She doesn't have the needed cardiac reserve. The heart is also more susceptible to the effects of anesthesia. (This is not to say that geriatric dogs shouldn't undergo procedures requiring anesthesia. They should. The vet simply has to take age into account when administering the anesthetic.)

It's the same for the lungs, which function in close concert with the heart. The elastic fibers in a dog's lungs allow them to expand and contract with each breath. But as a dog grows older, some of the fibers are replaced by scar tissue, diminishing her ability to breathe as efficiently as possible. Lung secretions also change, which translates to a diminished capacity for oxygen to cross from the air the dog breathes into her lungs and then to the rest of the body. Thus, just as those who are used to exercising with their dogs need to recognize that an older dog can't exercise in extreme temperatures as well as when she was younger, they should recognize that, say, five years is going to change a human's exercise capacity much less dramatically than a dog's. A jog or brisk walk with a dog by your side may need to become significantly slower as the dog progresses through older ages. (And we don't like to see a dog of *any* age tethered to a bicycle. Imagine not being able to stop running when you needed to.)

**Hormonal changes.** The network of hormones and the glands that secrete them is called the endocrine system. While age-related changes vary from gland to gland, overall there tends to be some degeneration. For instance, the response of the hormone insulin to clear sugar from the bloodstream after food has been eaten might not be as vigorous. What's "normal" for thyroid hormone values differs in older dogs, too, which is significant because the hormone coming from the thyroid gland is instrumental in the regulation of metabolic activity. These changes don't automatically translate to disease states, but aging dogs have to be watched more carefully for hormone-mediated conditions such as diabetes and hypothyroidism, both of which affect the body cells' ability to do what they have to do.

One study has shown that the normal thyroid level for a female beagle puppy is 4.3 milligrams per deciliter of blood, while the normal level for the same dog at age twelve would be 2.6.

**Changes in the reproductive system.** There is no menopause in the canine world. Female dogs never lose their ability to bear puppies. But fertility does decrease with age, resulting in smaller (and fewer) litters. Also, puppies born to older dogs often have congenital defects, and there can be complications with whelping (labor). Of course, we recommend that most dogs be spayed by the age of six months, anyway. Females are significantly more prone to developing cancerous tumors of the mammary glands if they are not spayed before their first heat (which generally occurs between the ages of six and twelve months).

Older male dogs, like older men, are prone to prostate problems resulting from enlargement. The greatest difficulty for dogs with enlarged prostates is an increased susceptibility to infections, which can lead to illness that is accompanied by fever. An enlarged prostate can also make it difficult to go to the bathroom, but whereas in men it's about urinating, in dogs it's sometimes about difficulty with bowel movements. The difference is likely due to differences in anatomy between the two species.

*Note:* Enlargement of the prostate occurs in male dogs who have not been neutered — a good reason to have them neutered before they reach their first birthdays, just like their female counterparts.

**Gastrointestinal slowdown.** No doubt if you've ever gotten up close to your dog (which you most assuredly have), you know where the term "dog breath" comes from. You don't like it, but you live with it — your dog may not love all of your scents, either. Sometimes, though, a dog's bad breath may not just be unpleasant, it could be a sign of dental disease, particularly in an older dog. Why? While GI function in older dogs remains pretty much intact in the stomach and intestines, there's a decrease in gastrointestinal action in the mouth, which is the beginning of the GI tract. Specifically, there is a decreased production of saliva, which helps clean the oral cavity. And the less clean the mouth, the more likely that problems with the teeth will occur.

Almost universal in older dogs is the development of dental tartar and periodontal, or gum, disease. That frequently makes eating difficult and increases the incidence of infections in the *gingiva*, the medical term for the gums. Some research has suggested that those infections can precipitate heart and kidney infections. It's not well-documented, but gingival infections certainly can be painful, and older dogs whose dental needs are not tended can lose their teeth.

It used to be that as dogs grew older and ended up with compromised teeth, the teeth were pulled as a matter of course.

## Avoid the Most Common Cause of Premature Death: Overfeeding

Too many calories, leading to excess weight, will hasten a dog's death. In a seminal study proving the point, researchers tracked two groups of dogs from puppyhood through old age. One group was given enough food to keep them trim and healthy. The other group was fed 25 percent more food—not even enough to make them fat, but enough to make them overweight throughout their lives. A full fifteen years later, the thinner dogs were less likely to have developed hip dysplasia and osteoarthritis. Even more dramatic, they lived, on average, two years longer than their overfed counterparts.

Today, a dog can undergo a lot of the same procedures people do in order to save their teeth—and their ability to chew and enjoy their food. (Chapter 3 covers saving your dog's teeth in greater detail.)

**Decrease in liver size.** The liver has two main functions. One is to manufacture proteins, which are the building blocks for all the tissues in the body. The other is to break down toxic substances and deposit them in bile, which makes its way to the intestinal tract and is then excreted in bowel movements.

As a dog ages, she actually loses liver cells, which makes her liver smaller. That, in turn, translates into a decrease in liver function, which means a diminished capacity to detoxify. For instance, because the liver helps metabolize drugs, an older dog might not handle a particular drug dose as well as she would have when she was younger. Even dietary supplements may be metabolized more slowly in an older dog.

This is not necessarily something you will ever end up dealing with. A shrinking liver with advanced age is a fact of life. But your veterinarian might very well end up taking liver capacity and function into account when prescribing drugs (including anesthetics) or advising you about supplements, which is why you should not only tell your veterinarian if you're giving your dog supplements, but also tell what amount, so she can let you know if the dose is too much of a liver burden. There's no simple test for liver function, so the vet won't be able to prescribe drugs for an older dog according to a precise formula. But various blood tests, considered in combination with the dog's age, allow for a reasonable, safe estimate of proper drug doses.

**Decrease in kidney and bladder function.** A dog, like a person (and almost all other animals), has two kidneys. And each kidney is composed of thousands of nephrons, sub-units that help filter waste from the blood and send it out of the body through the urine. Long story short: kidney function decreases with age.

Unfortunately, as with the liver, there's no single perfect test for kidney function. The screenings most commonly used don't show any abnormality until a dog has already lost 75 percent of her kidney capacity, which means a dog's kidneys could be in pretty bad shape, even though the numbers on a lab test might look normal. (More on detecting kidney problems — and what to do about them — in Chapter 7.)

The other major organ of the urinary system is the bladder. If her bladder doesn't function properly, a dog may end up dripping or leaving puddles where she has been sleeping. The condition has the same name as it does for humans — urinary incontinence. Older female dogs, predominantly those who have been spayed, are the ones to end up afflicted with urinary incontinence. There's a drop in levels of the hormone estrogen with spaying, which weakens the tone of the sphincter that controls urination and affects dogs more as they age. Between 20 and 50 percent of adult, spayed female dogs develop some degree of urinary incontinence.

The problem has traditionally led some owners to bring their older dogs to the pound, where they often meet the fate of euthanasia. But now incontinence can be treated much more successfully than it used to be. (Urine soiling, and how to solve it, will be discussed in some detail in Chapter 3.) Incontinence resulting from cognitive dysfunction ("canine Alzheimer's") can be dealt with, too.

**Bone loss.** Like people, aging dogs often undergo a decrease in bone density. Fortunately, because dogs have a shorter lifespan than people, they tend not to develop osteoporosis. Their loss in bone mass is rarely enough to cause problems such as a fracture upon falling. If a dog does break a bone, it usually signifies disease of the bone at that location rather than decreased bone density throughout the body. We call that a pathologic fracture.

**Neurologic decline.** Falloff in this area divides logically into two categories: a decline of the senses, including smell, sight, and hearing; and a decline in the function of brain cells. Both happen as a matter of course. It's the degree to which they occur that determines whether a dog's everyday life becomes significantly compromised. It's also important to pinpoint which parts of the neurologic, or nervous, system are causing a problem. Sometimes a neurologic deficit could seem like a decline in brain function when it is not.

Consider that a decline in the function of cells in the ear canal can lead to hearing loss. Easy, right? But such a sensory deficit might also lead to behavior that looks like senility, yet isn't. If your old dog isn't turning around when you call, you might suppose she's gone daft, when she simply can't hear you. Some degree of hearing loss is, in fact, quite common in older dogs. That's why it's important not to automatically assume your older dog has a canine version of Alzheimer's if her behavior has become erratic or she seems not to understand as much as she used to. Veterinary testing is key here.

Sometimes a screening at the vet's office will reveal a problem that has nothing to do with a root problem in the nervous system. For instance, a brain tumor could be causing a dog to act differently, less engaged or perhaps more erratically, from the way she used to. The earlier it's caught and treated, the less damage it will do.

Note that decreased eyesight, very common in aging dogs because of degenerative changes in the fluid of the eyes' back chambers along with degenerative changes in the lenses, tends not to be as serious for a dog as it would be for a person. You might not even notice. Why? Dogs are generally not involved in the fine visual detail work of, say, driving a car or reading the newspaper; they don't surf the Net. If the squirrel gets away, it's no big deal, and neither your dog nor you will suffer for it.

## WATCHING FOR TRUE ILLNESS

Just as it is important to understand the natural changes that occur in a dog as part of the aging process, so as not to become unduly alarmed and mistake age for illness, it is equally important not to dismiss true illness as a garden-variety symptom of old age. For instance, we've had people bring in old dogs who had always been active and now have great difficulty getting around. One owner of a particularly sweet black Lab/Border collie mix named Ellie told us, "It's okay. She's just getting old." But it wasn't okay. It's one thing to slow down a bit, but a barely ambulatory dog is a dog with a problem that needs tending, no matter what her age. Once Ellie, age twelve, had necessary knee surgery, she was, with no exaggeration, spry again. It happens all the time.

Likewise, if your dog starts to do something she didn't used to do, or stops doing something that has always been a habit, a visit to the veterinarian is in order. Any change that persists could be the sign of a problem and requires a professional look.

Don't be afraid to take your older dog to the vet because you don't want to hear bad news. Very often, we're able to tell people,

"This is nothing to worry about. We can take care of it." People's minds are put at ease more often than they're presented with alarming findings.

Then, too, if you bring your dog in at the first sign of what appears to be trouble, more will be able to be done for her if there *is* something wrong. For instance, to give an obvious example, a small lump on a dog's flank is a lot less complicated to treat than one that has grown quite large and may have invaded surrounding tissue. There's no problem that isn't more easily dealt with when it's dealt with early.

It can be a bit of a balancing act. Some people with older dogs, understandably nervous about their pet's age, rush to the veterinarian's office when it's not necessary, say, if the dog throws up after eating grass (which she probably always did) or merely sneezes a few times in a row. Others delay when a problem needs immediate attention, sometimes trying to make a diagnosis themselves by going on the Internet or talking to a friend or breeder, which potentially deprives the dog of timely treatment.

How to walk the middle path? That's what the rest of this book is about—taking sensible preventive measures against disease and acting quickly and appropriately if something does go awry. We'll keep you from falling prey to some popular faulty notions about senior dog care, too.

Keep in mind, chances are that the end of your dog's life will most likely be a very, very small part of your time with her. Because veterinary advances keep coming fast and steadily, you will have years of wonderful, happy experiences with your older pet—more good years than ever before possible.

# 2 | How to Make Sure You're Choosing the Right Diet

"FORMULATED SPECIALLY for your senior dog's nutritional needs"; "Antioxidants to help retard the aging process"; "Optimal protein level helps older dogs maintain lean body mass"; "Vibrant maturity 7+ Senior Formula"; "Essential nutrients and high quality protein to help support strong muscles including a healthy heart."

Walk into any pet store, or down the pet food aisle of a supermarket, and there's no end to the claims on packages of dog food, enticing you to buy just the right one for your older pal. The wording often has a scientific cast, such as "exclusive antioxidant blend . . . to help boost the immune response of your older dog to healthy adult levels."

But scientific it's not. We've seen so-called senior foods significantly compromise dogs' health.

A case in point: Lola, a lovely Heinz 57 of a dog with a little bit of a lot of breeds thrown in, was switched to a "senior" diet by her owners when she was diagnosed with heart disease at age nine. But the food made it even harder for her to cope with her condition, because it happened to be higher in sodium than the food she had been eating, and that made her require more medications to control her disease.

Beau, a dignified golden retriever who had reached the ripe age of fourteen, also fared worse once his owners, with the best of intentions, put him on senior rations. He had been diagnosed with kidney disease, and his family thought a senior diet would be gentler on his organs. It turned out Beau's new diet was higher in protein and phosphorus than the diet he had been on previously, and that only stressed his kidneys even more.

How can such scenarios occur? The answer is that there's no legal definition for senior dog rations, so levels of protein, sodium, calories, and other nutrients are all over the map. Tufts Cummings School board-certified veterinary nutritionist Lisa Freeman, DVM, has seen too many dog owners learn this the hard way. "I've commonly had people come in and say, 'My dog has gained weight, and I don't understand why,'" she says. "It turns out their pet turned eight or nine, so they switched him to a senior diet, often in the belief that a senior diet has fewer calories than other dog foods, since dogs slow down as they age. Then I analyze the two diets and find the dog has gone from four hundred calories a cup to four hundred and fifty.

*There is no legal meaning for "senior" dog food. The label means whatever the manufacturer wants it to mean, so don't be swayed.*

"On the flip side, someone comes in because their dog is experiencing unanticipated weight loss. You worry with an older dog that there's an underlying medical problem. Lots of money is spent on lab tests to find out what's wrong. But then it comes out that that dog, too, was switched to a senior diet—and has gone from four hundred calories a cup to three hundred and fifty."

So what *is* signified by all those claims on packages of food marketed to guardians of older dogs? The answer: whatever each company wants them to signify. By law, a *puppy* food must have specific levels of various nutrients to support a dog's growth until he reaches adulthood. Law also dictates that a food meant for adult dogs in general must contain minimum amounts of various vitamins and minerals to support healthy maintenance once growth has stopped. But *senior* food? There's no legal definition for it because, while studies on the nutrition requirements of older dogs are ongoing, there's not yet enough of a knowledge base to support one. There's not even a legal senior age. A company may call seven years old "senior," or it may define ten as senior—a problem in itself since a seven-year-old Great Dane is aged but a seven-year-old Chihuahua is not. A company may not even list its cutoff age on the package of a senior food, leaving you with absolutely no way of knowing whether the contents are intended for your older companion.

Added into the muddle are various ingredients not on the list of those known by the scientific community to be essential for canine health, but which some dog food manufacturers say will help older dogs remain healthy—everything from omega-3 fatty acids to antioxidants to oatmeal. The rationale for those add-ins? It runs the gamut from provocative-but-inconclusive research to pure marketing gimmick. (One manufacturer sells a senior food containing "sun-dried tomatoes . . . and sweet potatoes.")

The silver lining here: a food that is designed to be complete and balanced and is marketed for older dogs will not have less of all the vitamins and minerals that by law have to be in any food meant for adult dogs. There are minimums that must be met. Still, the proportions of nutrients may not be optimal for an older dog. Furthermore, some of the added ingredients not required by law might be of unknown value and, in some cases, have the potential to do more harm than good.

Following is a guide to finding a good, appropriate food for your older canine companion, with suggestions on what and how to feed him should your geriatric friend fall sick.

## FEEDING YOUR HEALTHY, OLDER DOG

On paper, human nutrition requirements shift a bit as an adult ages. For instance, while the vitamin D requirement remains the same from ages fifty-one through seventy, the need for that nutrient increases afterward. That does not mean, however, that on a person's seventy-first birthday, he automatically begins to prepare breakfasts, lunches, or dinners any differently from the way he has been for years. Chances are that if someone is healthy and has been eating a nutritionally balanced diet — plenty of vegetables and fruits, whole grains, and lean sources of protein and calcium — he will be just fine continuing along those same lines. The changes in requirements are just minor tweaks to an overall nutritious diet, not a wholesale overhaul.

It's the same with an older dog. As long as he is healthy, there's no reason to believe that the moment he turns geriatric by chronological age something must change in the way he is fed — which should be a load off for anyone who wants to do right by an older dog. That is, even though the veterinary community has not yet reached consensus on how to tweak the diet of a dog getting on in years to make it uniquely suited to his age category (although research should yield answers in the coming years), continuing to feed him the well-balanced adult diet he has been eating since he grew out of puppyhood should, by and large, continue to satisfy his nutrition requirements, as long as he is healthy and does not develop specialized dietary needs.

How can you ensure choosing the right food for your dog throughout his adulthood? The answer lies not in the claims blasted in large type across the front of the package, but in the fine print on the back or squashed into the folded sides.

## THE STATEMENT OF NUTRITIONAL ADEQUACY

The single most important piece of information on a bag or can of dog food is the Statement of Nutritional Adequacy, which is not a marketing ploy but a legal requirement set for manufacturers. The statement will tell you three things:

1. Whether the food is complete and balanced.
2. Whether the food is appropriate for *maintenance* as opposed to *growth* (for puppies) or *gestation and lactation* (for pregnant/lactating dogs).
3. Whether the food was actually tested on dogs in feeding trials for proof of how it works in their bodies, or simply formulated to meet a standard for various nutrients without the hard work of seeing whether dogs did well eating it.

The toughest part about the Statement of Nutritional Adequacy is not understanding the information it contains but finding it on the package. It doesn't have a heading that says "Statement of Nutritional Adequacy." And it doesn't stand out from much of the less relevant fine print on dog food packages, such as where the product was manufactured or who owns the brand trademark. It's not in an easy-to-find spot, either. For instance, on a fifty-pound bag of dog food, it won't necessarily be on the front or the back panel but somewhere on one of the skinny side panels, perhaps hidden in a fold of the bag.

So how do you access it? Start by looking for a sentence that contains the words "Association of American Feed Control Officials (AAFCO)." This body regulates the production, labeling, distribution, and sale of animal food. It also strives for uniform

*The Statement of Nutritional Adequacy, which you need to read
to determine if a food is right for your dog, can be hard to find.*

pet regulation and sets nutrient profiles — the canine equivalent
of the Dietary Reference Intakes established for people.

The sentence should also say the food provides "complete and
balanced nutrition." Just about all commercial dog foods do, but
a few are "for intermittent or supplemental use only" and should
be avoided unless you buy them directly from a veterinarian
who is treating your dog for a particular illness in which more
or less of certain nutrients may be beneficial (as in less protein
should your dog have advanced kidney disease).

You'll also need to look for the word "maintenance." That signifies the food is appropriate for adult dogs rather than puppies or pregnant bitches. The phrase "for all life stages" may also
be okay for an older dog. It means the food is appropriate for
growth, reproduction, *and* adult maintenance. It will probably
contain more nutrients than a senior dog needs but, in most
cases, it won't hurt the dog. (If your dog has a medical condition,

be sure to talk to your veterinarian or a veterinary nutritionist for guidance on whether these nutrient levels are appropriate.)

Finally, make sure the wording includes something about how the food went through "animal feeding tests using AAFCO procedures" rather than simply was "formulated to meet the nutritional levels established by the AAFCO Dog Food Nutrient Profiles." It's perfectly legal to create a food according to the accepted formula. But it means the food was never actually tested in dogs with an AAFCO feeding trial.

Such trials have certain built-in limitations, so they are not in and of themselves a complete guarantee, but they do provide a

---

## What the Label *Must* Say Versus What It *May* Say

While the large print in thick, bold letters on packages of dog food generally falls under the heading of "marketing," the small print is a legal document that *must* appear somewhere on a bag or can of dog food. Here are the items that, by law, have to be on every bag, box, or can.

• Product name (and brand name, if any)
• Net weight
• The fact that the food is intended for a dog (animal species intended for)
• Guaranteed analysis (a dry-versus-canned matter; see page 33)
• Ingredients statement
• Statement of Nutritional Adequacy
• Feeding directions
• Name and address of manufacturer or distributor. This is perhaps the second most useful piece of information after the Statement of Nutritional Adequacy, because it's your entrée to information that's not on the label, including levels of various nutrients.

measure of assurance that the food will support a dog's health. For instance, they can detect whether the vitamins and minerals are being digested and absorbed by dogs. They will also help to identify whether there are any interactions between nutrients that could affect nutrient absorption or utilization.

Never assume that if one food from a particular manufacturer has been subjected to animal feeding tests that all of their dog foods have. There are variations within as well as between brands, so you need to check the Statement of Nutritional Adequacy whenever you're checking out a new food.

## WHAT BRAND ARE YOU BUYING?

Along with checking the Statement of Nutritional Adequacy, be sure to buy a product made by a reputable, well-known company that has been making dog food for many years. New dog food manufacturers crop up literally every month, and while they might be very earnest about producing a quality dog food, they simply don't have the financial backing as start-ups or the years of research on dogs that a well-known company has. You want a food that was carefully formulated and fed to literally thousands of dogs before you offer it to yours.

Consider these criteria for what qualifies as a reputable, well-known company:

• Employs at least one full-time nutritionist (ideally, more) who formulates the food and monitors the feeding trials.
• Conducts ongoing research both to continually improve its line of foods in the particular and to advance knowledge of pet nutrition in general.
• Has its own manufacturing plant as opposed to leaving oversight of pet food production to others.
• Has good internal quality-control standards for ingredients, the end product, shelf life, and accountability, that is, tracking of products in the case of a recall.

• Has the ability (and willingness) to answer any questions you ask when you call its consumer help line (with, for example, questions on nutrient levels, the manufacturing process, etc.).

Not sure if the company whose dog food you buy meets these criteria? Call and ask! A lack of ready answers to your questions is a red flag.

## LABEL FABLES

"Holistic," "human grade," "premium," "organic." It would be reasonable to assume that terms like these on a package of dog food have precise definitions. After all, there are strict, federally mandated rules for labeling a food meant for people with the word "organic." Not so for dogs. What "organic" and all these other terms signify on dog food is the manufacturer's call. Sometimes they mean nothing more than "buy me."

There is one term on dog food labels governed by law, however: "natural." The question is, is "natural" dog food better for your pet? And what about the term "byproducts"? Should you steer away from a dog food that has any? Finally, how to make heads or tails of health claims?

"Natural" means the product doesn't contain any ingredients synthesized in a laboratory except, perhaps, for nutrients. If lab-synthesized nutrients are present, the package must say "natural, with added vitamins, minerals, and other trace nutrients." Synthetically produced nutrients will often have multisyllabic, complex-sounding names, like pyridoxine hydrochloride (a form of vitamin B6) and ferrous sulfate (iron). Don't let the science-y terms scare you away. They're just part of a chemist's lexicon for describing vitamins and minerals essential to your dog's health. And they're just as safe and effective as the same nutrients found in nature.

Most people are not, in fact, terribly concerned about whether the nutrients in their dog's food are natural. We find they have many more questions and fears about *preservatives* that aren't natural, wanting to steer clear of those produced in a laboratory.

The worry is understandable; lab-made preservatives have been called the cause of canine cancer, kidney disease, arthritis, even hair loss and blindness. But fear of synthetic preservatives is unfounded. No proof of harm has *ever* been scientifically documented. Even a synthetic preservative called ethoxyquin, which causes the most concern for some dog owners who believe it can harm their pets, has never been shown to cause adverse health effects, not even in well-conducted studies in which high doses were fed to dogs.

Quite the opposite. Preservatives, synthetic or natural, *must* be added to dry food to keep it safe for dogs. (Canning, on the other hand, makes for airtight storage that protects dog food without preservatives.) The ingredient in dry dog food that necessitates the addition of preservatives is fat. Fat, which is found in relatively high concentrations in dog food, is more susceptible to spoilage than other ingredients. Not only would rancid fat make food less tasty and less nutritious for your dog, it would also make the food unsafe to eat.

Among the most commonly used synthetic preservatives in dog food are chemicals known as BHT and BHA (which are also used in food for people). If the thought of feeding your dog synthetic preservatives gives you the heebie-jeebies—despite no proof of their ever having caused harm—by all means look for natural ones, such as vitamin E (often listed on the ingredients statement as tocopherols), vitamin C (which is sometimes listed as ascorbic acid), and rosemary. But be aware that they are not as powerful as the synthetic ones, so they won't protect the food from spoiling for as long. You must therefore buy smaller quantities of naturally preserved dog food at a time. And make certain the store where you buy it has good shelf turnover.

In the next five years or so, dog food with natural preservatives is likely to become pretty much the only kind of ration you're going to be able to find. Even though synthetic preservatives are perfectly safe and have been keeping dogs healthy and thriving for decades, consumer pressure is causing dog food manufacturers to switch to natural.

## STEER CLEAR OF BYPRODUCTS?

A lot of people don't like the *idea* of byproducts, associating the word with ingredients unfit for human consumption and, by extension, unfit for their beloved canine companion. These people are, pardon the expression, barking up the wrong tree. To the contrary, ingredients used as byproducts in the United States are considered delicacies in other countries, and even prized for their taste by some people here. They include sweetbreads (thymus gland), tripe (cattle stomach), tongue, heart, and various other tissues.

What makes a byproduct a byproduct is that it's not part of the muscle meat of an animal, but instead comes largely from the organs, including not just those mentioned above but also the liver and spleen. These parts of an animal are nutrient rich. Thus, if your old buddy's food has byproducts and the quality of that food can be vouched for by virtue of the fact that it has been manufactured by a well-known, reputable company, he is eating a high-quality diet, not a substandard one.

## SORTING THROUGH HEALTH CLAIMS

There is only one health claim allowed on dog food, and it has to do with improved oral hygiene because of the food's abrasion, or scrubbing action, on the teeth.

Other than that, health claims on packages of dog food are illegal. So how do manufacturers get away with label claims such as "Boosts the immune response of your older dog"? It's because such phrases are not health claims per se but, rather, structure/function claims.

How can you tell the difference? A health claim links a food to a specific outcome down the line—feed this food and your dog's mouth will be in better shape. But a structure/function claim is nothing more than a statement that can be made for *any* food—it cannot state in any way that the food will prevent, cure, or treat a condition or disease. For instance, what dog food *wouldn't* help boost the immune response of your older dog? Without protein, vitamins, and minerals, a dog's immune system wouldn't work at all. But no source of nutrients or any particular ingredient can be said to put the immune system to work to vanquish cancer or any other condition. That would be an illegal health claim.

---

## Should You Buy Dry or Canned Food?

A part of the label called the "Guaranteed Analysis," often situated near the Statement of Nutritional Adequacy, shows the percentage of protein, fat, and fiber in the food. That percentage is always much higher for dry food than for canned, leading many dog guardians to conclude that dry is more nutritious. Not true. The concentration of nutrients in dry food is greater only because dry food contains relatively little water. If you feed your dog according to package directions, the actual amounts of nutrients he eats are the same either way. He's just getting more water with his nutrients if the food comes in a can.

Note that dry food is less expensive—and better for your dog's teeth (although it doesn't relieve you of the responsibility of brushing his teeth every day). On the other hand, moist food renders urine more dilute—a good thing if your dog is predisposed to bladder stones. But don't fret about which to choose. Go with the one your dog likes and that works for you. Many people feed all dry food, but if your dog prefers a little canned food mixed in to moisten the dry stuff, that's okay, too.

Take structure/function claims with a grain of salt. That's about what they're worth—on labels of people food as well as dog food.

## SHOULD YOU SKIP TRADITIONAL COMMERCIAL DIETS ALTOGETHER?

Despite the questionable, slippery-slope validity of some of the wording on packages of dog food, we cannot stress enough that commercially prepared dog food that has been through AAFCO feeding trials and is produced by a reputable, well-known company will prove safe and nutritious for your dog. Nonetheless, some people are not convinced that what they can find on the shelves is good enough, or safe enough, for their older pal. They decide that what's fit for their dog can come only from nonmainstream diet sources—or from their own kitchen. We understand the concern, but we have serious reservations about the more popular alternative and home-designed diets making the rounds these days, including raw food diets and vegetarian regimens.

### Raw Food Diets

You can find site after site on the Internet—as well as brochures and other print media—with exhortations to feed your dog a raw food diet, or at least a diet with raw food as its centerpiece. This includes whole raw chicken and other types of meat, often still on the bone. Claims for the benefits of raw food abound—everything from an improvement in your pet's energy and deportment to a stronger immune system, fewer allergies, less arthritis, and a lower risk for cancer.

People who argue in favor of raw food diets often say that dogs are carnivores who evolved in the wild eating raw meat and nothing else, and that the heat processing involved to make most commercial foods destroys nutrients and enzymes essential to a dog's health.

Not true. First, dogs are *not* carnivores. Like humans, they are omnivores whose systems thrive best on a mixed diet of animal food and plant foods. Furthermore, while heat does degrade certain nutrients, such as the B vitamin thiamin, nutrient deficiencies do not abound. Pet food manufacturers compensate so that the product that reaches your dog's bowl still has sufficient levels of vitamins and minerals. (There would be a lot of lethargic, malnourished pet dogs walking around if it didn't.)

It's true that the ancestors of today's pet dogs, wolves, did eat raw meat. But we should not take our feeding cues from them. Wolves in the wild, as opposed to dogs who live in human homes, survive for only a few years.

If raw food does provide any benefits, it has nothing to do with its lack of cooking. For instance, raw food diets are said to give dogs a better-looking coat. But that's because raw food regimens are typically very high in fat—which can be true for a food whether or not it has been heated. Similarly, raw food diets may reduce symptoms in dogs with urinary problems. But that's a result of raw food's high moisture content, which, like a high fat content, is easily achievable with commercial diets.

What does stand out about raw food diets are their many downsides. Eating bones often left in raw meat, for instance, can result in obstructions of the gastrointestinal tract, broken teeth, and an inflammation of the GI tract called gastroenteritis. Plenty of dogs have appeared in our emergency room because they needed costly surgery to have bones removed from their throat or esophagus, fractured their teeth on raw food, or needed to be admitted as an inpatient in our intensive care unit because their GI tract was damaged.

In addition, there is a very real risk for bacterial contamination, just as there is for humans who eat meat uncooked and therefore don't kill harmful bacteria in the food by heating it first. Sometimes, a foodborne illness arising from bacterial infection of meat causes vomiting, diarrhea, and dehydration, and owners are chagrined to learn that their dog is sick as a result of being fed a raw food regimen. But sometimes the complications are much more serious. There have been published reports of death resulting from blood infections caused by bacteria in raw food diets. The risks are significantly greater for an older dog than a middle-aged dog. They may not have the immune systems of a younger adult dog to fight the offending bacteria, and they are less able to withstand the sometimes severe effects of dehydration and other effects of contamination.

The dogs aren't the only ones at risk. So are the people in the home. Harmful bacteria may not be cleaned thoroughly enough from utensils, dishes, counters, hands—anything used to feed the dog. The very young, the elderly, and anyone dealing with an illness (even a cold) are especially vulnerable, because the immune systems in those groups do not work as well as in other people to fight bacteria.

The bacterial culprits that affect dogs are the same ones you hear about when you hear of bacterial contamination of human foods. Researchers at Tufts and the University of Pennsylvania analyzed five different raw food diets (two of them were actually commercially prepared rather than made in home kitchens) and found that one of them tested positive for *E. coli* 0157:H7, a particularly harmful form of *E. coli* that is the leading cause of kidney failure in children (and has even caused deaths). Several other recent research projects found widespread contamination of commercially available raw meat diets with various forms of *E. coli,* salmonella, *Campylobacter,* and clostridium bacteria. All can make a susceptible person, as well as a susceptible older dog, quite sick.

Freezing, incidentally, will not kill the bacteria—it will just slow their growth. But bacterial growth isn't the end of the problem. Raw food diets might also very well be nutritionally inadequate. When the Tufts and Pennsylvania scientists examined the nutrients in the five raw food diets (including the two that were commercially prepared), they found shortfalls in a wide variety of minerals, including iron, zinc, potassium, manganese, calcium, and phosphorus, as well as vitamin E. Furthermore, some of them contained *too much* vitamin D and the mineral magnesium, in addition to other nutrients. Such nutrient imbalances can result in a large number of health problems, including (but not limited to) skin conditions, anemia, and orthopedic complications. Again, old dogs are going to be more vulnerable than middle-aged dogs.

### Vegetarian Diets: A Thorny Issue

There are a lot of sound, even honorable, reasons for a person to follow a vegetarian diet. These include the belief that it's wrong to eat other animals; the desire to reduce the risk for diseases associated with diets high in animal foods, including heart disease, hypertension, and prostate and various other types of cancer; and a wish to eat in a way that's easier on the planet. Growing plant foods takes much less of a toll on the land than raising cattle, chickens, and hogs.

We support any person's decision to go vegetarian. But their concerns do not make good reasons for keeping meat out of a *dog's* diet. Dogs, much more than people, require a meat-based diet to maintain their health. While not impossible, it is extremely difficult to keep a dog in the best shape on a diet that eschews all meat.

Meat-free diets, even ones that are commercially available, have been found to be deficient in a host of ingredients essential to healthy canine living, including the protein building blocks taurine and carnitine, among others. In one study of two commercial vegetarian foods meant for cats (but with similar implications for dogs), Dr. Freeman and colleagues found numerous deficiencies of amino acids in addition to vitamins and minerals — despite claims from the manufacturers that the foods were complete and balanced and formulated to meet the required AAFCO profiles! Such deficiencies leave older dogs particularly vulnerable to everything from heart disease to anemia, skeletal problems, and skin disorders.

Consider, too, that dogs do not have the same health concerns that drive some humans to give up animal foods. For instance, while they get certain forms of heart disease, their arteries do not clog as human arteries do, so it is not necessary for them to avoid the saturated fat in animal foods that helps make the "gunk" contributing to blockages in human blood vessels. To the contrary, we have seen dogs develop heart disease *because* they're eating a vegetarian diet that does not adequately support the functioning of the heart. One Rhodesian ridgeback, Sadie, had progressed to heart failure by the time she was brought to our offices after an extended time on a vegetarian diet that her well-meaning but misguided owner fed to her.

The bottom line: while health and ethical concerns and even a particular philosophy can validly inform a person's decision to become a vegetarian, health in itself is a matter of science, and "vegetarian" and "healthy" do not go together for a dog.

## Homemade Diets

Nothing says "attentive" and "caring" like "homemade," so it's no surprise that some people assume that their dog, particularly their older dog, will thrive on a tastier, more nutritious diet if they make the dog's meal themselves. Something like a stew with chunks of beef and vegetables, they reason, has got to be better than kibble you can buy in a twenty- or fifty-pound bag at the store. The sentiment is commendable; the practice, though, is lacking.

Your delicious, affectionately prepared homemade diet, even with top-grade ingredients for people, might be nutritionally deficient for a dog. An older dog, in particular, could be very sensitive to even small nutrient deficiencies, leaving him at risk for falling ill. The longer the shortfall in nutrient intake goes on, the less able he'll be to bounce back in the event that he does become sick. That's why we strongly advise you to buy your dog's food rather than prepare it—even if you prepare it from recipes offered on the Internet. Just because someone has taken the time to type out the recipe is no guarantee that it is nutritionally adequate.

That said, if you feel your dog simply *must* be fed a homemade diet, make an appointment with a board-certified veterinary nutritionist (see Resources) rather than decide on your own what to cook. He can tell you exactly what ingredients you need to mix, in what proportions, to keep your older companion in the best health possible. Some veterinary nutritionists will also provide consults through your veterinarian, which are particularly helpful if your geriatric pet develops a condition such as kidney disease. The right diet could actually help slow the rate at which the condition progresses.

## No Matter What the Diet, Add Water

Water must *always* be left in a bowl for your dog to quench his thirst at will. Unlike food, you cannot safely give water at mealtime, then take it away when the dog seems done. That will not only make your dog uncomfortable but also more prone to dehydration.

Adult dogs need roughly an ounce of water per pound of body weight each day to meet their water losses in urine, feces, and elsewhere, largely from the lungs during breathing. Of course, the exact amount of water any dog requires depends on such factors as whether he is eating wet or dry food, how much and how often he pants, how hot the weather is or to what degree he exercises vigorously, and how often he feels under stress. But don't put his needs to the test. Always make sure the water is there, and when the bowl is getting closer to empty, add more.

Make sure the water is clean, too. Change it daily, even if your dog doesn't make much of a dent in what's there, and use multiple bowls if you have multiple dogs. Ensuring access to fresh, clean water is particularly important if your pet has an illness for which he receives medications, such as bladder stones, kidney failure, or heart disease. Some of these medications make dogs urinate more, so they need to drink more.

## DOES YOUR OLDER DOG NEED SUPPLEMENTS?

There's no question that older dogs are more vulnerable to various medical conditions than younger ones. Therefore, it might seem reasonable to give your older pet supplements prophylactically. At the very least, you may want to feed your geriatric friend a dog food that has supplements added.

But there's no reason for a healthy dog, including a healthy older dog, to take supplements. Dog food that has undergone AAFCO feeding trials truly contains everything your pet needs to maintain good health.

Truth be told, supplements can create problems where there hadn't been any before. For instance, they can interact with a medicine in a way that causes adverse effects—everything from gastrointestinal problems like vomiting and nausea to more serious outcomes that can affect health over the long term. They can also cause side effects by themselves. And sometimes supplements contain contaminants that cause side effects.

At least as important to consider is that, unlike foods and drugs, supplements require no review prior to marketing to test for product efficacy or safety, meaning that a supplement may not do what its manufacturer says it does and, worse still, may be bad for your pet. In fact, while drug manufacturers have to prove their products are safe and effective before putting them on the market, the Food and Drug Administration must prove a supplement *un*safe in order to remove it from the marketplace. With ever-dwindling government funds earmarked for such testing, and thousands of supplements reaching the market today, such an event is unlikely to happen.

Okay, now you know why you don't need to—and often shouldn't—give your older dog supplements. But the marketing pressure, not to mention pressure from various websites and chat rooms on the Internet, can make it difficult not to at least consider them.

The three most popular supplements, or supplemental ingredients, for dogs that fall into the "senior" category are antioxidants, glucosamine, and omega-3 fatty acids.

**Antioxidants.** With antioxidants, as health food stores for people go, so goes the pet food aisle. There are literally dozens of dog foods with boosted levels of antioxidants, not to mention antioxidants in the form of supplements. Some dog guardians even give their dogs antioxidants intended for humans, which means those dogs are getting awfully high doses, since dogs tend to weigh significantly less than people. Even half the amount intended for humans is too much. Among the more popular antioxidants people buy for their pets are vitamins C and E, often with the assumption that extra doses of those nutrients will help stave off cancer and heart disease.

But in the vast majority of cases, there's no inherent reason to make sure an older dog ingests antioxidants beyond the levels of vitamins C and E already in dog foods. Vitamin C is not even required by dogs (as compared to people, monkeys, and guinea pigs, all of whom do require it in their diet). Its value in dog food is primarily as a preservative. In fact, at high levels it acts as an oxidant, wreaking metabolic havoc on cells and possibly causing chemical reactions that could potentially contribute to *causing* diseases such as cancer. It can also increase the risk for certain types of bladder stones. And too much vitamin E can predispose a dog to excessive bleeding. In addition, antioxidants may be detrimental by interfering with other treatments. For example, they can interfere with the effectiveness of chemotherapy or radiation therapy during cancer treatment.

Keep in mind that even in people, clinical studies have not shown unequivocally that a specific antioxidant confers a particular health effect. That is, scant research has ever indicated that taking $x$ amount of $y$ for a certain period of time prevents disease $z$. The large bulk of the evidence comes from epidemiologic studies in which eating patterns were simply observed in large populations. In those kinds of studies, it's hard to tease out whether it's a particular antioxidant or some other chemical in the overall diet—or some other aspect of people's lifestyle—that appears to go hand in hand with good health. All scientists can do in these cases is make associations rather than prove any cause and effect between a single substance and a particular health outcome. The evidence for any antioxidant's benefit in dogs is even more tenuous (although there has been some provocative, albeit inconclusive, evidence regarding certain antioxidants to treat signs of the canine version of Alzheimer's disease — see Chapter 9).

**Glucosamine.** When it comes to glucosamine, a supplement used to quell arthritis pain, the evidence is a little more compelling, with the emphasis on *a little*. That is, the science showing any benefit is not nearly as strong as word on the street.

Note that as an ingredient in store-bought food, there will probably never be enough glucosamine to have a therapeutic effect. That's true even for therapeutic foods you can get only at the doctor's office. Yes, they are analyzed so that glucosamine levels indicated will be in the food. But most do not reach levels that may have potential therapeutic benefits. Glucosamine must be taken in the form of pills to reach a therapeutic level.

Specifics on choosing glucosamine for an arthritic dog will be addressed in Chapter 4, but be aware that even if you do choose to give your arthritic dog glucosamine supplements, whatever it does for him won't be a drop in the bucket compared to the benefit of helping him get into optimal body condition, meaning helping him to lose weight if he's overweight. Lifestyle-wise, that's the number one thing you can do to lessen an arthritic dog's pain.

**Omega-3 fatty acids.** A kind of fat found in oily fish such as salmon, omega-3 fatty acids are said to help dogs who have heart disease, arthritis, certain types of cancer, and certain types of kidney failure. Is there anything to it?

It appears there very well may be, at least when it comes to heart disease. But the mechanism is very different from the mechanism by which omega-3 fatty acids work in people, mainly because the most common type of heart disease people get is different from canine heart disease. In a person, plaque builds

## Improving Quality Control

The maze of government regulations for the manufacture of supplements is confusing and arcane — often more protective of the marketers who stand to profit from them than the consumers who want to keep their dogs healthy. But there is one area where improvements are now on the legal books and have been required to be implemented by all companies, both large and small, since June 2010: quality control. Supplements will be required to be processed in a consistent manner and to meet quality standards. For example, the amount of an ingredient stated on the label must actually be in the pills, and the pills must contain no contaminants (this must be true for both canine and human supplements).

Significant limitations still abound. For instance, a consumer will continue to have no sure way of knowing whether the supplement is safe for a dog or capable of doing what it is purported to do. Furthermore, the onus will still be on the FDA to determine that a company is not in compliance rather than on a company to prove it is, so buyer beware.

up in the arteries and can cause a blockage that leads to a heart attack. Omega-3 fatty acids help prevent this by thinning the blood, so to speak. Specifically, they make blood platelets less likely to aggregate, or clump together, and thereby less likely to contribute to a life-threatening clot.

Dogs, on the other hand, rarely develop plaque build-up, or atherosclerosis. They more commonly end up with heart valve malformations that lead to congestive heart failure, wherein the heart ceases to do its job well enough and fluid accumulates in the lungs or abdomen.

A concurrent complication for dogs with congestive heart failure is that they produce high levels of substances called cytokines, which are extremely detrimental because they lead to decreased appetite and directly result in a loss of muscle, including heart muscle. Here's where omega-3 fatty acids enter the canine picture. In research conducted at Tufts, we found that certain breeds of dogs given omega-3s had less muscle loss. (More on the possible benefits of omega-3s for heart disease in Chapter 6, including which breeds benefit for which reasons.)

On the issue of cancer, the evidence for omega-3s is thus far equivocal. While some studies in laboratory settings have shown that omega-3 fatty acid supplementation helps keep cancer cells from growing and spreading, trials in actual dogs, away from lab-bench tissue samples, have shown no benefit.

That said, omega-3s are in fact recommended for certain dogs with cancer, just as they are now being used by veterinarians in dogs whose heart disease is severe. But they should not be used by anyone trying to *protect* their dogs from either of those ills. There is simply no evidence that omega-3s will ward off heart disease and cancer, only temper their progression.

In fact, you could create more problems than you are trying to avoid by supplementing your healthy dog with omega-3s without the advice and consent of a veterinarian. Omega-3s, like vitamin E, can cause bleeding problems in high doses. That's why the vet *always* needs to be involved in decisions about omega-3 supplementation. Your dog's doctor is in a much better position than you to make an informed decision about the amount that might be right for your dog. In some cases, no amount is right. Consider that dogs with platelet problems or certain types of cancer may be at increased risk for bleeding, and in these dogs, omega-3 fatty acid supplementation would be contraindicated.

A veterinarian will also be able to talk to you about the appropriate *form* of omega-3 fatty acids. Cod liver should not be used as a source, because it could end up delivering to your dog toxic amounts of vitamins A and D. Flaxseed oil should also not be used, because the plant-based omega-3 fatty acids in flaxseed oil have to be converted to the omega-3 fatty acids that you'd find in fish oil, and dogs, like people, are inefficient at making this conversion. Long story short: there are too many variables with omega-3s, some unknown even to most educated laypeople, for you to go it alone with omega-3 supplementation in caring for your older pet.

## KEEPING AN OLDER DOG'S WEIGHT STABLE

Gaining excess pounds is all too common in older dogs. So is unintended weight loss. Neither is good for your pet, especially in his advancing years. That's why monitoring your dog's weight is of key importance as he ages. Too many pounds can exacerbate heart disease and arthritis and can *cause* problems, too — diabetes, back pain, and other orthopedic ills. It can also bring on arthritis where there had never been any. In addition, excess weight on a dog can make anesthesia riskier, especially if the dog is very obese — an important point because anesthesia is more likely something a dog is going to need in his later years. Excess weight can even shorten a dog's life — significantly — as we explained in Chapter 1.

A loss of too much weight is just as concerning, because it can harbinger creeping frailty. And just as with people, a frail, weak old dog is more likely to fall ill — and to succumb to whatever illness befalls him. Think of how a hale, robust older person seems much younger than his actual age, whereas "birdlike" older people often seem as though there's not too much time left before they give out.

Too thin — or too heavy — is so important when it comes to dogs that veterinarians don't even call their proper weight "ideal" or "healthy" body weight, as doctors do for people, but rather "optimal body condition."

Why is it not as easy for older dogs to keep their weight stable and thus maintain proper body condition? And what can be done to stop a slide in either direction?

## IF THE ISSUE IS WEIGHT *GAIN*

As the nation's people go, so go its canine pets, with nearly 50 percent of them overweight. Exacerbating the epidemic of canine overweight further is that a number of dogs tend to slow down in their golden years, which reduces their calorie burning.

What's the best way to tackle the issue? The first thing to do when you think your dog has gained weight is not change his diet but make sure he is, in fact, overweight. Looking down at the dog from above, you should clearly be able to see his waist behind his ribs. And you should be able to see a clear-cut abdominal tuck, at least when looking at your companion from the side. Finally, when you touch your pet on his sides, the ribs should be easily felt, without too much fat covering them.

Referring to the Body Condition System will help you make an assessment. It's a scale developed at the Nestlé Purina Pet Care Center that rates dogs from 1 to 9. "Ideal" is a score of 4 or 5. Higher than that, and your dog is too heavy for his size. (See page 47 for the complete scale, with illustrations.)

If it turns out your dog is overweight, it's important to figure out why. Once in a while, the reason for excess weight is medical—a condition such as hypothyroidism or Cushing's syndrome. In the case of Cushing's syndrome, the adrenal glands put out too much of the hormone cortisol, which can cause not only weight gain but weight redistribution, with a loss of muscle mass and an accumulation of fat in the form of a pot belly.

But truth be told, the reason for the weight gain is usually not medical but environmental—attributable to what or how you're feeding your older friend, or a change in his exercise level. Maybe you and others in your household are sneaking the dog extra treats, and each thinks he or she is the only one doing it. Still, you should take your overweight dog to the veterinarian for a checkup to rule out any medical causes for his weight change, as well as to get medical confirmation that your dog is indeed overweight.

If the issue is not something like hypothyroidism (which can be controlled with medication), the veterinarian can review with you strategies for reducing your dog's excess poundage. A discussion dedicated to the subject might reveal that extra snacks

# Nestlé Purina Condition System

**TOO THIN**

**1** Ribs, lumbar vertebrae, pelvic bones, and all bony prominences evident from a distance. No discernible body fat. Obvious loss of muscle mass.

**2** Ribs, lumbar vertebrae, and pelvic bones easily visible. No palpable fat. Some evidence of other bony prominence. Minimal loss of muscle mass.

**3** Ribs easily palpated and may be visible with no palpable fat. Tops of lumbar vertebrae visible. Pelvic bones becoming prominent. Obvious waist and abdominal tuck.

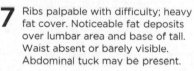

**IDEAL**

**4** Ribs easily palpable, with minimal fat covering. Waist easily noted, viewed from above. Abdominal tuck evident.

**5** Ribs palpable without excess fat covering. Waist observed behind ribs when viewed from above. Abdomen tucked up when viewed from side.

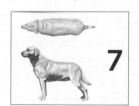

**TOO HEAVY**

**6** Ribs palpable with slight excess fat covering. Waist is discernible viewed from above but is not prominent. Abdominal tuck apparent.

**7** Ribs palpable with difficulty; heavy fat cover. Noticeable fat deposits over lumbar area and base of tail. Waist absent or barely visible. Abdominal tuck may be present.

**8** Ribs not palpable under very heavy fat cover, or palpable only with significant pressure. Heavy fat deposits over lumbar area and base of tail. Waist absent. No abdominal tuck. Obvious abdominal distention may be present.

**9** Massive fat deposits over thorax, spine, and base of tail. Waist and abdominal tuck absent. Fat deposits on neck and limbs. Obvious abdominal distention.

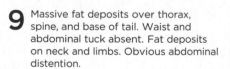

**Courtesy of Nestlé Purina.**

## Calories Contained in Commercially Available Treats

Treats can be part of any loved dog's life, but snacks for dogs do not have the same nutritional balance as dog food. Thus, treats should not add up to more than 10 percent of a dog's total calories. You'll be amazed, looking at the following chart, just how many calories certain treats supply. Some have hundreds of calories per treat, so that if one treat was 10 percent of a dog's diet, he'd have to be consuming thousands of calories a day—more than a tall man—for the snack to constitute just 10 percent of his calories. Another way of putting it: some commercially available treats can never be appropriate for a dog, even a large dog, without being broken up into several smaller treats and doled out over the course of a few days.

Don't forget that table scraps count as treats, too. There's nothing inherently wrong with occasionally letting your dog have some scraps at the end of a meal. But some dogs—and you probably know if yours is one of them—consume much too high a proportion of their calories from the chicken cutlets, meatloaf, and other dishes you've cooked up for yourself. Family-style is nice, but for the sake of a dog's health, it should have its limits.

The best treats, from a weight-management point of view, include nonstarchy vegetables such as carrots or green beans. (Fruits contain more calories than vegetables, and grapes and raisins are toxic to dogs, anyway, as are onions and garlic.) Your dog won't care too much that they're not rich-tasting. For your friend, it's the love the treats represent that counts, not so much the actual taste. Dogs have only about two thousand taste buds on their tongue, on average, compared to some nine thousand taste buds for people. That's why, in part, dogs gulp down their food rather than savor it—they're not getting an intense taste sensation.

*continued on page 49*

have been creeping into your dog's daily routine (does the dog walker need to be told to stop slipping him too many tasty morsels?), or rounded helpings of dog food are being served when the servings used to be level. Maybe the dog—and you—have to get off the couch a little more. Maybe you took in a cat, and the dog needs to be kept away from Kitty's kibble.

Perhaps the solution for your pet is a food that is lower in calories than the one he has been eating. A dog that weighs forty pounds should average roughly 1,000 calories a day. We say "roughly" because calorie needs vary depending on the forty-pound dog in question. A very active, muscular dog is going to require more calories than a sedentary, pudgy one. Muscle requires more calories to sustain itself than fat does.

| Calories Contained in Commercially Available Treats, *continued from page 48* | |
| --- | --- |
| **TREAT** | **Calories per treat*** |
| Charlee Bear | 3 |
| Snausage | 25 |
| Beggin' Strip | 30 |
| Old Mother Hubbard Couch Potato Biscuit, Small | 33 |
| Milk-Bone Biscuit (Medium) | 40 |
| Greenie (Regular) | 90 |
| Rawhide Chew | 100 |
| Milk-Bone Biscuit (Large) | 120 |
| Old Mother Hubbard Couch Potato Biscuit, Large | 137 |
| Milk-Bone Biscuit (Extra Large) | 215 |
| Purina Busy Bone | 655 |
| Baby carrot | 3 |
| Green bean | 2 |

* These were the calorie counts as we went to press. Manufacturers may change product formulations from time to time. Check with manufacturers for the most up-to-date calorie information.

No matter what your dog's calorie requirement, identifying a food with the appropriate calorie level to slim him down can be tricky. Unless a food is labeled "light," "low-calorie," or "reduced-calorie," pet food manufacturers are not required to put calories per serving on the label—and they generally don't. Even the cal-

## Calorie Counts for Popular Brands of Dog Food

Your veterinarian should be able to identify a food that has the right calorie level for your dog. This chart will help, too. It gives the calories per cup in ten of the most popular brands of dog food on the market today. As you'll see, senior brands run the gamut from being relatively high to rather low in calories. The word "senior" is not a surefire guarantee of anything.

If the food you feed or a brand you're considering is not on the chart, contact the manufacturer or check the company's website. If the company withholds calorie information, consider it a very red flag.

| BRAND OF FOOD | Calories per cup* |
|---|---|
| Royal Canin MEDIUM Aging Care 25 | 315 |
| Iams ProActive Health Active Maturity | 334 |
| Eukanuba Large Breed Senior | 336 |
| Eukanuba Senior Maintenance | 341 |
| Purina Active Senior 7+ | 351 |
| Science Diet Mature Adult Active Longevity | 363 |
| Iams ProActive Health Active Maturity Small and Toy Breed | 383 |
| Eukanuba Small Breed Senior | 396 |
| Purina ONE Vibrant Maturity 7+ Senior Formula | 403 |
| Pro Plan Senior Chicken and Rice Formula | 408 |

*These were the calorie counts as we went to press. Manufacturers may change product formulations from time to time, so check with the manufacturer for the most up-to-date calorie information.

orie contents listed on many diet foods are not correct, as Tufts research has shown.

In a 2010 study of nearly a hundred commercially available pet food diets that Dr. Freeman published in the *Journal of the American Veterinary Association,* she found that foods vary greatly in the number of calories they contain. Thus, a dog owner may be making a well-meaning and conscientious effort to slim down an overweight dog by putting him on "diet" food, but not actually be decreasing the amount of calories the pet takes in.

On the contrary, the dog's calories may inadvertently be *increased* with a food switch. Weight-loss foods can differ in calories by twofold — anywhere from 200 calories per cup to nearly 450 calories, more than in a number of nondiet dog foods. Muddying the issue further still, following the feeding directions on packages of weight-loss dog food can cause many dogs to gain rather than lose weight even if there's no change in calorie density, because the amount of food recommended per day is often too high for dogs' needs.

While most brands of dog food give a range of portion sizes, even the portion on the low end of the range may be a bit much for your dog. That's why, especially when starting a new food, it's important to begin with the low end of the portion size suggestions (perhaps even making it a scant portion), and go from there. Remember, your dog most likely gets treats, too.

Monty is a perfect example of a dog whose caretaker tried to do right by him by feeding the amount specified on the label but who ended up severely overweight. The handsome beagle weighed thirty-eight pounds when he should have weighed twenty-five, which meant he was 50 percent over the right body weight and was therefore clearly obese.

Monty was getting only about fifty calories per day from treats and was being fed his regular meals in exactly the amount recommended on the label for a dog his size. But that amount, in combination with Monty's low metabolic rate, was simply too much for him. When his dedicated owner worked with Dr. Freeman to reduce his portion sizes, he gradually slimmed down to a trim twenty-five pounds. He was even allotted some special dog treats here and there—they were incorporated into the overall calorie-controlled plan in order to keep him (and his guardian) happy.

The bottom line: there needs to be a broad-based strategy in place for weight loss. Whatever that strategy (or, in some cases, combination of strategies), it's better than simply choosing a new kind of dog food in the hope that it offers fewer calories when, in fact, it may not—and when fewer calories from meals may not be the issue in the first place.

Just as important is implementing a plan for monitoring your dog's weight once you design an intervention with his veterinarian. We recommend weighing the dog every two to four weeks during a weight-loss program to ensure that steady weight loss is achieved (and continues) until your dog has reached his ideal weight. If weight loss is not happening, the calories need to be reduced again—don't just continue to weigh and accept that the weight is staying the same. You'll be very happy if you stick with the program.

"I can't tell you how many times I've heard people say, 'He's like a puppy again,' once they've slimmed down their overweight dogs," Dr. Freeman says. "Owners often assume an older dog's sluggishness is due to age, but when we succeed in getting the dog to lose enough pounds to achieve ideal body condition and he becomes active and spry again, people are shocked that what was causing the problem was reversible rather than a function of the years going by."

## IF THE ISSUE IS WEIGHT *LOSS*

If a younger dog loses weight, the weight lost will primarily be fat. But for geriatric dogs, the weight loss is often muscle, particularly if they have heart or kidney disease. A loss of muscle associated with aging is called sarcopenia, a term coined by the esteemed Tufts nutrition researcher Irwin Rosenberg, MD, and it generally goes hand in hand with gradually worsening weakness that plays into an inability to withstand illness and other problems associated with old age.

If your dog is losing weight, find out the underlying cause rather than go straight to trying to feed him more calories. Sometimes the problem is a serious medical one, such as cancer, heart disease, kidney disease, or liver disease, which is why a dog losing weight should be taken to the vet for a professional checkup—both a physical exam and, in most cases, some blood work. If it turns out your pet does have an illness, diet therapy will become one of a number of treatments he will undergo.

But sometimes the reason for an older dog's weight loss is not so grave. For instance, he may have dental problems that cause pain from chewing and thereby affect his willingness to eat. Maybe, with age, his perception of taste and smell has diminished to the point that the food he has always eaten simply doesn't interest him anymore. If this is the case, putting some low-salt chicken broth over his food may impart the stronger flavor he needs to get his appetite into higher gear. Harry, a mellow Shih Tzu who came through our offices, loved the broth, and put on a couple of necessary pounds as a result. (Note that this is the one instance where you should definitely go with homemade. Even chicken broth labeled low-sodium is still high in that ingredient.) Some dogs may benefit from smaller, more frequent meals—the same overall amount of food in three or four meals a day as they have always gotten in two meals daily—because they get full more easily than they used to.

Sometimes, the problem is similar to one that causes an older dog to become overweight. In an effort to do right by a dog, his owner switches him to a senior food because he has crossed a certain age threshold, but the new food has significantly fewer calories than the one he has been fed for years. Or the person switches to a homemade diet in the belief that his older pal would do better on home-cooked meals rather than meals from a bag or can. But that diet, too, may have too few calories, or a nutrient imbalance that doesn't let him *absorb* enough calories.

In a number of cases, dietary supplements cause unwanted weight loss. People give their older dogs all kinds of supplements that aren't medically indicated, and supplements such as selenium and iron, as well as zinc, can cause GI upset and thereby diminish appetite. That's true whether these nutrients are given singly or as part of a multivitamin. In addition, lots of supplement pills administered together, or even throughout the day, can have interactions that affect appetite.

Perhaps it's not what the dog is consuming but some unaccounted-for change. For example, he may have developed back pain that doesn't allow him to lean down comfortably, and therefore he cannot enjoy his food (in that case, place it on a low stool for him). Or there are three dogs in the house, only one of which is old, and the younger two eat the food in all three bowls in forty-five seconds, while the older dog needs two minutes to eat. That affects calorie consumption dramatically. We've seen it happen—the solution is to make sure the older dog eats separately in an area the other pets can't get to while he has his repasts.

Of course, old dogs, like some old people, can just get more finicky, or less interested in food, so you have to come up with ways to entice them. You might try a different food (with your veterinarian's advice and counsel) or add a small amount of canned food to dry. That alone may solve the problem. Be sure to change any food gradually to avoid upset in your aging dog's GI tract. Or try experimenting with the *temperature* of the food. Your dog may eat it only at room temperature, or only warmed, or only cold. Getting a new food bowl might help, too. Your pet may detect a smell on his bowl that he finds objectionable, even if you put it in the dishwasher every single day. A dog can detect smells at concentrations one hundred times less than a human can, and in some cases (certain hounds, for example) at concentrations a *million* times less.

## IF DISEASE DOES STRIKE

If a grave medical situation arises, with or without a change in weight, significant dietary modifications will often be required as an adjunctive therapy to other medical interventions, either to help change the course of the dog's disease or to at least slow its progression and improve quality of life.

This is *not* the time to switch to a diet off the Internet or on a friend's recommendation out of desperation. In such cases, a veterinarian *must* be involved to ensure that nutrition is an integral part of your dog's medical care. One reason is that if a dog has a serious illness, the levels of nutrients he will need more of—or less of—often won't be found on store shelves or, for that matter, in your pantry. He may have to follow a therapeutic diet that is specifically designed with his condition in mind and is available only at the doctor's office. It is as if the food he eats becomes prescription medicine.

Four companies make most of the therapeutic diets available only at veterinarians' offices: Hills, Iams, Purina, and Royal Canin. An advance in veterinary nutrition research has led to the development of many such dietary formulations, sometimes even for a single health problem. It used to be thought that for disease A, you fed diet B. It's now known that what a dog should eat depends on the *stage* of his disease as well as on his symptoms and lab values. A dog with advanced kidney disease, for instance, requires significant protein restriction, while too much protein restriction early on in the illness can contribute to muscle loss. Likewise, a dog with heart disease, depending on how severe the level of disease and what medications he's taking, may need mild, moderate, or severe restriction of sodium.

The illnesses for which diet becomes a particularly important part of therapy include liver disease, skin disease, dental disease, bladder stones, diabetes, cancer, heart disease, kidney disease, and arthritis. The nutrition therapy for many of these will be discussed in later chapters, where those conditions are discussed at length. Note that no matter what the illness, between-meal snacks have to be discussed with the veterinarian as carefully as the quality of the meals themselves. The wrong snack can counteract the benefit of a therapeutic diet, as can using inappropriate foods to administer medications. As an example, a dog in the advanced stages of kidney disease who has been placed on a low-sodium, low-protein, low-phosphorus diet should not be given any medication rolled up in deli meat, which is high in all three of those nutrients.

## GETTING A SICK DOG TO EAT WHEN HE HAS LOST HIS APPETITE

Like sick people, sick dogs often don't feel like eating. A therapy such as chemotherapy may be making them nauseated, for example, or they're just too weak for their appetites to kick in. It's a particularly vexing problem because a very sick dog needs his food to keep up his strength as he fights the disease.

Try the following if your old friend becomes sick and has lost his lust for eating.

• Keep dry dog food in a treat jar rather than its original package, and feed your dog from there. Dogs often feel treats are "better" than their regular food, because it's not really about the taste of the food. It's that the dog's owner is treating him *special* by going outside the daily routine to make things nice.
• Feed your friend on one of your own dinner plates. Chloe, a shy Greater Swiss mountain dog we fell in love with, ate significantly more when her victuals were served to her on the china from which her family ate. (It's very important for dogs to feel they're part of the pack.)
• When you eat, keep the dog's bowl or plate of food next to you on the table. As soon as you finish, give the dog his meal. We have found that nine times out of ten, the dog will eat when he has been refusing food before. (But once you start this routine, you can't go back to feeding your dog the old way—it'll be too

hard to retrain him. That's why you should save this trick for a serious medical condition.)

## INDIVIDUALIZE IT

If your dog is healthy, don't change his diet just because he has turned a certain age; a meal plan that isn't broken shouldn't be fixed. Don't start supplementing him with various substances, either, despite the siren call of claims that they will keep him young in old age. Chances are relatively high that such substances will not be helpful, or even useless, but harmful.

Only if your dog's body condition has undergone a significant change or he has been affected by a harmful condition or disease should there be any consideration about changing his diet, or including dietary supplements. And that consideration should be gone over with a veterinarian who can gauge the course of his illness and determine appropriate dietary changes or supplements. If your veterinarian is uncertain about the direction to take, he can contact a veterinary nutritionist who has been board certified by the American College of Veterinary Nutrition. (See Resources.) Just as there are veterinary specialists in areas such as cardiology, oncology, and dermatology, there are specialists in clinical nutrition.

In other words: don't play dietitian if your older dog is healthy, and don't play doctor should he fall ill. Let his medical professional determine the particular dietary shift that would be right for him, or seek specialized help, making changes as necessary. That's the best way to treat your dog as an individual whose health and safety deserve tailored care, rather than the one-size-fits-all approach recommended via ads and marketing.

# 3 | Five Common Medical Conditions of the Older Dog

NOBODY COULD get near Pierre Jade—or PJ, as his owners called him. He bit his groomer. He snarled at anyone who tried to stroke him. He even bit or tried to bite his veterinarian every time she tried to get near him, which was often, since he had a heart murmur and diabetes that she frequently needed to check. He was adorable—a silvery miniature poodle, thirteen years old—but I hate to say it, he was not a nice dog.

Finally, he was brought to me for a dental checkup, and I discussed with his family that four of his teeth were so far gone they needed to be removed. They consented, and within days of the extractions, he became calmer, pettable.

The cardiologist, the oncologist—they save lives all the time. It's all very dramatic. The dog is close to death, then lives after treatment. I don't save lives, but I definitely make lives better.

—*Jean Joo, DVM, Residency Training in Dentistry and Oral Surgery*

ANY DOG, AT ANY AGE, can come down with any number of conditions. But there are five chronic conditions, as opposed to immediately life-threatening, that commonly tend to strike old dogs. The earlier you identify possible signs, and the sooner you take your dog to the vet for treatment, the better the chance that the problem can be tended to early in the disease process, affording your pal more healthy—and happy—years.

## DENTAL DISEASE

Some dogs have the most horrible breath despite beautiful teeth. You might find that unacceptable as you and your dog sit together on the couch to watch television, but from a health standpoint, it's perfectly acceptable. Dogs who have awful breath in combination with loose teeth and pus, on the other hand, have dental disease. It means the bone anchoring the teeth is eroding. If the problem progresses unchecked, the jaw can weaken to the point that arteries beneath the bone become damaged and bleed, allowing a pathway for bacteria to enter the bloodstream.

Ideally, you've steered clear of advanced dental disease by brushing your dog's teeth once a day, every single day, from the time you brought her home. That's the best way to keep her mouth healthy, although even today not all veterinarians impress upon owners the importance of daily brushing. But it's never too late to start.

Consistently brushing your pet's teeth will not stave off cavities, as dogs don't usually get cavities. One of the reasons may be that they have fewer pits and fissures in their teeth to grind food, and such indentations, or occlusions, are where food particles and the cavity-causing bacteria that feed off them tend to accumulate. Also, the types of bacteria that accumulate in dogs' mouths may be less prone to be involved in the cavity-causing process.

Rather, regularly brushing your dog's teeth will help stave off gum disease, also known as periodontal disease. Gum covers the bone that anchors a tooth in place. If the gums are not kept clean, they recede, and then the bone under the gums recedes, no longer able to keep the teeth stable.

Some dogs tolerate a toothbrush meant for people extremely well. Others will accept only a child's toothbrush with soft bristles, or a finger toothbrush made especially for dogs—a thimble-shaped piece of rubber with bristles at the end that you put over your fingertip. You can even use gauze wrapped around your finger, if need be.

The aim is to disrupt the layer of plaque that forms a film over your dog's (and your) teeth every day. The sticky film contains microscopic food particles, bacteria that feed off the food and wear away teeth, and a layer of slime that holds it all together. To best break the chemical bonds that allow the plaque to stick to the teeth, try to angle the toothbrush where the teeth and the gums meet. A lot of people focus on the white part, which is important, but you really need to get to that gum/tooth juncture, which is where so much of dental disease takes place.

Go particularly for the back teeth, which are the main chewing teeth and therefore the teeth on which dental disease tends

## Teeth-Saving Dog Food?

If a dog food has an abrasive action on the teeth — which virtually all dry foods have — wording on the label along the lines of the contents being able to "cleanse, freshen, or whiten teeth" is allowed.

Some dog foods also have a seal from the Veterinary Oral Health Council (VOHC), which recognizes products that meet standards for plaque and tartar control. The council does not test products itself, but awards its Seal of Acceptance if data from trials conducted according to its protocols pass muster. (See Resources for information on how to find a list of products that have the seal.)

Note that some pet foods bear claims for plaque or tartar reduction or prevention without the VOHC seal. Technically speaking, that means the product is misbranded, but if the claim is made with respect to a product's abrasive action, enforcement is a low priority. The Food and Drug Administration's Center for Veterinary Medicine is exercising discretion by not objecting to these types of claims at this time. Still, *no* dog food may claim to be able to prevent or treat dental diseases.

to occur. Also, on all the teeth, focus more on the outsides. This will make brushing easier, but that's not the reason to do so. It's that the insides of a dog's teeth have more contact with saliva, which has its own plaque-attacking chemicals.

You can, but aren't required to, use toothpaste. That said, some toothpastes for dogs contain an enzymatic cleanser to help disrupt the plaque layer. Look for ingredients with the suffix "ase"—that means it's an enzyme. The ones you're most apt to see are lactoperoxidase and glucose oxidase. Flavor choices are often poultry, malt, or seafood. (Dogs are not usually fans of mint.) Use veterinary toothpaste only. Dogs don't spit out the paste, and the ingredients in human toothpaste can upset a canine stomach.

Along with brushing your dog's teeth regularly at home, make sure her oral hygiene is checked by the veterinarian as part of her regular annual exam. You know your dog, but you definitely need a fresh set of eyes—professional eyes—to identify gradual changes.

The vet should do more than lift your dog's lips and take a quick look. She should also look at all the soft tissues of the oral cavity—the cheeks, tonsils, tongue, and so on—for evidence of tumors, which are sometimes cancerous.

In addition, the doctor should search for evidence of missing or broken teeth. You can check for broken teeth on your own periodically, too. They're important to identify because they can abscess (form pus-filled cavities, potentially taking an infection from bad to worse) and cause other problems as well. The way to see whether a broken tooth has abscessed (which can cause a dog a lot of pain that she stoically won't show) is to X-ray it. That will tell, too, whether a root canal is needed.

The veterinarian should also check for gum recession as well as calculus, or tartar. That's plaque that has been hardened by various minerals in saliva, and it actually protects the offending bacteria that lead to gum erosion. It's a particular problem for dogs with diseases that make it hard to vanquish bacteria—the bacterial loads in their mouths can affect their overall health. Consider, for instance, that dogs with diabetes have weakened immune and circulatory systems that increase their load of harmful bacteria, and compromised teeth and ensuing dental infections from the bacteria in tartar can make their diabetes harder to control. Diabetes or not, tartar should be removed, which can only be accomplished with a professional cleaning.

Some older dogs need a professional teeth cleaning once a year as a matter of course; others, less often. A groomer who takes

## Canine Root Canal

Root canal treatments are performed to treat dead teeth that may or may not have abscessed. Most dogs end up needing root canal treatments because of tooth fractures rather than cavities and related decay, which are more common in people.

The procedure itself is done the same way it is in people, but with special instruments because of the long, deep roots in dog teeth. (A German shepherd or Labrador retriever can have roots as long as thirty-five millimeters, even up to forty, whereas human roots are closer to twenty or twenty-five millimeters.) First, a hole is drilled into the tooth to expose the pulp cavity. Then, all the diseased pulp and dentin is removed, and the canal is flushed with a bleach solution or other antiseptic solution to disinfect it. Afterward, the pulp cavity is dried and filled with a material called gutta percha. Finally, the access hole is filled with composite—the same material used to fill cavities in people. That seals the disinfected canal, preventing bacteria and bacterial products from making their way into the pulp cavity.

Most dogs don't need crowns placed on teeth that have been treated with a root canal. For those who do, gold alloys are recommended, as they are strong and more durable for dogs.

---

## Little Dogs, Big Dental Problems

Toy breeds need particular attention paid to their dental care. If a small dog's teeth are in bad shape, her jaw can snap while she's playing. In addition, toy breeds are predisposed to dental disease. They may need to go for a cleaning every six months rather than once a year or less. On the other hand, some big dogs—chewers who are constantly scraping material off their teeth with chewing action—may need to go for a cleaning only every other year.

---

a scaler and cleans off the tartar on the teeth is *not* providing a professional cleaning. Removing that tartar is not a bad thing, but it doesn't address the more significant problem, which is tartar under the gum line. That's what directly causes periodontal disease and what needs to be removed by a veterinarian.

Getting under the gum line requires anesthesia (we haven't yet met a dog who will open wide for a thorough cleaning and polishing), which means your older pal has to be cleared for the procedure. Specifically, there will be lab work to provide an indication of your dog's overall health, including kidney and liver function, and a check to see if your dog has developed a heart murmur. None of these issues will usually keep your dog from being eligible for anesthesia that will allow the cleaning to go forward. The vet just needs to know about them so the anesthesia can be adjusted as necessary to accommodate your dog's condition. Rest assured that just about all dogs go through the teeth cleanings with flying colors and with a guarantee of improved oral health.

Note that veterinary dentistry is rather new, having been in the mainstream for only the last five to ten years. Even the American Veterinary Dental College has been in place for just about twenty years. The field is still emerging. If your dog requires more intense dental care than your regular veterinarian

## Is Your Dog Too Old for Anesthesia?

We have found that a lot of dog owners, owners of older dogs in particular, are afraid of anesthesia. In fact, too many dogs don't get the various treatments they need because of fear of anesthetizing, and the dogs die sooner than they need to, or at least live out the remainder of their lives uncomfortably. In one of the first cases Dr. Joo ever saw at Tufts, a fifteen-year-old Italian greyhound was brought in with rotted, bleeding teeth. He had had them for some time and clearly needed dental work, but because he had a heart murmur, his owners kept saying, "Let's not risk it." They had let him have his yearly cleanings when he was younger but stopped when the dog entered old age, believing he could no longer survive being put under. The lack of an annual cleaning was no doubt the reason the dog's problem became as bad as it did. "Finally," Dr. Joo says, "the bleeding from the dog's mouth became uncontrollable. Bone under the teeth completely eroded away. The owners consented to the necessary dental work, and the dog did great afterward. No more bleeding episodes. An ounce of prevention really *is* worth a pound of cure. Letting a dog undergo anesthesia when necessary instead of waiting helps avoid really dramatic, sad stories at the end."

The reason older dogs can undergo anesthesia safely is that good monitoring and appropriate selection of drugs by the veterinarian keep down any risks. (You can do your part by making sure your dog is not obese — very overweight dogs don't breathe as well under anesthesia.) Most of the time, gas anesthesia will be used on an older dog, because that makes it easier to control the depth of the anesthesia.

If a dog needs to undergo anesthesia for surgery on a particular organ, the vet can also pick a drug that's easy on that organ, further tailoring the anesthesia to the dog. Even in the past twenty years, anesthesia has become much more sophisticated in its ability to prevent pain associated with surgery.

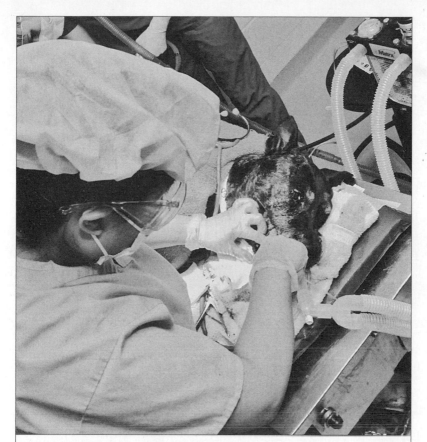

*Dr. Joo extracts the dead tooth of a twelve-year-old mixed breed.*

can provide, you may want to look up the American Veterinary Dental College for a board-certified diplomate in veterinary dental medicine. Short of board certification, there are special certification programs and training programs that give practitioners a bit of an edge; you can ask your vet if she has been through one. (See Resources.)

## If Your Dog's Teeth Must Come Out

If you're reading this chapter very late in the game and it's not possible to save your dog's teeth with cleanings or more involved

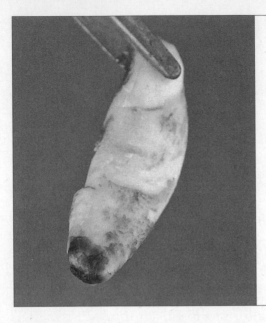

*A close-up of the tooth that Dr. Joo extracted. The dark spot at the root is the beginning of an abscess.*

procedures like root canals, your veterinarian may recommend extracting them. It is sometimes the right call. Diseased, unsavable teeth are not good to have around.

The silver lining here is that even though a dog is always better off with a set of healthy teeth, she can continue to have a good quality of life without them. Some old, toothless dogs are even able to continue to get down kibble rather than just wet food. As you've no doubt noticed, dogs wolf down a lot of their food, rather than chewing it. By taking care of your dog with the decision to have her teeth removed in a severe situation, you've done right by her by stemming the spread of rot and infection.

## LARYNGEAL PARALYSIS

The larynx is what people refer to colloquially as the "voice box," because it houses the vocal cords that provide a dog with her bark (and a person with her voice). But the larger function of the larynx, a long, cylinder-shaped organ made of cartilage that lies between the mouth and the trachea, is to open up widely when a dog (or person) breathes in so that air can get to the lungs and then the rest of the body.

In some older dogs, however, like Bucky (the obese, velvety chocolate Lab from the beginning of Chapter 1, who had so much trouble breathing that his tongue turned blue from lack of oxygen), the larynx becomes paralyzed near the mouth end. That leaves a dog struggling to inhale. The condition is called laryngeal paralysis. It almost invariably strikes dogs twelve and older, and those dogs are almost invariably large breeds, such as Labs and golden retrievers. You'd be hard-pressed to find a dachshund with the problem.

Sometimes owners know something's wrong because their dog becomes cyanotic, meaning she turns blue at the gums from a lack of oxygen and collapses. Another sign might be a change in the dog's voice—a weakening of her bark. Other dogs have laryngeal paralysis diagnosed when their owners bring them to the vet with a condition known as aspiration pneumonia, which occurs when food or water gets into the lungs. Consider that just as the larynx is supposed to open for inhalation, it's supposed to close completely during swallowing. If it is functioning poorly, that complete closure won't occur.

But the most common sign of laryngeal paralysis is simply the struggle for air, the inability to breathe in effectively. Veterinarians refer to this as inspiratory dyspnea. It's usually a struggle that runs a slow, progressive course, perhaps exacerbated by exercise. But it can also come on very acutely or get much worse in hot weather. Consider that dogs don't sweat over their whole bodies; they cool themselves by panting. If a dog can't pant because her larynx won't move, she becomes very hot, which makes her anxious and stressed, so she struggles even harder to take more breaths, and it becomes a vicious cycle.

Once the veterinarian confirms the diagnosis (a laryngoscope with a light attached is put at the back of the dog's mouth while she is under light anesthesia, and the doctor sees that the larynx is not opening like it should), an operation is performed. It does not fix the paralysis per se. With laryngeal paralysis, the nerves that allow the larynx to open and close are damaged, and no medicine or surgery will make them work again. Instead, the operation is designed to mechanically hold open the larynx permanently.

The most commonly performed surgery to accomplish the task is called a laryngeal lateralization, or laryngeal tie-back. That's exactly what it is. The veterinarian reaches the larynx through an incision in the neck and places a suture that holds open the front of the larynx on one side, keeping it tied back, so to speak.

The other side remains closed to lessen the chance that food will go down into the lungs and cause aspiration pneumonia. There *is* a 5 to 10 percent risk for aspiration pneumonia after a tie-back, but that risk is mostly in the first twenty-four hours post-op. The dog is still not totally awake from the anesthesia. For that reason, dogs are often kept off food for the first day. The risk remains for the rest of the dog's life after that, but it's low.

Note that a laryngeal tie-back doesn't make the dog "normal," but it does eliminate much of the breathing difficulty. A dog can essentially go back to her prior level of physical activity after the operation.

## DIABETES

HURRICANE'S OWNER was extremely devoted to him. When the dog, a schnauzer, turned twelve, she noted that he was drinking more water than usual and also urinating more. She took him to his primary care vet, who examined him, ran lab tests, and diagnosed diabetes. The doctor told her that the treatment for a dog with diabetes is an injection of insulin twice a day, every day, for the rest of the dog's life.

The vet was spot on in his assessment, but the woman brought Hurricane to us for a second opinion—fair enough for a serious condition like diabetes. She kept wondering whether there were pills the dog could take instead of getting injections, the way some people with diabetes do, or whether there were dietary tweaks that could be made to control Hurricane's condition.

After much explanation, she realized we weren't trying to avoid other treatments; there just wasn't any successful treatment other than insulin injections.

She started crying in the exam room, finally confessing that she didn't think there was any way she could give her canine companion shots; it turned out she was extremely needle-phobic, which was why she had come to us. She was looking for an out.

Gradually, we talked her into insulin treatments, making it clear the dog would die without the injections but would live quite well with them.

We kept Hurricane in the hospital for a few days, which we often do when we start diabetes treatment, in order to get blood sugar under control. Then we had the woman come back in. We usually allow about an hour to show people how to do the injections. This owner needed considerably longer just to get to the point where she could hold the syringe and handle the needle.

The techs were great at teaching her little tricks. They showed her that the needles are very, very tiny, explaining that many animals don't mind them at all. (I'm convinced some of them don't even feel it.)

After the woman could hold the equipment, we had her practice with a needle and a vial of water. Then we had her inject the needle into an empty plastic bag. When she was completely ready to go, we first asked her to inject Hurricane with water—not the actual insulin—as a kind of dress rehearsal. It was hard for her. Hurricane was jumping all over her, so glad to see her after having been cooped up in the hospital, but she looked kind of pale.

When she first went to give the injection, she jumped back. She just couldn't bring herself to put the needle through Hurricane's skin. We suggested she either pinch the skin really hard for a minute to kind of deaden it, or use an ice cube on the spot, which would do the same thing. Not all dogs need that — Hurricane didn't; he was not a reactive dog — but I recommended it in this case to make his owner more comfortable.

She chose the pinch, closed her eyes, and pushed in the needle with someone else holding Hurricane. As soon as she finished — it takes just a second — she said, "But he didn't do anything." We told her, "That's right, because you did it correctly."

She practiced a couple more times with a water injection, then gave Hurricane his evening dose of insulin. She and her dog were on their way.

For the first five days after someone takes home a dog newly diagnosed with diabetes, we call them to see how things are going. Each day the woman sounded a little calmer. She did say, "This is never going to be easy for me. I'll always have to get my nerve up." But she was so happy. Hurricane was eating well and feeling good.

— *Linda Ross, DVM, Associate Professor, Department of Clinical Sciences*

Your dog starts drinking more water and asking you to open the back door more often so she can relieve herself. You may not even notice the change at first — it can be relatively subtle. But then the dog starts waking you in the middle of the night to be let out — something she hasn't done since she was sixteen weeks old. In addition, you're finding puddles in the house, and you also find yourself filling the water bowl more frequently.

Take your dog to the vet — she could very well have developed diabetes, a condition of too much sugar in the blood that can affect dogs starting as young as middle age — six to seven years old.

The reason diabetes causes more thirst and urination is that in an effort to rid the blood of excess blood sugar, also called glucose, the sugar spills into the kidneys, pulling water with it and thereby leading to the creation of more urine. Where glucose goes, water follows. And the more a dog urinates, the more she's going to want to drink. (Increased sugar in the bloodstream also stimulates receptors in the brain to increase thirst.)

Another sign of diabetes you may notice is that your dog has a great appetite but appears to be losing weight. That's because her cells are starving—they can't take in the glucose from the bloodstream even though she is eating enough. In some cases, the dog actually becomes weak, not just because she's "starving," but also because the excess blood sugar—hyperglycemia—can adversely affect nerve conduction. She may have a harder time getting up and exhibit intolerance to exercise.

The condition occurs if the pancreas stops producing insulin, a hormone that's key to making sure sugar is properly transported from the bloodstream to all the cells that make up the various body tissues. Normally, the pancreas secretes just the right amount of insulin based on what is eaten, in a very tight range, from the day your dog is born till the day she dies. But if the insulin-producing cells in the pancreas give out, the dog simply doesn't make enough to handle the sugar that ends up in the bloodstream after meals, and blood glucose levels creep up.

Once your dog's doctor makes a diagnosis of diabetes—using the results of a blood test and a urinalysis—your friend will need insulin injections twice each day, forever. Dogs don't respond to the medications that a lot of people with diabetes take by mouth to stimulate insulin-producing cells to work harder; once dogs have diabetes, they lack enough insulin-producing capacity to work with.

At first, as experienced by Hurricane's owner, twice-daily injections may sound onerous—and scary. Some people practice on an orange before they inject their dogs. But within about a week, you'll likely feel like you were doing it your entire life—handling the needle, the syringe, the vial. It's a subcutaneous injection, just under the skin, with a very small needle. Most frequently, your dog's vet will teach you to administer it in the floppy skin a little bit behind the scruff of the neck, between the shoulder blades. Many dogs, like Hurricane, don't even notice they're being given a shot. And dogs don't have needle phobias themselves, so there will be no barking, whimpering, or other forms of resisting if she does realize what's going on; there's no anticipation on the dog's part that would make giving the shot more difficult.

The vet will usually start your dog on a relatively small amount of insulin and work up from there, if necessary. The aim is to avoid a hypoglycemic crisis—blood sugar that crashes too low and can induce life-threatening seizures or a diabetic coma.

It can take several weeks to get the dose to where blood sugar comes into the normal range, so there will be a number of visits to the veterinarian's office for the fine-tuning. Hurricane actually needed to have his dose increased in the first month. Your vet might also talk to you about monitoring glucose at home with a blood glucose monitor, similar to the kind used by people, but instead of pricking a fingertip, you prick the dog's ear for a blood sample. Some vets will also advise you to use little dip sticks to check for glucose in the urine.

Within a month or two, your dog's diabetes should be well regulated, at which point her doctor might want to see her two to three times a year for re-checks. She can then go on to live for years, although as a dog with diabetes, she will be more likely to develop some complications along the way.

Most commonly, she will be predisposed to developing infections, very often urinary tract infections. This happens with males as well as females. (If your diabetic dog keeps having to dribble a few drops, take her in to be checked.) Also, wound healing isn't as quick or strong in a dog with diabetes (high blood sugar is immunosuppressive). Most dogs with diabetes will also go on to develop cataracts, which are caused by the build-up of sugar molecules within the lens of the eye. A cataract makes a dog more likely to get glaucoma, a painful condition that can cause blindness; thus, a discussion with your dog's veterinarian on whether to have a cataract surgically removed is in order.

Note that you will *not* have to put your dog on a carbohydrate-restricted diet, as is the case with people. Most canine diets are relatively carbohydrate restricted in the first place, and diabetes is not a lifestyle issue for dogs, anyway. It does not occur because of the kinds of food a dog eats.

Living with a diabetic dog, you will have to make a commitment to be an active member of her healthcare team. And you'll need to pay extra attention to her care. Making sure your dog gets an injection of insulin twice a day at twelve-hour intervals doesn't just happen. For instance, if you leave your dog with diabetes with a pet sitter, you need to make sure the person knows

---

## A Particularly Dangerous Diabetes Complication

If your diabetic dog has been doing fine but then skips two meals, perhaps because she isn't feeling well, get her to the veterinarian's office right away. She is at risk of going from feeling just a little bit unwell to being deathly ill very quickly. That's because she may develop diabetic ketoacidosis. It occurs when a dog with diabetes doesn't eat and therefore builds up ketone molecules in the blood that indicate starvation. These molecules are broken-down fat that can be used for nutrition but, at the same time, are toxic, particularly to the brain. They make the animal feel even sicker, therefore less likely to eat, and that creates a vicious cycle leading to the creation of more ketones.

The treatment is a constant infusion of insulin and fluids at a twenty-four-hour facility. The insulin pumps glucose into cells, which causes ketone production to stop. It's necessary because once a diabetic dog is sick, the insulin you inject at home is not enough.

Death can still ensue, even with treatment, but by taking your dog in, you're giving her the chance to make it through.

exactly what she or he is doing. Because of the way the syringes are marked, it's all too easy to give a tenfold overdose—say, fifty units of insulin instead of five. Furthermore, the difference in those two numbers amounts to less than a tenth of a teaspoon difference in volume, so it's not something you can see.

You also need to make sure you always have enough insulin on hand. We can't tell you the number of people who call on Christmas Eve to say they don't have enough insulin to get their dog through the holiday. Sometimes the solution may be as easy as getting a prescription filled at the local chain drugstore, but the particular insulin your dog uses may be mail-order only. And you can't switch back and forth; they're all different formulations.

That said, once you become used to folding the extra care and attention into your routine, you will have ensured that you'll have your pet with you a lot longer than you would have otherwise.

## CUSHING'S SYNDROME

I INITIALLY brought MacGyver in because I thought he had a skin condition due to his age, which was nine. His skin kind of seemed paper thin, and he had also lost a lot of hair. He appeared to be getting more sluggish, too, which I also thought was about his age.

The vet started asking questions. Is Mac drinking more water than usual? (Yes.) Has his energy level gone down a lot recently? (Also yes.) With questions like those, I had a feeling we were talking about more than a skin condition.

—*Owner of a nine-year-old Tibetan terrier*

The constellation of symptoms this man was talking about—changes in skin, loss of hair, drop in energy, drinking more water than usual (and also urinating more)—points to a very common condition in older dogs. Called Cushing's syndrome, it often strikes dogs in the eight- to ten-year range. Owners pick up on one or two of the symptoms—sometimes it's the excess drinking and urination, and they think it's diabetes—but when you put them all together, Cushing's should be suspected.

Cushing's syndrome is the release of too much of the hormone cortisol, the body's natural steroid. The cause is most often a tumor in the pituitary gland, which sits at the base of the brain. The pituitary signals the adrenal glands (one in front of each kidney) to secrete cortisol, and they secrete an excess if the pituitary is not functioning correctly as a result of the growth. The other cause of excess cortisol release is a tumor in an adrenal gland itself.

The excess cortisol of Cushing's syndrome arrests production of new follicle growth. That's why dogs with the condition get a very thin, sparse coat of hair.

Signs besides those already mentioned include increased panting and a pot belly. Owners often assume the bigger tummy is simply a result of age-related weight gain, but the pot-bellied appearance isn't about that. It occurs because Cushing's causes the muscles to atrophy; the muscles in the abdomen no longer hold in all the organs as tightly (stomach, intestine, and so on), and they push the belly outward.

For all the possible outward signs, definitive diagnosis of Cushing's syndrome tends not to be as straightforward as diagnosis of diabetes. For instance, your dog's veterinarian might suspect it when she looks at the results of blood work for preoperative screening for a totally unrelated condition. If a liver enzyme called alkaline phosphatase is elevated, that can be a sign that there's increased cortisol in the blood. (This is not true for people.)

The doctor will then go on to measure cortisol in your dog's body via a number of different blood tests, but equivocal results are common. For that reason, the vet may also perform an abdominal ultrasound. It could identify an adrenal tumor, which requires different treatment for Cushing's than a faulty pituitary gland.

Even after the veterinarian diagnoses Cushing's syndrome definitively, some people are tempted not to treat it because the signs tend to be a little less acute, less alarming, than those of diabetes. Not treating it is a bad idea. In one study, almost half of dogs untreated for Cushing's died of complications. Among the most common are blood clots that cause strokes or pulmonary thromboembolisms (clots that develop in the lungs). Another complication of Cushing's is a predisposition to developing severe infections, because cortisol, like other steroids, is immunosuppressive. What might be a minor infection without Cushing's syndrome can suddenly become a life-threatening condition for a dog who does have it.

The good news is that in many ways, Cushing's is easier to treat than, say, diabetes. There are no injections, so there is less worry about the timing of doses; the disease won't regiment your life the way diabetes does. Also, if you treat Cushing's, the problems go away—no more pot belly, thin skin, or panting. With diabetes, treatment delays complications but doesn't dispel them.

Pituitary-dependent Cushing's, the kind MacGyver had, is treated medically—with drugs—whereas adrenal tumor–dependent Cushing's is often treated by means of surgery (although medications can be used in some cases, too). The two drugs used are mitotane (Lysodren) and trilostane (Vetoryl). Your vet's experience and preference will dictate which she prescribes. For either, the major side effect is underactive adrenal glands—a kind of overshooting the mark. The life-threatening clinical signs of underactive adrenal glands include severe vomiting and diarrhea, seizures, and electrolyte imbalances, causing weakness.

For that reason, your dog's doctor, in starting either of these drugs, will monitor your pet very closely for the first several months to make sure the dose is right. Once your friend is on maintenance, she'll generally go for a follow-up appointment twice a year.

Mac was put on Lysodren, and his owner was over the moon

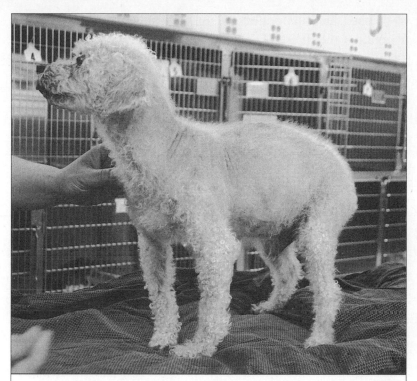

*The distended belly and thinning hair are characteristic signs of Cushing's syndrome.*

with the results. It took more than six months for the dog to get completely back to normal, but even before that, the man was saying, "He's like the dog we had four years ago." Mac's owner had thought his dog was just getting older and was thrilled to learn there was a solution for what was slowing him down and causing so many symptoms.

## URINARY INCONTINENCE

More than a few of us remember Mike, a man beside himself because his collie-shepherd cross, fourteen-year-old Mollie, was leaving urine around the house. Mike was out of a job, feeling depressed, and thought maybe his old girl was picking up on his mood and retaliating by not waiting till she got outside. He had been on the Internet checking out different recommendations and even tried giving her a "holistic" diet. It didn't help. Neither did limiting her water.

He was afraid he was going to have to put the dog to sleep, which darkened his mood even more—he thought it was all his fault—but he came to see us as a last resort. The visit was no small thing, since money was so tight.

After examining Molly and talking with Mike, it became clear that she was not urinating on purpose but having episodes of incontinence. That is, she was passing urine in the house but not actively trying to void; it just dribbled out. There was a history of puddles of urine on the spot where she slept and urine that made its way down her hind legs.

Except for the incontinence, Molly was in excellent health. We put her on a medication for her condition, and the problem was solved. Mike's eyes filled knowing that he hadn't traumatized Molly and, more important, that he wasn't going to have to lose her.

As it turns out, up to one in five older female dogs—and an even higher proportion of older *large* female dogs—develops urinary incontinence. The dog does not feel the urge to urinate, as is the case with conditions such as Cushing's disease or diabetes, but instead passes urine without realizing it—usually while lying down or sleeping.

Urinary incontinence can strike any female dog who has been spayed, but Dobermans and giant schnauzers appear most commonly affected. (Male dogs who have been neutered can develop urinary incontinence, too, but it's much less common. More on males in a bit.)

It's almost always the loss of estrogen that is responsible for the problem. When a dog is spayed, the removal of her ovaries causes a precipitous drop in estrogen. The less estrogen, the lower the tone of the urethra's sphincter muscle, which is what controls the release of urine from the body. The tone becomes lower still when a dog is sleeping, which is why accidents often occur then.

The problem can do more than ruin your carpet (one woman we know even had to replace some of her hardwood flooring). It can predispose a dog to developing urinary tract infections. The weakened sphincter makes it easier for bacteria to come up into the urethra. Lying in a wet puddle of urine also makes it easier for bacteria to spread. A dog with urinary incontinence who lives outdoors can end up, too, with urine scald — skin that becomes inflamed, even infected, because the urine proves very irritating.

The condition is diagnosed largely with your help. The vet will ask if you see your dog posturing to urinate indoors. If you do, it's not urinary incontinence, because that means your dog feels the urge to void, signifying a different medical condition (or behavioral problem). For urinary incontinence to be diagnosed, you should see urine trickle out while your dog is lying down, perhaps asleep, or at least find puddles in the spots where your dog normally sleeps, such as Mike reported with Molly. The veterinarian might also ask whether you find the rear quarters or the side of your dog wet with urine. That could be a sign as well.

Once a diagnosis is made, treatment is easy: drugs either in the form of phenylpropanolamine (PPA) or an estrogen compound to replace the estrogen that's missing. PPA, the drug Molly was put on, works by strengthening the sphincter muscle.

If the word "phenylpropanolamine" sounds familiar to you, that's because it used to be commonly available in over-the-counter cold medicines for people. Most companies took it off the market years ago because in women, there was a slight increase in stroke risk associated with its use. But it is still available for veterinary use, and it's usually very effective. The disadvantage is that at high doses, it can make a dog hyper-excitable or very anxious; it's somewhat related to amphetamines chemically. It

---

### If the Problem Does Not Originate from a Loss of Estrogen

Sometimes, an older dog's urinating indoors is a function not of urinary incontinence but of canine cognitive dysfunction (sort of a dog's version of Alzheimer's disease) or, in even rarer cases, a neurologic disease of the lower spine or a tumor in the spinal cord. In those instances, neither drugs nor the surgeries discussed above are going to help the problem, and further diagnostic testing will be necessary. (See Chapter 9 for a discussion of canine cognitive dysfunction.)

---

may also slightly raise an animal's blood pressure (which may be the reason for the higher stroke incidence seen in women). Thus, the veterinarian may not want to prescribe it if your dog has another condition in which blood pressure might be abnormal, such as heart disease, kidney disease, diabetes, or Cushing's disease. (Mike was able to give it to Molly, since she was in excellent health.)

Note that phenylpropanolamine needs to be given one to three times a day for the rest of the dog's life, because it has a short half life. But that's an inconvenience, not a danger.

If the vet chooses an estrogen compound over PPA, it's often diethylstilbestrol (DES), which comes in a very small, easily administered tablet. The doctor will start with what is known as a loading dose for a certain number of days, then scale back to the minimum needed to keep the dog from piddling unawares. Some owners have to give the drug only once every two weeks; others, twice a week.

The reason it's so important for the dog to take as little as possible is that high doses of estrogen can cause suppression of the bone marrow, which produces the red blood cells necessary for life. On a secondary note, giving too much can also have the side effect of making the dog act as if she's coming into heat.

## When Drugs Don't Work

If medication fails to do the trick, or your dog cannot tolerate it, surgery might be the next step. One option is a colosuspension—a surgical procedure in which the vagina is pulled forward and tacked to the body wall. In the process, the bladder and urethra are moved, too, and that causes intra-abdominal pressure on the bladder-urethra juncture. That juncture is where the sphincter is, so the greater pressure there helps with continence. More than half of all dogs who undergo the procedure are helped by it; it some cases, the operation eliminates incontinence completely.

In a very few cases, your dog may have collagen injected into her urethral sphincter to make the opening smaller. It's a new treatment that has been available for only a few years. But it requires anesthesia and special equipment, and it's not inexpensive. It's usually reserved for younger dogs who have a congenital problem with their sphincter, rather than older ones whose lack of estrogen catches up with them.

Another new treatment is to surgically place a cuff around the urethra to tighten it. The cuff is called a hydrolic occluder. But again, this is most commonly performed in younger dogs.

If urinary incontinence persists despite surgical measures or drugs, or because the usual treatment routes must be ruled out, there are now products on the market to make living with the problem easier. For instance, you can buy diapers designed specially for pets. Even regular baby's pull-up diapers work nicely and might be less expensive (although you sometimes have to cut a hole for the tail). Just like for babies, a diaper on a dog will wick away urine and protect from infection, except instead of diaper rash, you're protecting against scald.

If your dog won't tolerate diapers (some rip them off), you can at least purchase flat pads that also wick away urine and that you can keep in her bed or underneath her as she lies in her favorite spots. There are also companies that make low-level beds on short legs, sort of like a hammock a few inches off the floor. The beds are made of a special fabric that's solid tissue, not like a screen, but still has many holes that allow the urine the pass through. That protects the dog from scald, and if you put a tray underneath to catch the urine, it protects your floor.

## With Males, the Problem Is More Often the Prostate

Male dogs develop urinary incontinence much less frequently than females for the simple reason that they have longer urethras — the longer length allows more pressure from tissue surrounding the urethra to keep the urine in.

In the rare instance that an older male dog does develop urinary incontinence, he can be treated with testosterone (rather than estrogen). But testosterone as a drug can be toxic to the liver, so the dose has to be managed carefully. Phenylpropanolamine is another option, just as for female dogs, with the same risks of over-anxiousness and high blood pressure.

Because urinary incontinence is so uncommon in males, the veterinarian will probably check for other conditions that could be causing it, rather than just prescribe a drug and seeing if that clears the problem, as would happen for a female dog.

A much more common problem for geriatric male dogs, just as for geriatric male people, is an enlarged prostate, known as benign prostatic hypertrophy, or BPH. But it's seen virtually only in males who have not been neutered. Every intact male dog will have some degree of it.

Sometimes the enlarged prostate doesn't cause any problems whatsoever. In rare instances, it causes difficulty starting the urine stream, as it does in men. But in most dogs, an enlarged prostate causes straining during bowel movements. Because of differences in anatomy between men and male dogs, an enlarged prostate in a dog puts pressure on the rectum, literally pinching it. In fact, a male dog with a very enlarged prostate may actually cry when trying to have a bowel movement.

Your dog's veterinarian will evaluate his prostate with a digital exam during the course of his annual physical (although in

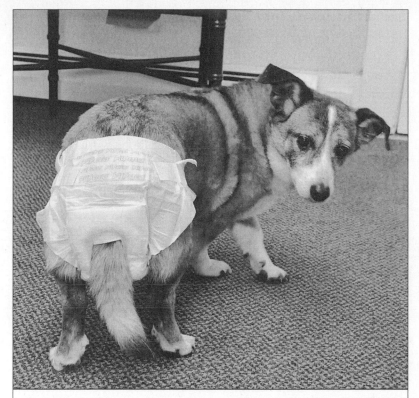

*Sometimes, for urinary incontinence, diapers can serve as a last resort.*

a very small dog, under fifteen pounds, it may not be physically possible). If his prostate is enlarged and it appears simply a function of age, the doctor will not recommend any action unless the dog is straining to defecate or urinate, in which case the best solution is neutering. That causes the prostate to shrink. (Dogs can also be given drugs to shrink their prostates, like men can, but they're expensive.)

If the vet suspects a prostate-related problem other than BPH (perhaps, in addition to an enlarged prostate, the dog has a fever or generalized illness), she will do some further diagnostic evaluations. The prostate may be infected (prostatitis), and the infection can develop into a serious abscess. The prostate can also develop a malignancy—cancer.

An infection, just like BPH, can often be cured by neutering the dog—and by treating with antibiotics. But that won't cure prostate cancer. And surgery to remove a cancerous prostate is not usually an option, as it is for men, because when you remove the prostate, you remove the urethral sphincter, rendering the dog severely, permanently incontinent. (Unlike in men, the prostate wraps around the sphincter.) Furthermore, by the time prostate cancer is detected in a dog, the tumor itself is usually too big to be amenable to surgical resection.

Thus, the treatment for a dog's prostate cancer is generally a combination of radiation therapy, chemo, and medical management. The prognosis, unfortunately, is poor.

It should be mentioned that prostate cancer can occur in either a neutered or an intact dog. That said, the benefits of neutering—no prostate infections and no BPH that can lead to incontinence or straining—far outweigh the risks. Therefore, unless neutering is simply not an option, say, because a dog is a breeding specimen, we highly recommend it.

# 4 | Protecting Joints Stops Pain

CHEN JUNJIE was born in China and lived there with his "father," but the man's family lived in western Massachusetts, and he would bring the dog with him sometimes when he came to visit. There were no quarantine restrictions, because the owner had proof of an up-to-date rabies vaccination and a recent health certificate from the dog's veterinarian.

A black Lab of about seventy pounds, Chen Junjie (which means "pure, handsome man") had a lot of arthritis pain in his two front legs when he was finally brought in to us — two bad "elbows." One "elbow" was really destroyed. He could walk for only about five to ten minutes before stopping.

We tried a new operation on him called a sliding humoral osteotomy. It's not widely available yet. A group of about fifty surgeons in the world interested in elbow joint disease has been invited to participate in the development of the procedure and follow cases to see whether it's really working. You take a special training course, then your data on dogs who have undergone the surgery are pooled with other surgeons' data to get a fuller picture.

The surgery involves putting a plate on the elbow that's designed to take weight off the inner part of the elbow joint and redistribute it to the outer part. Between that procedure and medical management — drugs and lifestyle changes — Chen was able to go from walking five to ten minutes at a time to more like thirty or forty. The wife was so happy she told the husband he couldn't take the dog back to China anymore. Chen had become too much of a good walking buddy.

We're still working out kinks. There have been changes in the implants and the instruments because we've had some problems with plate and screw loosening. We had to change the style of the screws. But I suspect the operation will be released for wider use within the next couple of years.

—*Michael Kowaleski, DVM, Associate Professor of Orthopedic Surgery*

As we said in the Preface, advances in canine orthopedics are comparing very well with those of human orthopedics, so much so that sometimes we can do for dogs what we can't do for people. It's no small thing, since owners often come in worried that their only choice will be to let an orthopedic problem progress until they have to put a lame dog down.

The scenario goes as follows. A beloved older pal begins to limit his physical activity, running around less often and climbing and descending the stairs less frequently. Before long, he doesn't want to jump into the car—and resists being hoisted onto the seat. He also starts to have a harder time getting up from a resting position, finding it difficult to bring his legs underneath him as he tries to stand.

His arthritis has clearly gotten the better of him. Perhaps it's one of his back hip joints or an elbow joint that's causing the problem, keeping him from moving about without great difficulty.

But treatment of arthritis, in addition to other aspects of canine orthopedic problems that contribute to arthritis, has come very far, as Chen's outcome illustrates. A dog with increasing trouble making his way around is by no means at the end of his tether.

## THE NATURE OF ARTHRITIS

The arthritis that most dogs develop is called osteoarthritis. Unlike rheumatoid arthritis, a disease in which the body's immune system attacks the lining of the joints, osteoarthritis develops when the cartilage surface, joint lining, and/or ligaments and tendons of which a joint is comprised deteriorate and ultimately cause painful rubbing of bone on bone. Osteoarthritis tends to affect the large joints — those in the hip, knee, elbow, or shoulder.

Osteoarthritis is also the most typical kind of arthritis in people, representing four out of five cases of the disease. But it comes on for very different reasons in the two species. In people, osteoarthritis is a wear-and-tear condition that's part and parcel of the aging process. The more decades someone uses his joints, the creakier they're going to get.

But in dogs, who live only a decade or two, arthritis is not simply the result of wear and tear. It frequently develops because of a developmental joint malformation. In most cases, that problem is a dysplasia, meaning the dog has a joint misalignment that he inherited from one or both of his parents. Two bones don't fit together properly.

Sometimes the dysplasia and attendant arthritis resulting from it will cause great pain even when the dog is still a puppy, so he undergoes a surgery to treat it. And the operation will be quite successful in bringing the joint into better alignment, often preventing the worsening of arthritis down the road, or at least reducing its severity. But while an operation can make a joint closer to normal, it cannot completely turn a compromised joint into one that acts as if there was never an alignment problem in the first place. Thus, a number of dogs who go through joint-correcting surgeries will end up with progressive arthritis later in life, because cartilage and bone in affected joints never line up exactly right and finally give way to pain.

Of course, not all dogs with joint dysplasia are operated on early in life. Sometimes they simply don't exhibit signs of pain until middle or older age. And it's not always a dysplasia that causes the arthritis. A number of other underlying conditions can also cause the bones in a dog's joint not to line up properly and predispose him to arthritis later on.

Sometimes it's not a developmental condition at all but,

rather, an injury early in life that sets up a dog for arthritis. For instance, by the time they reach middle age some dogs rupture a ligament in the knee called the cranial cruciate ligament. It's the canine version of the anterior cruciate ligament torn by athletes such as football players and skiers. But whereas in people, the rupture of that ligament is sudden and causes excruciating pain that must be tended to right away with an operation (think of football games where a player crumples to the ground and is out for the rest of the season), in dogs, the rupture occurs slowly, chronically, over time, until finally it results in a complete tear. Lameness typically starts out mild, then progressively worsens as the ligament tears more and more. Like a dysplasia, a ruptured cranial cruciate ligament may be operated on to slow the progression of knee arthritis in a dog (the arthritis begins the moment the ligament begins to tear), but again, it doesn't ensure that arthritis will never become worse.

Whatever the underlying reason for your dog's arthritis, here he is now, in a great deal of pain from the condition, and he needs to be tended to. What can you do to restore his quality of life and slow disease progression?

## LIFESTYLE AND MEDICAL MANAGEMENT

No matter what the joint and no matter how the problem began, slowing the course of arthritis—pushing back pain as much as possible, for as long as possible—is a five-pronged approach, with the first two prongs being the cornerstones of treatment. In fact, sometimes tending to those two alone is enough to reverse clinical symptoms. Even if a dog ends up undergoing surgery to correct a joint problem, these steps remain critical. The surgery works in conjunction with lifestyle and medical adjustments, not in place of them.

1. **Weight control.** Keep your arthritic dog thin, as in runner or triathlete thin, a little thinner than average. When a dog walks downstairs, the pressure on his joints might nearly dou-

ble. When he jumps, he puts 150 percent of his weight on his front limbs. The less weight, the less pressure, and the less pain. Refer back to Chapter 2 for steps toward slimming down an overweight dog.

## Other Types of Canine Arthritis

Large joints are not the only ones affected by arthritis in a dog, and the arthritis does not always result from a problem that began early in the dog's life. Sometimes osteoarthritis occurs in the "wrist" (carpus) of a forelimb or the "ankle" (tarsus) of a hind limb, and this usually *is* a wear-and-tear condition resulting from use after a number of years. It's generally treated medically rather than with surgery. One option is to periodically inject the compromised joint with hyaluronic acid, an important component of joint fluid that helps keep the joint lubricated. But if the problem becomes severe enough, the joint might simply be fused in an operation so that it no longer bends, which makes the discomfort disappear. Dogs function extremely well with fused ankles and wrists.

In addition to wear-and-tear osteoarthritis in smaller joints, dogs sometimes get a type of arthritis that is virtually identical to human rheumatoid arthritis. An autoimmune disease, it tends to affect small to medium breeds, Shetland sheepdogs in particular, and is dramatically painful, affecting multiple small joints. Some dogs also develop lupus, another type of autoimmune arthritis, and some develop idiopathic arthritis, meaning the cause is unknown. All of these, treated medically rather than surgically (the rheumatoid type of arthritis calls for the steroid prednisone and/or immunosuppressants), are relatively uncommon. We might see one case every two months in our clinic, whereas in the same time frame we might see two hundred cases of osteoarthritis of the hip, knee, or elbow born of joint dysplasia.

**2. Exercise moderation.** By moderation, we do not mean "restriction." Restricting activities causes loss of muscle, which only makes the joints need to work harder. Consider that the muscles surrounding all the joints act as shock absorbers, taking the brunt of the pressure that comes with each step. Only rarely do the muscles fail to do their job, with the joints ending up absorbing the shock instead. If muscles aren't regularly used, however, they atrophy, making them less able to do their job and leaving more impact absorption to the joints, which will degrade them even further if they already are arthritic. That said, if the arthritis is severe, try to help your pal avoid high-impact play that includes running and jumping, which can only make lameness from arthritis worse. Instead, go for leash walks and, if possible, swimming. The bottom line: arthritic dogs should have moderate amounts of nonstrenuous exercise every day.

**3. Nonsteroidal anti-inflammatory drugs (NSAIDS).** These drugs, if deemed necessary in addition to lifestyle measures, should preferably be taken on an intermittent basis, perhaps after periods of activity that are more intense than usual, or even prophylactically, in anticipation of a very active day. Ideally, they should not be taken daily because they can have significant side effects, including liver and kidney damage, gastrointestinal upset, and GI ulcers.

Make sure to get a prescription for your dog, because NSAIDS intended for people, including over-the-counter aspirin and ibuprofen, cause gastric ulcers more commonly in dogs than in people. There are a number of NSAIDs your veterinarian might prescribe, including deracoxib (Deramaxx), etodolac (Etogesic), firocoxib (Previcox), carprofen (Rimadyl), and tepoxalin (Zubrin), all of which are tablets. There's also meloxicam (Metacam), which you squirt over your pet's food. Rimadyl is one of the most commonly ones used, for historical reasons. It was the first one licensed, and veterinarians became used to prescribing it. Any of these preparations make reasonable choices, though. In fact, some dogs respond better to one NSAID than another,

# Recognizing Arthritis Pain

Sometimes, unfortunately, arthritis pain is not always recognized. For instance, if the elbow joints in both front legs hurt equally, there may not be a telltale limp. Instead, the gait abnormality will be symmetrical. The dog will shorten his stride, shuffling to limit the amount of time on each limb. (That was the case with Chen.) If the two back legs are affected, rather than traveling forward with his spine straight, the dog will swing his back and sort of waddle right and left to help advance the limbs rather than move them at the compromised joints. The dog can go years perhaps before the pain gets the better of him and the problem is picked up.

But waddling and shuffling, just like limping, are not normal. Limping, of course, is always a sign of pain, just like it is in people, even if the dog isn't constantly holding his leg in the air or whimpering in discomfort. The whole point of a limp is to mitigate pain.

Finally, if a dog keeps holding up his front paw, it may not be his paw that's hurting. It could be his elbow, and he's holding his limb in an unusual position to relieve joint pressure.

Once the pain is recognized for what it is, people often ask us to take periodic X-rays to see if the arthritis has worsened. But radiographs are actually a poor indicator of how a dog is doing. For instance, the arthritis might look worse on an X-ray, but the dog, through treatment, might be faring better. On the flip side, two X-rays taken six months apart may show no change, but the dog may be in much worse pain. The best way to determine the course of a dog's arthritis is through the owner's observations along with clinical exams by a veterinarian. Following the progression of arthritis radiographically is of secondary importance.

so many veterinarians stock a number of them and work with the patient until they find the medicine that causes the greatest relief with the fewest side effects. In general, these preparations act by decreasing inflammation in the joints, thereby alleviating pain and increasing mobility.

**4. Slow-acting, disease-modifying osteoarthritis drugs.** For arthritic dogs, these drugs are composed of the supplements glucosamine and chondroitin sulfate, available together in a single pill. One brand, Cosequin, is often prescribed by veterinarians.

As we said in Chapter 2, much of the evidence on glucosamine is anecdotal, but current thinking is that the combination supplement may help protect cartilage that is damaged but not yet destroyed, and in that way stave off the bone-on-bone contact that causes pain. Cosequin also acts like an anti-inflammatory right in the joint (although nowhere near as well as NSAIDs) and is believed to help return joint fluid to its proper consistency. Normal joint fluid is thick and viscous, but as arthritis progresses, it becomes watery and therefore a poorer lubricant.

Word on how well the supplement works in total is equivocal, but we do know that it doesn't work overnight, so don't administer it for a week or ten days and then give up in frustration. You need to commit to giving it to your dog for six to eight weeks — or even longer — and *then* evaluate whether it's helping. The supplement does not help every dog, so if it isn't making your dog feel better or move around more easily after a couple of months, discontinue it and save your money. (For the average Labrador-sized dog, Cosequin averages about forty dollars a month.)

*Note:* Chondroitin sulfate is available in countless over-the-counter preparations for people with arthritis as well as for dogs. We recommend you stay away from them, even if their price or claims are attractive. Chondroitin is a supplement, not a drug, and supplements are not nearly as well regulated as medicines. That means over-the-counter chondroitin may not dissolve properly in the digestive tract to deliver the active ingredient to the blood and the rest of the body tissues. The manufacture of Cosequin, on the other hand, is well controlled. The company that makes it, Nutramax, has good quality control.

Your veterinarian may recommend other supplements in addition to Cosequin. There's even less definitive evidence that they work, but they're not likely to hurt your dog, either. One of the more popular ones is Adequan. Its active ingredient is polysulfated glycosaminoglycan, which is a constituent of joint fluid. Like Cosequin, it takes several weeks to see results, so don't give up too soon. Also, like the other supplement, other types of glycosaminoglycan are available over the counter but lack strict regulation and oversight, so it's hard to know that what the label says you're getting is what your dog is actually absorbing. Stick to the Adequan, which your veterinarian will inject into your dog's muscle.

No matter which arthritis supplement your dog may end up taking, he will not necessarily need to take it forever. Often, a dog will require a supplement for just a finite period of time to return him to the mobility he needs in order to have less pain and more independent movement. Some dogs are able to go on and then off supplements every so often. A lot of owners tell us that's the case. They play it by ear, stopping the supplement, watching for signs of pain, and bringing the pill back into the dog's routine if they notice a slowing down or out-and-out discomfort.

**5. Dietary modification.** There are some prescription dog foods that appear to help quell arthritis symptoms. One of the most popular is Hill's j/d, which has a higher ratio of omega-3 fatty acids to other fats than regular dog food. It has been shown that on this diet, dogs experience a decreased need for NSAIDs. The data aren't iron-clad, but the food can reasonably go into the might-help-can't-hurt category. Keep in mind, though, that it is high in calories. Use it only if you can maintain the dog at a very trim weight.

## OTHER TREATMENTS

If the five steps above don't ameliorate your dog's arthritis pain sufficiently, there are other steps you can take.

### Centrally Acting Pain Medications

If a dog's arthritis pain has become unbearable, medications that focus specifically on pain per se rather than on inflammation or other pain-related phenomena can be brought into the arsenal of drugs that will help keep your dog comfortable.

One drug that's now widely used in veterinary practices is called tramadol (available under a wide variety of trade names). An opioid in the same family as morphine, the drug is quite safe, can be given orally rather than injected, and is very well tolerated by most dogs. Like other opioids, it works by attaching to pain receptors in the brain, but it also affects other central neurotransmitter systems, for example, enhancing both serotonin and norepinephrine. Data on its efficacy in mitigating arthritis pain specifically are lacking, but it may provide additional benefit. *Note:* Tramadol is a sedative and can make some dogs drowsy.

Another analgesic drug used successfully to control pain in dogs is Neurontin (gabapentin). Taken commonly by people as an antiseizure medication, it slows down nerve conduction, blocking a type of pain called neuropathic pain.

Often, a dog will be prescribed supplements and NSAIDs in addition to a pain medication. It's a matter of working with your veterinarian—and your dog—to tailor the combination of drugs that do the best job in the lowest doses.

### A Role for Physical Therapy

One of the best things a person with osteoarthritis can do to keep his range of motion from deteriorating further is strength training, also known as resistance training, because it involves pushing the muscles against the resistance of weight (with weights or resistance machines) in order to keep them in good shape. As we mentioned previously, the stronger the muscles, the better able they'll be to absorb the brunt of any impact, rather than leaving that work to the joints.

It's the same for dogs. Exercising the muscles of a dog with arthritis better equips him to absorb pressure from movement and save his compromised joints from taking on more of that burden. But dogs don't lift weights or do sets and "reps" with resistance machines. So how can you help a dog strengthen his muscles via strength training? With physical therapy.

Physical therapy for dogs has evolved into a field called canine rehabilitation medicine. It is so new that it was approved only in the spring of 2010 as the latest specialty in veterinary

## Seeking a Pain Specialist

If your veterinarian has done all he can in terms of providing your dog relief from arthritis (or other) pain, you may want to seek the services of a veterinarian who specializes in pain management. Pain centers for animals are becoming more and more common. We have one at Tufts Cummings School of Veterinary Medicine, with at least 50 percent of the visitors suffering from arthritis pain (and many of the rest in chronic pain from cancer). A veterinary pain specialist will frequently be a diplomate of the American College of Veterinary Anesthesiologists, equivalent to board certification for physicians, and will be equipped to provide pain consultations that include using very specific combinations and amounts of pain-alleviating drugs.

A good place to start your search for a hospital that offers a veterinary pain management service is the International Veterinary Academy of Pain Management. (See Resources.) If you don't live in or near an urban area, you may not be near one, but often practitioners specializing in pain will do phone consults.

medicine. Veterinarians must receive specific training and take special boards to become diplomates in the field. A step below becoming a diplomate is to become certified. Veterinarians as well as veterinary technicians — the rough equivalent of nurses — can become certified in canine rehabilitation medicine by taking a series of classes and then passing a test.

It all began with humans' physical therapists who had an interest in veterinary medicine. They started applying physical therapy to animals they knew personally, and it grew from there. Admittedly, physical therapy has a longer history of use for dogs who have had an operation and need to regain strength as they recover, but there is an emerging role for dogs with worsening arthritis who have been moving around less and less in an effort to avoid joint pain.

One thing someone certified in canine physical rehabilitation might do is get his arthritic dog on an underwater treadmill. The benefits haven't been proven with a clinical trial, but, theoretically at least, the dog could strengthen his leg muscles by walking without having to bear his entire weight in the process; the water eases some of the burden. Your dog might be put on a regular swimming regimen as well. Again, the water would allow him to exercise his muscles without stressing his joints.

Your dog's physical therapist will probably also teach you extension/flexion exercises to perform on your pet at home. This is exercise that is done *to* the dog to increase his range of motion. For instance, you might be taught how to push against the dog's front legs in such a way as to extend and contract the muscles in his elbows, so it will be easier for him to walk if he has elbow arthritis. A dog bears 60 percent of his weight on his front legs, and the elbows thrust forward as he walks. If there is arthritis in the elbow joints, walking will cause pain, but your flexing the surrounding muscles on a regular basis with a series of repetitions will increase range of motion enough to give the joints a break.

Of course, this works only as well as you follow through. It's

*The muscles of this Lab mix are being strengthened through physical therapy to take stress off her joints when she moves about.*

*Walking on a treadmill underwater relieves pressure from the joints of a dog with arthritis while he exercises.*

one thing to take your dog to the "gym" so he can have his walking session on an underwater treadmill. It's another to carve out the time to engage him in passive strength training — training in which *you* do the work of bending his legs so that his muscle and joint flexibility increase. You have to make a real commitment, three to five sessions per week over the long term, and some breeds are easier to work with than others. A Labrador retriever will be perfectly happy to let you manipulate his legs; a terrier, maybe not so much.

But what you put into your canine charge's physical therapy can really give him back his life. Small, incremental changes in his muscle strength can make big differences in his daily life — allowing him to stand to go to the bathroom or walk over to his food or water when he is hungry or thirsty. You won't turn your dog into a puppy again, but you can nudge him back toward a place of more livable mobility.

Your veterinarian may be able to help you find someone who specializes in canine rehabilitation medicine, particularly if you live in an urban area, but there are also organizations that can help you find veterinarians certified in canine rehabilitation medicine — an important point since anyone can hang a shingle that says "canine physical rehabilitation." See Resources at the back of the book.

## SURGERIES IF PAIN CAN'T BE KEPT AT BAY

As we said earlier, often a dog has an operation early in life to deal with a dysplasia or other problem that has led to the arthritis. For instance, a dog with elbow dysplasia, very often a Labrador retriever, golden retriever, or Bernese mountain dog, may undergo arthroscopy, a surgery in which the doctor goes into the elbow with an arthroscope — a little telescope with a lens attached to a thin metal shaft on one end and a camera hooked to the other — and removes loose, bony fragments from the faulty joint, leading to immediate pain relief. (Chen Junjie underwent

that operation as well as the sliding humoral osteotomy.) A ruptured cranial cruciate ligament, which connects the thigh bone
(femur) to the shin bone (tibia), might be tended to with one of
several operations, for example, a lateral suture, which involves
stabilizing the joint with a two- to six-inch length of forty- to
one-hundred-pound test nylon fishing line.

Such operations are performed frequently even in older dogs,
perhaps those heading from middle age into old age. But some
operations are also performed on older dogs to keep arthritis
pain in check that are different from procedures they may have
missed while still young. They tend to be recommended when
medical management alone is not doing the trick.

For instance, sometimes after a dog undergoes surgery to sta-
bilize the knee following a rupture of the cranial cruciate ligament, he tears his meniscus, part of the joint cartilage in the knee.

## Is Acupuncture Worth a Try?

If your dog is in significant pain from arthritis and none of
the conventional treatments has provided enough relief, you
may want to consider acupuncture. The empirical evidence
for its benefit is not as strong as it is for other treatments, but
neither is it likely to do any harm.

Once you start exploring avenues of alternative medicine
such as acupuncture, you're headed into uncharted waters in
terms of standards of care and training of personnel. But the
International Veterinary Acupuncture Society, at least, is a
potential resource for finding someone reputable who won't
promise more than he can deliver. Most of the acupuncturists
listed are veterinarians who have passed a demanding course,
and they will perform acupuncture in addition to practicing Western medicine by prescribing drugs and so on. The
Eastern and Western treatments are synergistic rather than
mutually exclusive.

| A New Bone Plate for a Ruptured Cranial Cruciate Ligament |
| --- |
| In the last few years, a new bone plate was developed by a half dozen surgeons, including Dr. Kowaleski and Dr. Randy Boudrieau from Tufts, for one of the most commonly performed surgeries to treat a ruptured cranial cruciate ligament. The procedure is known as the tibial plateau leveling osteotomy (TPLO), and the newly designed plate stabilizes the tibia after it is cut and re-angled during the operation, and holds the bone in place until it heals. The device is now the most commonly employed TPLO plate in use. |

Such a tear can be painful for any dog but is most commonly identified in one who has already broken his cranial cruciate ligament. (Sometimes the meniscus tears at the same time as the ligament.) The solution is surgery to remove the torn portion.

A bad hip may benefit from femoral head ostectomy. The ball component of the hip's ball-and-socket joint is cut away, and the joint is eventually replaced by scar tissue. It won't make the hip normal again, but it will allow movement without pain. A femoral head ostectomy is not always an option for large dogs, who need their joints as well as their muscle to move their hips. But in those dogs up to thirty or forty pounds, the procedure can work quite well, with a low complication rate.

Total joint replacements are becoming more and more common, too, just as they are for people. A dog who develops severe arthritis of the knee some time after he has ruptured his cranial cruciate ligament can now get a knee replacement. A hip replacement also restores normal function quite reliably (in fact it makes hip function in dogs of all sizes superior to hip function after a femoral head ostectomy).

Even total elbow replacements are coming into play. The implant was designed by a veterinarian in Sun Valley, Idaho, who worked with an engineer, and a multicenter trial to see how effectively it works is currently taking place, with Tufts participating. Dr. Kowaleski has already put one of the manmade joints, composed of titanium, into a big yellow Lab named Harley, who could walk only a hundred yards before the operation and is now walking much better. "We don't know yet if there are any pitfalls in the system," Dr. Kowaleski says. "Only about fifty of these elbow replacements have been performed in the world so far. We have to wait to see if the implant wears out or develops other kinds of problems, so the company is waiting before selling it widely. But I think it will come down the pike for general use at some point."

Of course, any artificial joint wears out eventually, just as it does in people, but it can last in a dog seven to ten years—long enough in many cases to avoid a second joint replacement.

## A NEW LEASE ON LIFE

Whether it's medications to keep your dog's stiffening joints more supple, or appropriate weight loss to keep pressure off the joints as your dog moves about, or even a later-in-life operation, arthritis does not have to keep your friend in debilitating pain. Don't hesitate to speak with your veterinarian if you see your dog beginning to have difficulty getting around, because there are many treatment options that would not have been at your disposal even a few years ago. You and your dog can enjoy at least a couple more years of each other's company if you avail yourself of the therapies available.

# 5 Fighting Canine Cancer

HERE IS A tale of two dogs, behind which lies a tale of two dog owners.

**The Ordeal of King.** We once treated a German shepherd named King, who was brought in by his owners with severe weakness to the point of frequent collapse, along with abdominal distention. Upon physical exam, we found that he had very pale gums, almost white. He also had a very weak pulse. It became clear pretty quickly that he had a type of cancer called hemangiosarcoma. Specifically, it was splenic hemangiosarcoma, meaning his spleen was bleeding into his abdomen. That's what was causing the abdominal distention.

We explained to the owners that the first step would be to remove King's spleen. The couple was upset, crying, feeling under a lot of pressure to make the right decision, but not at all sure what to do. They really struggled with the idea of putting an older dog through surgery—King was twelve—especially with a likely outcome of three months' survival.

After jumping on the Internet and trying to get on top of the situation by learning as much about the condition as they could, they decided to go ahead with the procedure, which we scheduled for two days later. We removed the malignancy, giving King the anesthetic support and critical care he needed. He bounced back amazingly quickly and lived an additional six months — the equivalent of a few years in the life of a person. The owners were very proud of their decision. They were especially happy with every single day they got beyond the projected three months.

**The Story of Annie.** By the time Annie's owners brought her in, the mass on the fourteen-year-old shepherd's lower back was the size of a volleyball, literally. The tipping point for their making the hour-long trip from Concord, New Hampshire, to our hospital was that the tumor had ulcerated through the dog's skin, and she began bleeding around the house. The couple was fearful, all the more so when we explained that Annie's was a complicated case. She had a type of cancer known as a soft-tissue sarcoma, and it had reached the point that she would require one or two complicated surgeries and then three weeks of daily radiation therapy — entailing a two-hour round trip every time.

After finding out all that would have been involved to treat Annie, along with the fact that two surgeries and radiation might very well have presented complications of their own, they decided to go not with the most aggressive approach available, but with the kindest approach instead. So we kept Annie as comfortable as possible for as long as possible — six more weeks. When the time came, with our support, the couple decided on euthanasia. They felt very sad, but were glad for their many years with Annie and at peace about not putting her through what they felt would have been a series of risks with few to no guarantees.

The moral of these two tales: in a life-threatening situation, just because there's something technically that we can offer doesn't necessarily mean it's the right thing to do. What may be the correct step for one owner may not be the correct one for another. Ditto for their dogs. Our approach is not to try to shoehorn every dog through a particular treatment protocol or decision tree. You have to take each case as it comes.

With a young dog, the decision making is usually fairly straightforward. As John Berg, DVM, chair of our Department of Clinical Sciences, puts it, "The dog breaks her leg; she has ten good years left; the leg is going to heal if you fix it. The question is more of a straightforward financial one. With an older dog, the question becomes a lot more complicated, more nuanced, so a lot of times the money becomes a secondary consideration and the primary one becomes, 'What's the right thing to do for this faithful companion who has been with me for twelve years?'

"It's our job to guide owners in figuring that out," Dr. Berg says. "It involves working with clients beyond just giving them scientific information. It involves something more human."

Another way of putting it: we try to avoid triumphs of medical expertise over common sense. While it's true that just because a dog is old doesn't mean she shouldn't be treated for a life-threatening condition, it's also true that just because there's something that *can* be done doesn't always mean it *should* be. With their veterinarian's help, owners have to weigh their own ability to deal with difficult treatments or potential complications, in addition to considering their dog's strength and vigor and ability to withstand what might be arduous procedures.

That's what you want to be thinking about as you read through not just this chapter on cancer but also the chapters on heart and kidney disease that follow. We present the "facts," but applying the facts to your particular dog in treating a life-threatening illness is going to depend on your own situation.

By no means should that make you feel discouraged. Most dogs who have life-threatening illnesses are old. If we didn't treat them, we'd be cutting the number of animals we treat in half. And treatment is improving all the time.

Note that the proportions of life-threatening illnesses are somewhat different for people and dogs. In people, the three leading causes of death in old age are heart disease, cancer, and strokes, in that order. In dogs, it's cancer, *then* heart disease, and then kidney disease.

Cancer befalls an estimated 50 percent of dogs over age ten, whereas some 25 to 30 percent of dogs over the age of thirteen end up with heart disease, most often in the form of faulty heart valves that can lead to death through congestive heart failure. For kidney disease, the incidence increases from about two in one hundred for ten-year-old dogs to almost six in one hundred for fifteen-year-old dogs.

No matter what the order, hearing any one of these diagnoses from your dog's veterinarian is unnerving—which may be why we find that all too many people wait too long to bring their dogs in, no matter what treatment on which they ultimately decide. They *suspect* their friend has a dire condition and are afraid to have their suspicions confirmed.

It's an entirely understandable but unfortunate response. Often, depending on the nature of the illness and how early it is diagnosed, much can be done to alleviate pain and sometimes even slow the progression of disease, buying your friend not just more time but more time worth living. Here is a guide to helping your dog get the most out of life for as long as possible once a grave disease such as cancer is suspected and then diagnosed, even if you decide not to go the most aggressive route.

## A CANCER PRIMER

A couple of basic similarities about cancer in dogs and cancer in people:

1. The older the dog, just like the older the human, the more likely cancer is to develop. That is, the more likely a cell will undergo an unwanted mutation in a particular area of the body, run amok in its replication until it forms a mass, or tumor, and finally prove malignant—able to invade and destroy healthy tissue.

2. Not all tumors are cancerous. Many are benign, meaning they have nothing to do with malignancy. A cancer, on the other hand, might not invade only local tissue. It can also spread, or metastasize, when a few cells break off from the larger mass,

travel through the blood, and start multiplying in near or distant body sites, causing life-threatening damage some distance from the cancer's site of origin.

But while the mechanism is essentially the same for dogs and humans, the organs in which cancers, or malignant tumors, typically develop differ between the two species. In both species, cancer can occur anywhere in the body, but the most common cancers in people, in descending order, are those of the skin, lung, breast (women), prostate (men), and colon and rectum. In dogs, the most common cancers include those of the lymph nodes, blood, bones, mammary glands (in females who have not been spayed), and mast cells—cells involved in immunity found throughout the body but which most often form unwanted tumors in the skin.

That's not the biggest difference, however. The major difference comes in cancer *treatment.* In people, the goal is generally to cure. In dogs, a cure is desirable, of course, and frequently possible, as you will see. But the goal is often to extend for as long as possible the time until the cancer makes the pet feel too ill for life to be worth living. (Even King was not made cancer-free; we just pushed back the spread of the cancer.)

It frequently plays out in the way chemotherapy is administered. If chemotherapy is called for to kill tumor cells, dogs are frequently given less of it than people are. People are generally willing to accept the often debilitating side effects of full-force chemo for themselves, because it may buy them years, even decades. But pet owners generally don't feel they have the ethical right to make a dog feel very ill for three to four months with ultra-strong chemotherapy treatment that might buy their pet only a few more months than she would get with a moderate dose. With their veterinarian's guidance, they often approve enough chemo simply to keep the cancer (and the pain it engenders) at bay for as long as possible—anywhere from six months to a year and a half.

Don't be put off. Six to eighteen months wouldn't be much for a person, but for a dog, who has a much shorter life expectancy, it amounts to a significant extension of time. Even the addition of as little as four months could spell an extra spring, summer, or fall. For many devoted owners, an extra one or two good seasons with their dog are priceless.

Of course, before you even decide how to approach treatment, you need to determine that there's a problem.

## WHAT ARE THE SIGNS OF CANCER?

Although signs of cancer do occasionally appear very acutely, more often they are slowly progressive and somewhat insidious. Either way, the Veterinary Cancer Society has identified ten common warning signs that a dog may have cancer and should be taken to the veterinarian for a work-up.

Abnormal swellings that persist or continue to grow
Sores that don't heal
Weight loss
Loss of appetite
Bleeding or discharge from any body opening
Offensive odor
Difficulty eating or swallowing
Hesitation to exercise or loss of stamina
Persistent lameness or stiffness
Difficulty breathing, urinating, or defecating

It is not at all certain that your dog has cancer if she exhibits any of these signs. They are not specific to cancer and could also indicate other conditions, a number of which are not life-threatening. Furthermore, if a change is temporary and reverts back to normal within a few days, chances are cancer is not the issue. For instance, loss of appetite that resolves on its own is most probably not a sign of a malignant tumor. But if a problem lasts at least a week or two and shows no signs of abating, even if it's not on the above list, testing in a doctor's office is warranted. While by no means do all old dogs develop malignant tumors, any departure from normal health or behavior that lasts more than several days should be considered a red flag and checked out. Better to risk finding out your dog has cancer than to miss something until it's too late to treat her effectively. If Annie, the shepherd with the volleyball-sized tumor, had been brought in when her swelling first became apparent, she could have been treated less aggressively and would have had a much better prognosis. Her owners also would have gone through less agony, and perhaps less guilt, in the process.

## MAKING A CANCER DIAGNOSIS

The kinds of tests your veterinarian performs to check for cancer will vary depending on the signs. Diagnosis of a mast cell tumor in or under the skin, for example, may be relatively simple. If the doctor feels a lump, she can simply aspirate some cells and check their appearance under a microscope. Your dog does not need to be asleep or sedated for the procedure. The veterinarian simply sticks in a needle, pulls out some cells along with attendant body fluid, puts the fluid on a slide, and then stains it (the cells are transparent and difficult to see unless they're stained). Upon checking the appearance of the cells, she either makes a diagnosis or sends the slide to a lab for a determination by a board-certified veterinary pathologist—someone who is trained specifically to identify abnormalities in cells and tissues.

But not all bumps in the skin can be diagnosed with a simple aspiration of some cells (more on lumps and bumps later in the chapter). Nor can certain cancers in other parts of the body be definitively diagnosed using this technique. Many cancers cannot even be seen or felt. That's why a veterinarian will often order imaging in the form of X-rays, ultrasound, CT scans, or MRIs. (When a mass *is* found, the veterinarian will often palpate the local and regional lymph nodes. Swelling or enlargement of these nodes may indicate that a tumor has spread.)

None of the imaging tests is definitive for cancer; a mass identified on an ultrasound, for example, isn't automatically cancerous. But such tests can be highly suggestive that a malignant tumor is growing, because they are able to demonstrate features — for example, invasiveness — that suggest malignancy. If that is the case, a biopsy — the gold standard for cancer determination because it is the only truly definitive test — is often the next step.

Where a needle aspirate will collect individual cells, a biopsy is the collection of an actual piece of tissue. The tissue is always sent to be looked at by a board-certified pathologist, rather than the primary care veterinarian, in order to get a close read of the architecture of the tissue at the cellular level. Are multiple clusters of cells clinging together? Are they different shapes and sizes? If the answers to these questions are yes, the answer to whether cancer is present will often be yes. The diagnosis usually takes one to three days, as the tissue must be properly prepared before it is sent off, and then takes a bit of time to read fully.

A dog undergoing a biopsy is, at a minimum, sedated, but usually put under general anesthesia. A biopsy is not an "awake" procedure because removing a chunk of tissue hurts. A dog shouldn't be feeling it — or moving around while the tissue removal is taking place, for that matter.

Be aware that while a biopsy is the gold standard for detecting cancer, there are times when the interpretation is incorrect. The problem is usually one of human error — poor sampling, for instance. The veterinarian misses the tumor by not going in deep enough or taking out too small a piece of tissue. When that's the case, if the biopsy comes back negative for cancer but the doctor strongly suspects that cancer is present because of the dog's history or results of other tests, she will ask herself, "Does this result really fit with what I think is going on?" If it doesn't, the

## Blood Tests Will Not Detect Cancer

Some people have a hard time accepting the fact that blood tests will not screen for cancer. The common scenario goes as follows.

VETERINARIAN: I think your dog has cancer.
DOG GUARDIAN: He just had blood work a month ago.
    Wouldn't that have shown it?
VETERINARIAN: Unfortunately, no.

There's not even a blood marker for cancer of the blood vessels, known as hemangiosarcoma. A dog could have completely normal blood work, in fact, and die suddenly of hemangiosarcoma two days later. (This particular type of cancer can take everyone by surprise. Sometimes the only indication of its presence is a ruptured blood vessel in a vital organ that causes a dog to bleed to death from internal bleeding.)

vet may make a presumptive diagnosis—a diagnosis without biopsy proof but with an accumulation of circumstantial evidence culled from the other tests. Alternatively, the veterinarian may decide to repeat the biopsy.

Sometimes, in instances in which the diagnosis of cancer seems obvious and certain, and the suspected tumor is not treatable, or the owner does not desire treatment, the veterinarian may make a presumptive diagnosis to avoid putting a dog through a biopsy unnecessarily. Why subject a dog to a procedure if it isn't going to lead to a medical solution, anyway?

Note that the same tests used to make presumptive diagnoses can also be used to *stage* a cancer once it has been diagnosed. Staging involves (1) getting a handle on the size of the tumor, (2) learning which local bodily structures the malignancy is invading, and (3) determining whether the tumor has metastasized, or spread, to other parts of the body.

For instance, chest X-rays are very commonly performed because many cancers metastasize to the lungs. That is, in fact, why chest X-rays are the single most common radiograph we perform. Unfortunately, their sensitivity is limited because a tumor in the lungs has to be at least one centimeter (a little less than half an inch) in size before it can be seen. But for that very reason, if the doctor does see a mass on the lungs, it's a very good bet that a cancer in the dog's body is far along.

## Your Own Veterinarian Versus a Cancer Specialist

Your dog's veterinarian is her primary care practitioner, so to speak. Your canine loved one's doctor can handle all the routine exams, shots, and illnesses of her life. Some primary care veterinarians also feel quite comfortable handling certain types of cancer treatment. If your dog is diagnosed with cancer, however, a referral may be made to a veterinary oncologist. Veterinarians who specialize in diagnosing and treating cancer have advanced training in the treatment of malignant tumors. They also may have equipment you won't find in your veterinarian's office. For instance, while some veterinarians are equipped to administer chemotherapy, radiation therapy is virtually always limited to veterinary cancer centers. That's important, because radiation may be recommended after a bout of chemotherapy, before it, or instead of it, depending on the type and location of the cancer. Sometimes radiation is also recommended for benign tumors. If, say, a benign brain tumor is kept from growing via radiation, the mass will be slower to compress healthy brain tissue.

For dog owners who live in or near urban centers, getting to a veterinary oncologist's office isn't a problem. For those in rural areas, reaching the nearest veterinary oncology office could mean driving a great distance.

Indeed, we'll frequently even take a chest X-ray of a very old dog who does not exhibit any signs of cancer but needs an expensive procedure, say, a $2,000 surgery to fix an arthritic knee. If the X-ray suggests that a cancer has spread to the lungs from somewhere else in the body, we want to be able to apprise the dog's owner that the dog has a limited amount of time left — likely a few months or less — and that it may be unwise to elect an expensive or complicated procedure unrelated to the cancer.

Staging the cancer — finding out how large and invasive it is and whether it has spread and to what degree — also informs the course of treatment.

## THE THREE MAIN TREATMENT OPTIONS

Help most often comes in the form of one of the three main cancer fighting tools available: surgery, radiation, or chemotherapy (or a combination of the three).

A dog whose cancer has not spread may just undergo surgery to remove the mass or the affected organ, radiation therapy, or both. These treatments target the primary tumor — the site where the cancer originates   rather than secondary tumors   sites to which the cancer has metastasized.

Surgery — going in and removing the tumor via an operation — cures more cancers than radiation or chemotherapy. That's because cancers that are still small enough to be excised completely with an operation have often not invaded local healthy tissue or spread elsewhere. For that reason, early detection is best — it provides a better chance for saving an animal's life. Even shrinking a small, not-yet-out-of-control tumor with radiation or chemotherapy is easier than trying to shrink a large one that may have already begun to invade healthy tissue around it.

Radiation therapy consists of an invisible beam of radiation directed at the cancer by a sophisticated machine. Dogs have to be brought to a hospital or clinic to have their tumors radiated either every day or every other day (although generally not on weekends) for a period of about three weeks. Each visit doesn't take long and the treatment isn't in any way debilitating. An occasional side effect tends to be a superficial skin burn, akin to a sunburn, that may appear temporarily near the end of the course of radiation. There are also some site-specific side effects that may occur depending on where the tumor is located.

A cancer that has spread or is suspected of having spread may be treated with chemotherapy—the administration of drugs, either orally or intravenously, that destroy rapidly dividing cells throughout the body. Chemotherapy is also used for cancers that involve the blood or lymphatic systems, the most common

---

## Uncommon Cancers Common to Specific Breeds

Just a handful of cancers—lymphoma, mast cell tumors, bone cancer, and a few others discussed at length starting on page 115—affect most dogs. But a few cancers tend to cluster in certain breeds. Why this is so has not been worked out specifically—the molecular genetic evidence is only slowly emerging. But there most assuredly is a hereditary predisposition. Among the more unusual cancers:

**Bladder cancer.** Susceptible breeds: Scottish and West Highland white terriers and, to a lesser degree, Shetland sheepdogs. The risk is eighteen times higher for Scottish terriers than for mixed-breed dogs.

**Histiocytic sarcoma** (which strikes visceral organs like the liver, spleen, and lungs, often at the same time). Susceptible breeds: Flat-coated retrievers, Bernese mountain dogs.

**Cancer of the nail bed.** Susceptible breed: Standard poodle (almost exclusively the black standard poodle).

**Perianal adenocarcinoma.** Susceptible breeds: German shepherds and Arctic Circle breeds, including Siberian huskies and malamutes.

example being canine lymphoma, because by their very nature, they *start out* spread throughout the body rather than localized. Given at two- to three-week intervals, chemo administration takes anywhere from an hour to half a day.

Some of the rapidly dividing cells killed by chemotherapy are cancer cells, of course, but other rapidly growing cells include those that line the gastrointestinal tract and those of the bone marrow and the hair. The death of GI tract cells explains the diarrhea experienced by some people undergoing chemo, while destruction of bone marrow cells explains why anyone getting chemo is more prone to infections, and loss of hair cells speaks to chemo-induced baldness. Again, dogs get fewer of these side effects, because the chemo for them is a lower dose — it's intended to extend life but not necessarily be able to cure the disease. The extra six months to year and a half of life that's commonly achieved for a dog on chemo are often of a very good quality.

We should note that veterinary medicine has become much better than it was even ten years ago at predicting which dogs will be good responders to chemotherapy and radiation treatment. In practical terms, that means some patients likely to respond poorly can be spared the side effects of treatment, while their owners can be spared the costs.

Following is a rundown of the most common types of cancer in dogs, what the treatment for each generally entails, and how likely the particular cancer is to respond to that treatment. The list is by no means exhaustive — cancer can strike any tissue in the body — but these six types make up the majority of cancers that affect older dogs.

**Lymphoma (cancer of the lymph nodes).** In a special fluid, lymph, the lymphatic system carries immune cells called lymphocytes throughout the body to fight off disease-causing organisms such as viruses and bacteria. This system is a key part of the immune system. Running pretty much parallel to the circulatory system that carries blood, it drains tissues of fluid when necessary and deposits fluid as well. The nodes of the lymph system are little nests, so to speak, where lymphocytes are produced, and that's where the cancer occurs. Cancer of the lymph nodes (often mistakenly called glands) can metastasize to various tissues throughout the body, as lymph fluid carries cancerous cells along with it.

An estimated 80 percent of dogs who get lymphoma get what's called the multicentric form — tumors in lymph nodes throughout the body. Certain forms of lymphoma can also affect the GI tract, liver, and bone marrow.

*Breeds reported to have a higher incidence:* boxer, bull mastiff, basset hound, Saint Bernard, Scottish terrier, Airedale, bulldog.

*Signs:* You may notice hard, firm bumps on the underside of your dog's neck or limbs that she finds painful. These enlargements of the lymph nodes will develop over several days to a week. You may also notice that your dog is not herself. Perhaps she isn't eating as much, is losing weight, and is not as active as usual. The signs may be rather vague and nonspecific — but still, you sense that something is wrong.

*Diagnosis:* Often, the veterinarian will perform a lymph node biopsy, although the disease can also be diagnosed with a simple aspirate. The biopsy can distinguish between different subtypes of lymphoma, however, which helps guide treatment and can improve the accuracy of the prognosis.

*Staging:* An abdominal ultrasound will indicate whether the cancer has spread to the liver or other abdominal organs. Because lymphoma can involve the bone marrow, the veterinarian may also perform a bone marrow aspirate, which requires general anesthesia. The prognosis is generally somewhat worse for dogs with bone marrow involvement. That can affect the dog's ability to form red and white blood cells, as well as the platelets responsible for the clotting of blood.

*Treatment:* Because lymphoma most often occurs in its multisite form, chemotherapy is usually the only treatment possible.

*Prognosis:* The remission rate with chemo most often falls in the 70 to 90 percent range. All evidence of the disease is gone, and the dog feels good. The median duration of remission is five to ten months. But within weeks of coming out of remission, most dogs need to be put down. Vets often recommend against a second course of chemo, because it's harder to get a dog back into remission a second time. Even if a new round of chemo

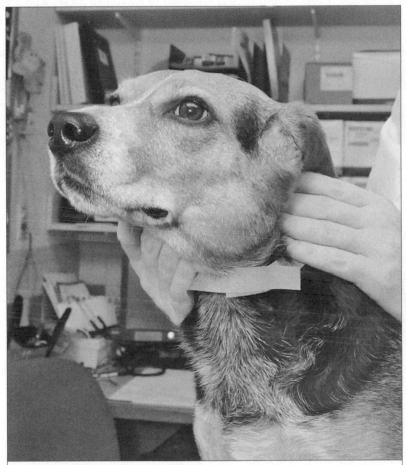

*Firm, hard bumps, usually on the neck or limbs, may be a sign of lymphoma.*

does work, the dog usually won't stay in remission that long on the second go-round.

**Hemangiosarcoma.** Hemangiosarcoma is a cancer of the cells that form blood vessels. It can originate in any tissue that contains blood vessels, but the most common location is the spleen, an organ in the abdominal cavity that stores red blood cells as well as lymphocytes and platelets, and also conducts "house cleaning" of old or damaged red cells. Four out of five cases of hemangiosarcoma occur there, as in the case of the German shepherd King profiled at the beginning of this chapter. Another relatively common site is the right chamber of the heart. Hemangiosarcoma can be particularly dangerous in that organ, because it causes bleeding into the pericardial sac around the heart, and even very small quantities of blood in the sac can affect the heart dramatically, keeping it from filling properly and perhaps leading to heart failure. In other words, it takes much less bleeding for cardiac than for splenic hemangiosarcomas to be life-threatening.

The incidence of the spread of hemangiosarcoma from the blood vessels to other tissues is virtually 100 percent. From the spleen, it typically spreads to the liver, and from the heart, it generally goes to the lungs.

*Breeds reported to have a higher incidence:* Most common in large-breed older dogs, especially German shepherds, golden retrievers, and Labrador retrievers.

*Signs:* Signs vary depending on where in the body hemangiosarcoma develops. If it's in the spleen, there are sometimes no outward symptoms. If it's large enough, however, you might be able to see for yourself that the abdomen is enlarged. The distention of King's abdomen was a telltale clue. A veterinarian is often able to feel it upon palpation of the abdomen.

Sometimes, if the tumor ruptures, it causes bleeding into the abdominal cavity, and the dog becomes weak (another sign that King was afflicted) and collapses or faints. The rupture itself may lead to immediate death. That's especially true if the rupture occurs in a hemangiosarcoma that has taken hold in the heart.

*Diagnosis:* Both types of hemangiosarcoma are presumptively diagnosed with ultrasound. The appearance of the disease is characteristic enough that a pretreatment biopsy is generally unnecessary.

*Staging:* An abdominal ultrasound, in addition to allowing a diagnosis, will suggest whether the cancer has spread from the spleen to the liver or other abdominal organs. A chest X-ray will give some indication as to whether it has spread to the lungs from the heart (and from the spleen as well).

*Treatment:* For splenic hemangiosarcoma, splenectomy — surgical removal of the spleen — is the prime mode of treatment. Just like a person, a dog does not need a spleen to live. If the primary site of hemangiosarcoma is the heart, surgery can be performed there, too, removing affected tissue. But we perform more splenectomies than hemangiosarcoma-related heart surgeries — not just because splenic hemangiosarcoma is more common, not because heart surgery is a little more involved (which it is), not because it costs a little more (which it does), and not because recovery takes a little longer (which it also does), but mainly because people are put off by the idea of heart surgery. People hear "heart" and "cancer" and often make a decision not to treat, even though dogs who undergo the surgery tend to do well and gain time as well as quality of life.

After surgery, chemotherapy is often recommended because the cancer so commonly metastasizes. Unfortunately, the data on whether chemo helps dogs with hemangiosarcoma are somewhat unclear, which probably means that if chemo helps, it doesn't help dramatically. A veterinary oncologist can guide you in making a decision on whether to treat a dog with chemo after her surgery.

*Prognosis:* Survival time after surgery is limited to about three to four months. But they're a very good few months, particularly after spleen removal. Recovery is quick, and the dog is good to go literally within days. Furthermore, during those months, the dog is not wasting away and getting worse. She'll be quite healthy until the cancer turns up somewhere else in the body, when the downturn will likely be fairly rapid and severe.

---

## Fear of Abdominal Surgery

While owners are often afraid of heart surgery for their older dogs, they can also be particularly afraid of abdominal surgery, including abdominal surgery to remove a cancerous spleen. They remember either their own or someone else's tenderness long after a similar operation. Indeed, it can easily take six weeks, and frequently longer, after an abdominal operation for a person to be able to walk again without pain. But that won't be the case for a dog who has had abdominal surgery.

Consider that when a person stands up to walk, she stands on two legs and uses her abdominal muscles to keep from tipping over. But because a dog walks on four legs instead of two, her legs do all the balancing. All her abdominal muscles have to do is hold in her organs, not expand and contract every time she takes a step. Thus, cutting through a dog's abdominal muscles to get inside to an abdominal organ like the spleen doesn't hinder her mobility. She's up and around pretty quickly, generally walking the day of the surgery and back to her normal self within a week to ten days.

*Note:* If surgery for hemangiosarcoma is performed on the heart rather than the spleen, the incision is through the chest instead of the abdomen. We used to wrap a dog's chest in bandages after chest surgery in the belief that it helped healing by contributing to a more comfortable recovery. But we found that wasn't the case. In addition, chest wraps inadvertently applied too tightly impaired breathing, and we wanted to avoid that mistake. Now, we just cover the incision, and the dog recovers much more smoothly, with a greatly diminished chance of having respiratory distress.

One caveat: not all tumors in the heart, or the spleen for that matter, are hemangiosarcoma. Before you make a decision to treat or not to treat, it's important that your veterinarian, or a veterinary oncologist, run tests that help to determine the nature of the mass. If a splenic tumor turns out to be benign, whatever the treatment, the prognosis tends to be quite good.

**Osteosarcoma (bone cancer).** One of the most painful types of cancer, osteosarcoma, or bone cancer, can occur anywhere in the body, although it most commonly affects the ends of the long bones of the legs, with the front legs affected almost twice as often as the hind legs. The long bone of the lower front leg—the radius—is the site most often affected. The disease causes great pain and lameness, which can occur all of a sudden or progressively. And in 98 percent of cases, the cancer spreads from the site of origin to other parts of the body—usually the lungs.

*Breeds reported to have a higher incidence:* Osteosarcoma is far more common in large to giant breeds than medium-sized and small breeds. Older dogs are not the only ones who get this type of cancer. The average age of onset is about seven, but dogs as young as a year old may become affected, too.

*Signs:* The telltale signs are lameness and a firm, often painful enlargement at the site of the tumor. The enlargement will be easy to see if the mass is in a bone in the lower part of the limb, where there is little overlying soft tissue. Tumors in the upper limb usually cause lameness, too, but are not visible to the owner.

*Diagnosis:* Diagnosis is often presumptive rather than based on biopsy. That is, if a characteristic bony abnormality is seen on an X-ray of a limb of a large-breed dog, and especially if the mass is in a classic spot like the distal radius, or "wrist," the veterinarian may advise treating for bone cancer without confirming the diagnosis with a biopsy. (That said, you, as caretaker of your dog, should always feel free to say you want a biopsy if you feel uncertain.)

*Staging:* Since virtually all bone cancers metastasize, and

## Cigarette Smoke and Other Environmental Carcinogens

A dog "parent" will often ask us this question in one form or another:

Q: I've had ten dogs, and eight have died of cancer. Is it something in the environment?
A: Possibly.

If anyone in your household smokes, so does your dog, in essence—and, apparently, the greater her risk for cancer. Research at Tufts's Cummings School has shown so far that cats living in homes with smokers are at increased risk for lymphoma, and perhaps oral cancer as well. Specifically, they are almost two and a half times as likely to develop lymphoma as cats in nonsmoking households, with the level of risk increasing with the duration and amount of exposure to environmental tobacco smoke. On that basis, it's more than reasonable to assume that dogs who regularly inhale tobacco smoke may be at a similar risk.

It may not just be secondhand smoke—smoke your dog breathes in after you exhale—that causes a problem. Evidence is starting to come to light that *third*hand smoke—the tobacco toxin leftovers that stick on skin, hair, drapes, and so on—can also make its way to your dog's lungs and set the stage for cancer.

Other environmental carcinogens to which your canine companion might be exposed include lawn herbicides and insecticides, in addition to other chemicals. Transitional cell carcinoma of the bladder, a common and difficult-to-treat tumor of the canine bladder, has been linked to insecticide and herbicide exposure. And a study in Italy showed a relationship between lymphoma risk and dog owners' use of chemicals such as paint and solvents.

*continued on page 123*

since the most common site for the cancer to spread is the lungs, the veterinarian will most likely recommend a chest X-ray. Ninety-five percent of the time, the X-ray will come back normal, because at the time of bone cancer diagnosis, the metastasis in the lungs is still microscopic. If a mass *is* seen in the lungs, the prognosis is worse than usual.

*Treatment:* The standard treatment for osteosarcoma is amputation of the affected limb. The amputation is to keep the dog comfortable. That is, it won't cure the cancer or ultimately save your dog's life, but it will eliminate the pain. That's key, because pain from bone cancer is extremely difficult to control even with

---

### Cigarette Smoke and Other Environmental Carcinogens, *continued from page 122*

Living in industrial areas also appears associated with increased lymphoma incidence. It isn't terribly surprising that, as is true in people, some canine cancers appear to cluster in specific geographic areas. The causes are unknown, but exposure to high concentrations of various carcinogens is a possible explanation.

Obviously, it's best not to allow smoking in your home, and your dog shouldn't be allowed on the lawn until after you can be sure the herbicides and insecticides you have applied have been absorbed and can't affect her. For safe measure, the same goes for lawn fertilizers.

It's not clear whether the chemicals get into the body through ingestion (perhaps dogs lick their paws after walking on the grass) or dermal absorption (absorption through the skin). Either way, why take any chances?

We'd like to be able to say that using organic materials makes the lawn safe, but while it sounds logical, the research hasn't been conducted. To play it safest, don't use chemicals on your lawn at all, and learn to live with some weeds and a less lush look.

medications. In addition, amputation completely eliminates the primary tumor—which prevents any possibility of the cancer recurring locally.

People are often understandably concerned about a dog on three legs; there's a psychological component with amputation that's not present for most other surgeries we do. But what's very important to recognize is that the psychological component is completely the person's. While appearance is emotionally very weighted for many people, dogs don't care how they look; cosmetic and aesthetic considerations are nonissues for our canine friends.

Many people ask us whether their dog will become depressed upon amputation, or whether their dog will be angry at them for having one of their limbs amputated. The answer, on both counts, is no. A dog would not even be able to connect what happens in the operating room with you—her logic and reasoning capabilities don't go that way.

Much more important than any aesthetic considerations on the part of a dog's owner is that a dog can usually adapt quite well after amputation, especially if it's an amputation of a hind leg, since she carries most of her weight on her front legs. Perhaps that's the reason that Dr. Berg says, "I've done many, many amputations, and I've never yet had someone who regretted the decision."

The only dogs who do not make good candidates for amputation are heavyset giant breeds, such as Saint Bernards or Newfoundlands, with a tumor in one of their front legs or dogs with *severe* orthopedic or neurologic problems unrelated to the cancer. They need all their legs. For such dogs, the trick is to remove the cancer but spare the limb.

A small number of cancer treatment centers offer limb-sparing surgery—surgery in which only the bone tumor and a small amount of surrounding bone and soft tissue are removed, rather than the entire limb. The challenge with this operation is that removed bone must be replaced, either with a bone graft or by moving a neighboring segment of bone into the defect. It's important to note that limb-sparing surgery is challenging, expensive, and somewhat complication-prone. That said, it can be an excellent option for the few dogs who are poor candidates for amputation.

*Prognosis:* After amputation, and with no chemotherapy, survival time ranges from three to nine months, with an average of about five. The quality of those remaining months is excellent. Even if the osteosarcoma has spread to the lungs, it has to become quite advanced before it makes a dog feel sick. If chemotherapy is applied after the amputation, average survival time goes up to about a year. (The evidence of chemo's benefit

*Amputation doesn't carry the same psychological weight for dogs as for people. They don't care how they look, as long as they can get around.*

in this case is clearer than with hemangiosarcoma.) A year is a long time in a dog's life—amputation followed by chemo is well worth considering.

**Mammary cancer.** A female dog has five pairs of mammary glands—ten nipples. The back glands—the four closest to the tail—are the ones most likely to end up with malignant tumors. People often don't realize how far back the mammary glands go. One standard poodle we came to know, a dowager named Rosie, wasn't referred to us until her owner noted a large mass between her hind legs while rubbing the dog's belly one day. Rosie had been leaving drops of blood around the house for several weeks, which the owner couldn't account for (and to which she turned a blind eye, because she was afraid of getting bad news). But when she saw the large, globular bump, ulcerated and dripping blood, there was no denying that the dog had to be brought in.

*Breeds reported to have a higher incidence:* It's not about breed so much as about whether the dog was spayed, and when. A dog who was spayed before her first heat has virtually no chance of ending up with mammary cancer, but her risk rises significantly if spaying takes place after her first heat. In fact, any potential cancer-sparing benefit is lost after the third heat—three estrus cycles, and a dog is just as likely to get a malignant tumor of the mammary glands as a much older dog who has been through many heats and has had multiple litters of puppies. That's why veterinarians don't see many cases of mammary cancer in the United States, while in Europe and other places around the world, it's more common. Spaying is much more the norm here.

*Signs:* You should give your older female dog "breast exams" every four months or so to check for unexpected lumps or bumps. Don't just check the nipple and right below it, but also the whole area surrounding it, feeling carefully beneath the skin. Any mammary bump is a potential cause for worry. Even small, potentially benign masses should be removed, as there is some evidence that they could become malignant.

*Diagnosis:* Most mammary masses are removed without a presurgical biopsy and are then submitted for pathologic examination.

*Staging:* A chest X-ray before surgery will look for metastasis to the lungs, but as with other cancers, any spread to the lungs might not be picked up at the time of imaging because there will still be too few cancer cells to form more than a microscopic mass. That said, if the tumor at the mammary gland is bigger than three centimeters (or around at least two inches), statistically, it is more likely to have already spread and prove fatal. The same is true if the cancer has spread beyond the mammary gland and into a nearby lymph node. Rosie's cancer, large as it was, hadn't yet invaded adjacent healthy tissue or spread.

*Treatment:* Surgery is the standard treatment. It's often relatively minor as surgeries go if just a single, small tumor is present. Large tumors and multiple tumors can require more major operations. Chemotherapy might also be advised for large tumors, as well as tumors known to have spread to lymph nodes or the lungs, tumors that have invaded blood vessels or the lymphatic system right at the site of the primary tumor, and tumors that appear to be highly malignant on microscopic examination. Unfortunately, to date, few data are available to say definitively whether chemotherapy is beneficial. In Rosie's case, the owner opted not to go with chemo, because we were able to remove the tumor in one surgery with clean margins.

*Prognosis:* With mammary cancer, there's a 50/50/50 rule. Out of one hundred dogs with a bump in a mammary gland, 50 percent will have malignancies. Of that 50 percent, 50 percent will spread to other body tissues and ultimately prove fatal. Translation: approximately 25 percent of bumps found in dogs' mammary glands are fatal. The ones that are not are usually small tumors that have not yet spread. So the prognosis for dogs with mammary cancer is highly variable, ranging from as little as a few months to a complete cure. Rosie was one of the lucky ones. She came through her surgery just fine and lived another year and a half before she developed kidney failure — the ultimate cause of her demise when she reached the ripe age of fifteen.

**Mast cell tumors.** Mast cell tumors are one of the most common cancers of dogs. Mast cells are found throughout your dog's body. They are immune cells that participate in normal inflammatory responses. Thus, mast cell malignancies can occur in virtually any tissue. But they most commonly originate in the skin or the subcutaneous fat just under the skin, appearing as lumps or bumps.

The majority of skin bumps in dogs are benign, but some can be very serious and difficult to treat. Deeper bumps — those beneath the skin rather than in it — are the ones that are most often cancerous. You can tell that a bump is beneath the skin if the skin slides over it. Also, in the case of a mast cell tumor, the bump may feel gelatinous rather than hard or fixed. If a bump moves *with* the skin, on the other hand, it's in the skin.

Mast cell tumors can have a variety of appearances; there's no set characteristic. For instance, those that are subcutaneous, or beneath the skin, are often ill-defined, while those within the skin are occasionally associated with skin reddening. In some cases, the tumor will grow rapidly, ulcerate through the skin, and bleed.

That said, you should never diagnose on your own. Bumps that look benign may not be, and vice versa.

*Breeds reported to have a higher incidence:* boxers, Boston terriers, Labrador retrievers, beagles, schnauzers, and Shar-Peis.

*Signs:* Any new lumps or bumps on your older dog's body should prompt a visit to the veterinarian. Even a small, seemingly innocuous bump may be the start of a malignancy that can invade surrounding tissue and spread to vital organs. Thus, part of your responsibility as the guardian of an older dog is to regularly go over her for new bumps, not just on her flank and other easily seen body parts, but also in all her nooks and crannies—her "arm" pits, in the folds of her neck, and so on. It doesn't have to be done every week, but it should be done at least every couple of months.

*Diagnosis:* The veterinarian will do a needle aspirate. Even in normal tissue there will be the occasional mast cell, since mast cells are everywhere in the body. But if it's a mast cell tumor, a stained slide will show sheets of mast cells. A needle aspirate may also show that the lump is simply a lipoma—a growth of benign fatty tissue.

It's very important here not to cut corners. We treated an eight-year-old boxer named Gus whose owners took him to their veterinarian because they noticed five smallish, similar-looking

---

### Is the Cancer a Sarcoma or a Carcinoma?

Why are they called hemangio*sarcoma* and osteo*sarcoma?* A sarcoma is a cancer that takes hold in connective tissue, such as bone or lymph tissue (or cartilage or muscle). The prefix gives the name of the specific spot in which the tumor has arisen. Thus, bone cancer is osteosarcoma ("osteo" is Greek for bone).

A *carcinoma* is a cancer of epithelial cells. These are cells that both cover the lining of any body surface, internal or external, and also comprise a number of internal organs, for example, the lungs, the liver, and the kidneys. Thus, for example, a carcinoma could arise in the lining of the oral cavity or, say, the GI tract or develop in the lungs.

There is also a third kind of cancer called a round cell tumor, because the cancer cells look round under a microscope. This type of malignancy generally arises from cells found in multiple tissues of the body. Lymphoma and mast cell cancer are common examples of round cell tumors.

## New Promise for Treating Mast Cell Tumors

A recent development in the treatment of mast cell tumors is the introduction of a new class of drugs that acts differently from chemotherapy. Whereas chemotherapeutic drugs work by directly damaging a cell's genetic material, these new drugs interfere with the body's messaging systems that control the division and proliferation of cells. In addition, unlike most chemotherapeutic agents, these drugs can be administered orally and therefore be given at home. One that has recently reached the market is toceranib phosphate (Palladia). It is beginning to be widely used by veterinary oncologists not just for the treatment of mast cell tumors, but also several other canine cancers.

lumps in various spots on his body. They were all soft and not painful to the touch. The vet aspirated two of them, saw that they looked fine under a microscope—no cancerous cells—and sent Gus home with a clean bill of health. But over a three-month-period, Gus's family found that two of the lumps that had *not* been aspirated doubled in size. The family brought Gus back to the doctor, who then aspirated the two growing lumps and found that they were indeed mast cell tumors. Precious time had been lost.

*Staging:* The veterinarian may order a chest X-ray to try to determine whether the malignancy has spread to the lungs. She will also palpate and possibly aspirate the regional lymph node(s) to check for metastasis. Along with working to stage the cancer, she will send a tumor sample to a pathologist to allow for grading based on the tumor's microscopic characteristics. Termed histolic grading, this step may be performed prior to surgery, or it may be performed once the mass is surgically removed. Grade 1 is the least serious tumor. The tumor typically doesn't spread; it tends to remain a local phenomenon, invading just the surrounding tissue. A grade 2 mast cell tumor metastasizes approximately 20 percent of the time, while a grade 3 mass almost invariably metastasizes. The overwhelming majority of mast cell tumors are grade 1 or 2. Both of Gus's, in fact, were a grade 2.

*Treatment:* Grade 1 and 2 tumors will be removed with wide margins of normal tissue around them — mast cell tumors are notorious for their ability to deeply invade nearby tissue. Whereas most tumors call for a one-centimeter margin around the cancer, in this case, we try to get a two-centimeter margin, almost a full inch. If we are unable to get a two-centimeter margin (perhaps the cancer is in a spot with very little adjacent tissue to allow closure of the wound, such as on the paw), we consider radiation therapy after the surgery to treat whatever part of the tumor might be left over. Mast cell tumors are very responsive to radiation. Gus did not require radiation treatment. We were able to get a two-centimeter margin around every side of each of the tumors, confident of having completely excised the cancerous cells.

Grade 3 tumors tend to be associated with short survival times and, for that reason, are not always treated; the expense and postsurgical recuperation are often not warranted. We don't want to put a dog through surgery for so little return. In addition, grade 3s tend to degranulate when they're operated on, meaning cells in the tumor break open and release histamine and other substances that can cause gastric ulcerations (even if the tumor is not near the abdomen), in addition to other problems. In those cases that surgery *is* performed on grade 3 tumors, antihistamines are often given prior to surgery to help prevent these problems.

*Prognosis:* If the tumor is grade 1 or 2, it is likely to respond well to surgery and, if necessary, radiation. And it will not tend to interfere with your dog's lifespan, whereas dogs with grade 3 tumors often live a few months at most, regardless of treatment.

As of this writing, Gus is eight months out of surgery with no sign of any mast cell tumor recurrence. But he has been marked as a dog who does develop them, so his owners will have to monitor his body particularly closely for the rest of his life to detect any lumps for timely aspiration as soon as they become visible.

**Soft tissue sarcoma.** Soft tissue sarcomas arise from connective tissue in muscles, nerves, and the like. They often appear in the limbs, trunk, head, and neck. Overall, soft tissue sarcomas have a 20 percent chance of spreading from their site of origin. They are locally invasive tumors, much like mast cell tumors, that can often be cured with surgery, sometimes with the addition of radiation therapy.

*Breeds reported to have a higher incidence:* Any dog breed may be affected by a soft tissue sarcoma.

*Signs:* Soft tissue sarcomas typically are soft to firm, steadily growing masses beneath the skin. They may feel immovable — fixed to deeper tissues. On occasion, they can extend through the overlying skin and cause ulceration and bleeding, as did Annie's, the fourteen-year-old shepherd mentioned near the beginning of the chapter. They typically don't cause pain, and owners don't necessarily bring in their dogs until the tumor is huge (again, like Annie's). That's a mistake. The bigger the tumor, the harder to treat, which is why a lump should be checked early.

*Diagnosis:* Occasionally, these tumors can be diagnosed with a needle aspirate. More often, however, the diagnosis is established by biopsy. Chest X-rays for potential lung metastases are obtained prior to treatment.

*Treatment:* Management of a soft tissue sarcoma is similar to that of mast cell tumors. The first choice of treatment is wide surgical excision. In some cases, amputation is necessary, particularly for advanced tumors located in the lower part of a limb. Surgeons attempt to obtain one- to two-centimeter margins of normal tissue around the tumor. Radiation is usually recommended for incompletely excised tumors.

New to the treatment arsenal for soft tissue sarcomas is metronomic chemotherapy. Traditionally, chemotherapy is administered intravenously at two- to three-week intervals, so that normal, healthy tissue can recover between doses. With metronomic therapy, low doses of drugs are administered orally and given daily or every other day. An advantage of metronomic therapy is that it can be administered at home, by the owner. Preliminary research results suggest that this form of therapy can dramatically reduce the risk for tumor recurrence following surgery. The value of metronomic therapy is also being investigated for a variety of other types of canine tumors.

*Prognosis:* The prognosis for soft tissue sarcoma is often excellent; surgically excisable tumors can potentially be cured. The response to radiation therapy can also be excellent. With adequate doses, the majority of tumors can be controlled well beyond a year. One dog we treated, a Labradoodle named Daisy, lived joyfully and actively for two and a half years after we removed a soft tissue sarcoma on her side and then administered radiation treatments.

# 6 Heart Disease: Not About Holding the Butter

PEOPLE FREAK OUT at the very concept of heart failure. They're used to the word "attack," as in "heart attack," but they hear the word "failure," and they assume they're going to have to immediately put the dog to sleep. They think it means the heart has failed completely and all is over. But once we sit down to explain that heart failure means fluid in the lungs because of a heart pumping problem, and that there are medications to get their pet through the crisis and also extend life and even quality of life, they become engaged in working through the treatment options. We can't tell up front whether it's going to be three months or three years, but with good care and dedicated monitoring, a dog can go on for a long time.

We are so happy to work with owners who are able and willing to be on the front lines (like the owners of Brandy in Chapter 1). You might even keep a dog out of the hospital, or at least potentially avoid repeat hospitalizations, if you give vigilant care and bring in the dog for scheduled monitoring appointments rather than through the emergency room.

— *Suzanne Cunningham, DVM, Cardiology Assistant Professor,
Diplomate of the American College of Veterinary Internal
Medicine (Cardiology)*

CANINE HEART DISEASE is rarely about the clogging of arteries with cholesterol-containing plaques, and rarely do dogs experience heart attacks, as Dr. Cunningham makes clear.

Rather, heart disease in most dogs is most often about a deterioration of the valves that control the flow of blood between the heart's four chambers (see box on page 139 for the exceptions). When a valve deteriorates, it no longer closes as tightly as it should after each heartbeat, so some blood ends up flowing backward instead of going forward and out from the heart to all the body's tissues, like it's supposed to. Through a stethoscope, the backward flow is heard as a murmur—a blowing or swooshing sound.

The gradual degeneration of heart valves is commonly called chronic valvular disease. It accounts for perhaps 75 to 80 percent of all heart disease in dogs and is quite common in older ones. In fact, by the time a dog turns ten, there's a one-in-five chance that he will have developed a heart murmur, and the cause is very often a faulty valve. Once the valve deteriorates to the point that there's a fluid backup in the body, it means that chronic valvular disease has progressed to heart failure.

## HOW YOU CAN TELL SOMETHING IS WRONG

While a veterinarian can pick up heart disease with a stethoscope, how can you tell there's a problem on your own? It's important to take your dog in right away rather than simply have the condition diagnosed during your pet's routine physical, which might be several months away. There are different signs to look for, depending on which side of the heart the valve problem occurs.

### Left-Sided Congestive Heart Failure

If the deterioration takes place on the left side of the heart, in what is known as the mitral valve (the valve that most often becomes diseased), the result will be *left*-sided congestive heart failure. High pressure in the heart's left atrium backs up into the lungs, causing fluid (pulmonary edema fluid) to leak out of the blood vessels there and into the air spaces of the lung. As edema accumulates in the lung, the dog may develop the following symptoms:

- Coughing (often at night)
- Fainting or collapse
- Becoming winded more easily
- More panting and exhaustion upon exertion

If the situation becomes bad enough, breathing becomes labored even at rest. In addition, the body as a whole does not receive enough oxygen, and death may ensue without emergency medical treatment.

### Right-Sided Congestive Heart Failure

Deterioration on the right side of the heart, in what is called the tricuspid valve, results in *right*-sided congestive heart failure, which manifests itself differently:

- Abdominal distention
- Difficulty breathing from fluid deposited not in the lungs but in the chest or abdominal cavity

No matter on which side the problem develops, the signs you notice at home won't say exactly where your dog is in terms of valvular disease progression. For instance, although a cough can result once congestive heart failure has taken hold, coughing in dogs with chronic valvular disease also often *precedes* the development of heart failure, as the enlarged left atrium can put pressure on the windpipe.

As chronic valvular disease leads into heart failure, your dog's breathing will become more labored, and he may exhibit a reluctance to lie down in certain positions, say, on his side, because that would make it more difficult to breathe. The condition is called orthopnea. Unwanted weight loss and muscle wasting can occur, too. This typically affects dogs with right-sided or end-stage heart failure.

Of course, you want to get your dog to see the vet well before that stage. Granted, none of these signs, not even any of the later ones, is specific to heart disease, but they all certainly warrant a visit to the doctor's for a listen with a stethoscope and, perhaps, follow-up testing.

## CONFIRMING THE PROBLEM

When you bring your dog to the veterinarian, he will place a stethoscope on different parts of your dog's chest to evaluate the sounds over the heart's four valves (just as your physician does with you). Veterinarians have a grading scale from one to six to quantify a murmur's severity, similar to physicians' grading scale for people. The louder the murmur, the higher the number.

And, not surprisingly, the louder the murmur, the more severe the backward blood leak often is, so tracking changes over time can provide important information and determine whether further evaluation, and possibly treatment, is necessary.

---

### Breeds Most Prone to Chronic Valvular Disease

While any breed may develop valvular heart disease, it is most common in small- to medium-sized dogs, particularly dachshunds, poodles, Malteses, cocker spaniels, miniature schnauzers, Chihuahuas, and Cavalier King Charles spaniels. Virtually all Cavalier King Charles spaniels end up with valvular heart disease; fifty percent of that breed develop a murmur by age five, and more than 90 percent by age ten.

Males are more predisposed to chronic valvular disease than females (small-breed males are up to twice as likely to get it as their female counterparts), and the disease may progress more quickly in males, although the reason for this is unclear.

The progression of chronic valvular disease is usually quite slow, and your dog may first show signs that are nowhere near out-and-out heart failure. Granted, a dog can develop a sudden worsening of the disease if he suffers a rupture of one of the chords that anchors the mitral valve in place. That may result in an abrupt onset of cough, difficulty breathing, or collapse, all signs of the need for emergency veterinary attention. But that is uncommon. Typically, valvular deterioration is a gradual process, occurring over the course of time. Many dogs live with it for several years and eventually die from something else altogether. We see that happen quite frequently.

In fact, if a murmur is only at a grade I or II, you won't even notice any signs at home that would prompt you to bring your dog in. The veterinarian may pick it up during a routine exam, and all he will often need to do is periodically monitor the situation — and make sure you are aware of it so you can check for behavior changes at home that could indicate a worsening condition and perhaps the need to initiate treatment.

On the other hand, a grade I or II murmur can be missed on a listen with a stethoscope, so *you* may very well end up being the "first responder" to your dog's heart disease by noticing new, untoward symptoms. By that point, the murmur will likely have already reached a grade III or IV. Once a dog's murmur reaches that stage, or if any more obvious signs of persistent cough, respiratory difficulty, or exercise intolerance are noted, further testing may be warranted in the form of a chest X-ray. A chest X-ray will allow the doctor to determine whether your dog's heart is enlarged and whether any evidence of actual heart failure is present. If the heart is not particularly enlarged, your vet may simply recommend further monitoring of the murmur and possibly repeating the chest X-ray every six to eight months.

If the chest X-ray does show significant heart enlargement, a visit to a veterinary cardiologist may be recommended, where your friend is likely to undergo an echocardiogram. That's simply an ultrasound of the heart that gives a more detailed look

## Not All Heart Disease in Dogs Is About Faulty Valves

While the lion's share of heart disease in dogs is chronic valvular disease, a couple of other types of canine heart disease also bear mentioning.

**Dilated cardiomyopathy** is a disease not of the heart valves but of the heart muscle, resulting in progressive enlargement of the heart chambers and a reduced ability of the heart to contract vigorously enough with each beat. That means not enough blood—and not enough of the oxygen and nutrients it carries—reaches all the body's tissues. Onset most often occurs in middle age rather than during the geriatric years. Dogs may develop weakness, intolerance to exercise, arrhythmias (irregular heartbeats), fainting, congestive heart failure, or even sudden death. Unlike with valvular disease, dogs most commonly affected are *large* breeds, including Doberman pinschers, Great Danes, Irish wolfhounds, boxers, and Newfoundlands (cocker spaniels are affected, too, the exception to the large-breed rule). As many as half of all Dobermans develop dilated cardiomyopathy, and up to half of them die suddenly, with that being the first and only sign of heart disease.

Because the disease is often not characterized by a loud heart murmur, it can be difficult to diagnose on a physical exam—which is why we feel strongly that older dogs of affected breeds should be examined by a veterinarian at least twice yearly. The doctor can look for potential signs of the disease other than a murmur, including alterations in pulse. If signs of a heart murmur or arrhythmia are in fact noted, further evaluation with diagnostic imaging is warranted. In the event of a diagnosis, your veterinarian may prescribe anti-arrhythmic medications, beta blockers, or ACE inhibitors. Beta blockers and ACE inhibitors have not been extensively

*continued on page 141*

than an X-ray can. It shows a picture of the heart pumping blood in real time, allowing an assessment of the degree to which the valves are functioning properly and to what degree blood is flowing backward rather than forward because of a valve's inability to close properly. An echocardiogram also allows for checking the vigor of the contraction of the heart muscle and may reveal enlargement of specific heart chambers or the presence of fluid around the heart—or lungs. The combination of findings from the echocardiogram and chest X-ray will allow the cardiologist to predict how close your dog is to heart failure and determine whether any treatment or lifestyle changes are necessary. An ECG and a blood pressure measurement may also be included in the mix to help make a determination about how to proceed with treatment.

## TREATMENT OPTIONS

Unfortunately, as of yet, no treatment has been proven to *cure* chronic valvular disease or even to delay the onset of congestive heart failure. Treatment is more about improving your pet's quality of life by helping the heart muscle function in spite of the incompetent valve. For instance, if your dog coughs after the development of valvular disease but prior to the onset of heart failure, he might be prescribed a cough suppressant and have a limit put on his exercise. You may also be advised not to pick up your dog from underneath the chest, as that will only push an enlarged heart upward and put more pressure on his airways. And the vet might suggest using a head halter or harness instead of a neck collar to avoid eliciting a cough by exerting pressure on your dog's trachea.

If chest X-rays determine that your dog has fluid in his lungs and therefore has progressed to heart failure, diuretics such as furosemide (Lasix) might be prescribed to get excess fluid out of circulation and relieve the lungs of their excess fluid burden. An ACE inhibitor like Enalapril may be prescribed as well. It will di-

## Not All Heart Disease in Dogs Is About Faulty Valves, *continued from page 139*

studied in dogs in the early stages of dilated cardiomyopathy, but since they have been shown to dramatically slow the progression of the disease and delay the onset of heart failure in people, a fair number of veterinary cardiologists, including those at Tufts, are willing to give these drugs a try. As long as the veterinarian makes the decision to prescribe on a case-by-case basis after careful consideration, it's a reasonable approach. The medications must be started slowly, particularly beta blockers, with a careful increase in dose over time. Some dogs actually do worse on beta blockers, at least initially.

Be aware that because dilated cardiomyopathy is an inherited disease, affected dogs should not be bred.

**Arrhythmogenic right ventricular cardiomyopathy,** also called boxer cardiomyopathy, is primarily seen not only in middle-aged to older boxers (as many as one out of three boxers are estimated to have some form of this disease) but also in bulldogs. Like dogs with dilated cardiomyopathy, dogs with this condition may develop enlarged heart chambers. But many dogs with structurally normal hearts end up with life-threatening arrhythmias, specifically, premature heartbeats from the lower chambers of the heart. The arrhythmias can result in symptoms ranging from weakness to fainting to sudden death. If your veterinarian detects an arrhythmia with a stethoscope, we strongly recommend further evaluation and monitoring. You may be referred to a veterinary cardiologist, who might get a twenty-four-hour ECG with a small device called a Holter monitor that your dog will wear at home. That will gauge the severity of the arrhythmia and help assess whether it requires medical treatment.

We have had some very good results with dogs diagnosed with boxer cardiomyopathy. One of them was Sparky, who

*continued on page 143*

late constricted blood vessels and help further relieve the work the heart has to do. As a preventive measure, some veterinarians may even recommend an ACE inhibitor once severe heart enlargement is noted, but before it's clear that the lungs are holding fluid. Research has not shown a clear benefit to prescribing an ACE inhibitor at that stage, but numerous studies at Tufts and elsewhere *have* shown that ACE inhibitors help control heart failure and improve the quality of life in dogs afflicted with it.

Some drugs given to dogs with congestive heart failure directly improve the ability of the heart to pump. These include digoxin (Lanoxin and Digitek) and a newer one called pimobendan (Vetmedin). Digoxin, derived from the foxglove plant, has been used to treat heart failure for centuries, but it is associated with several significant side effects and requires close monitoring. Pimobendan has been on the market for only a couple of years, but it has dramatically improved the treatment of heart failure in dogs (including Brandy the dachshund). In Japan, it's even allowed to be used for people.

Skepticism of the use of pimobendan in people persists in the United States as well as other countries, because although it was shown to improve quality of life for those with heart failure, similar drugs have such dangerous side effects that they can cause death before heart failure does. Also, in dogs with chronic valvular disease, the heart muscle often maintains its ability to contract, or pump blood, fairly normally until the very late stages of congestive heart failure, so why give a medication to improve its pumping ability?

The answer: recent studies have shown that pimobendan improves not only quality of life but also survival times in dogs with congestive heart failure. (In one multicenter trial, dogs given pimobendan lived twice as long as dogs who weren't.) We have seen many a dog on the verge of being euthanized by their human guardians because of concerns about quality of life with congestive heart failure—but who were granted a second lease on life with this drug.

## Not All Heart Disease in Dogs Is About Faulty Valves, *continued from page 141*

we first started seeing in 2005. He was out walking with his owner and collapsed suddenly on the sidewalk. The owner, a petite woman without the strength to carry a dog, had to leave Sparky where he was, go home and get the car, then get help moving him into the back seat for a ride to the emergency room.

We put him on the usual drug therapy, but he wasn't responding, so we put him on another combination of drugs that stabilized his arrhythmia. He went, literally, from having a near sudden death episode to almost going into a remission of sorts. His energy level was always high; Sparky bounced around every time we saw him.

After almost four years of doing well, he came in with what looked like fainting spells. But he wasn't fainting. The episodes were found to be seizures, having nothing to do with his heart. Sparky was now thirteen and had developed a brain tumor.

The owner did not have the money to proceed with radiation, which was the treatment needed (she had already spent so much over the years taking impeccable care of his heart), so we helped her get the money from an "angel fund" (see Chapter 8 for more about paying for dog care). The dog lived another six happy months after that, with his heart holding out perfectly well while he was anesthetized for radiation treatment. When he finally succumbed, it had nothing to do with heart disease.

Another boxer, Elvis, also came to us with boxer cardiomyopathy. We brought it under control, but then documented long pauses in heart rhythm—a different kind of arrhythmia—that were causing the dog to collapse. The owner opted for a pacemaker, which we inserted on Christmas Eve 2006, and Elvis lived another whole year.

## The Anatomy of Canine Heart Disease

A dog has four heart valves, just like a person: the *mitral* valve, which separates the two chambers on the left side of the heart (the left atrium and the left ventricle); the *tricuspid* valve, which separates the chambers on the right (the right atrium and ventricle); the *aortic* valve, which leads from the left ventricle to the aorta (the artery that pushes blood to the rest of the body); and the *pulmonic* valve, which leads from the right ventricle to the pulmonary artery (the artery that pumps blood to the lungs).

These valves are involved in the flow of blood as follows. In a healthy dog, once blood has been pumped out of the heart and has delivered oxygen and other vital substances to every cell in tissues throughout the body, it returns to the heart via the right atrium and flows through the tricuspid valve and into the right ventricle. From the right ventricle, the blood is pumped through the pulmonic valve and pulmonary artery into the lungs, where it takes up more oxygen. The newly oxygen-rich blood then returns to the heart via the left atrium and flows through the mitral valve to fill the left ventricle. When the heart contracts (it's a muscle that contracts with every beat), the mitral valve closes so that blood is propelled forward through the aortic valve and into the aorta, from which it is once again pushed out under high pressure to all the tissues of the body.

Problems arise when there is irregular thickening and shortening of the valve leaflets that close once blood passes through them. That thickening and shortening—the hall-marks of chronic valvular disease—are the very things that keep the valves from closing as tightly as they should after each heartbeat, causing some of the blood that should be moving forward through the heart to regurgitate, or leak backward. Specifically, blood backs up from the ventricles (lower heart chambers) into the atria (upper heart chambers).

*continued on page 145*

Cody was one of them. This super-friendly, super-loved eleven-year-old Cavalier King Charles spaniel had severe, late-stage chronic valvular disease with fainting episodes and was likely to die imminently when his people brought him to see us. But he derived immediate benefit from pimobendan and, in the hands of his highly dedicated owners, lived another two years and two months before finally being euthanized for heart failure. (The average increase in lifespan with pimobendan is closer to six to nine months; Cody's, like Brandy's, was an exceptional case.)

---

## The Anatomy of Canine Heart Disease,
### continued from page 144

Over time, whichever atrial chamber is affected by a faulty valve will enlarge to accommodate this extra blood flow (that's why it's not good for a person, or a dog, to have an enlarged heart). Furthermore, the leak will continue to worsen as a valve progressively degenerates, and the entire heart will have to work harder.

The body works to maintain normal distribution of blood despite the backward flow. One way it does this is by retaining more salt and water, which increases the volume of blood and thereby increases the pressure with which it travels through the blood vessels. It also constricts the blood vessels so that the extra blood volume has to make its way along even tighter spaces, bringing more pressure to bear. But all the increased pressure is not good for the dog. It increases the workload of the heart, which contributes to a worsening of the valve leak, which creates a vicious cycle by making even more blood flow backward.

Indeed, eventually the increased salt and water in the body, combined with the worsening leak and heart enlargement, overwhelm the ability of the heart to pump blood properly. The result is congestive heart failure, either on the left or the right side of the heart, depending on which valve has the defect.

Yet another part of treatment for dogs with congestive heart failure, particularly for dogs in whom the disease is advanced, is a reduced-sodium diet, which can be obtained from your veterinarian. Because sodium draws water, restricting sodium intake serves to reduce the amount of water the body retains. That's clearly beneficial. Research at Tufts has shown that sodium-restricted diets leading to less fluid retention reduce the size of the heart in dogs with heart failure—their hearts don't need to pump as hard when the blood volume is reduced. Conversely, many dogs with heart failure develop worsening signs of congestion after holidays or family gatherings during which salt-laden table scraps are thrown to Fido.

Whether to restrict dietary sodium after valvular disease develops but before congestive heart failure takes hold is controversial. The evidence is equivocal at best. In fact, excessive sodium

---

## Fish Oil for Heart Disease

Supplementation with omega-3 fish oil capsules may help with several types of canine heart disease. Here at Tufts, researchers tested omega-3 fatty acids in dogs with boxer cardiomyopathy and found that those given the treatment for six weeks had reduced arrhythmia, while those given flax or sunflower oil showed no change.

In another Tufts study on large-breed dogs with heart failure resulting from dilated cardiomyopathy—Great Danes, Labrador retrievers, and Doberman pinschers, among them—we found that those given omega-3s had less muscle loss and an increase in appetite. Dogs with congestive heart failure caused by valvular disease—Cavalier King Charles spaniels, poodles, and dachshunds, for instance—appear to get the same benefit. That is, certain effects of heart failure resulting from any condition appear to be attenuated with omega-3 supplementation. Speak with your veterinarian about brands and dosages.

## What About Valve Replacement?

If a person has significant valve disease, he can undergo open-heart surgery to get a valve replacement (or repair) that stops the progression of heart disease before heart failure has a chance to develop. This treatment essentially cures a person with valvular disease — at least until the valve needs to be replaced again years down the line.

The same technology is available for dogs, but it is available at only a few treatment centers at this point. Moreover, the operation costs more than $10,000, and sometimes more than $15,000, when all is said and done. And it's precluded in very small dogs because they are not large enough to undergo cardiopulmonary bypass — the bypass tubes may actually hold more than the dog's entire blood volume. Even in larger dogs, it is associated with a significant risk of death.

There is hope that in the future, minimally invasive surgical techniques will be available to fix dogs' faulty valves — a much safer procedure than an open-heart operation. A catheter would simply be fed into the dog's heart via a small incision in the neck or groin, and, with special instruments attached, valve leaflets could be reconfigured to some degree or the size of the area the valve needed to close off during blood flow could be reduced. Such catheter-based procedures are currently being researched.

restriction at that stage may actually result in more harm than good. It can *lead to* water retention because the body will detect reduced blood volume (through reduced blood pressure) and will activate other compensatory mechanisms to restore the status quo.

Early sodium restriction aside, once congestive heart failure develops from chronic valvular disease, the average dog given optimal medical treatment and a sodium-limited diet can be expected to live about six months. If he's given pimobendan in addition to other drugs, his lifespan may be extended by at least a few more months. And some extraordinary dogs with particularly dedicated people to take care of them may live another twelve to eighteen months, or even longer. Such people take their beloved pets for frequent visits to a veterinary cardiologist, where they are monitored closely and prescribed any necessary medication adjustments. The closely timed visits to a veterinary cardiologist are analogous to "heart failure clinics" visited by people with congestive heart failure.

Still, while medical management can significantly improve quality of life and prolong survival, valvular disease resulting in heart failure remains a progressive condition no matter what. Eventually, the dog will reach a point where his heart failure becomes refractory to further medical treatment, or the kidneys will not respond to further increases in the dose of a diuretic. The end result is an inability to breathe comfortably even at rest, and nothing more can be done. At that point, you can at least take comfort knowing you have done everything you could to keep your pet reasonably comfortable for as long as possible.

# 7 | When the Kidneys Start Giving Out

IN ONE RESPECT, treating a dog's kidney disease at home may be similar to treating diabetes. The owner of a dog with kidney disease may also need to give injections. But that's where the similarities end. With diabetes, the amount of insulin the owner has to inject is so tiny. With kidney disease, if it gets to the point that the dog needs subcutaneous fluid at home, the needle is larger, which makes it harder for some people. Also, you're administering a large quantity. The dog has to sit still and the needle has to stay in place while perhaps a whole pint of fluid goes in. It can take five or ten minutes. Even with that, however, people adjust. They're so glad to be able to do something for their pet.

—*Linda Ross, DVM, Associate Professor, Department of Clinical Sciences*

WITH KIDNEY DISEASE, often more than with other grave illnesses, the dog owner is thrown into the role of veterinary nurse practitioner. Much of what happens to keep the dog comfortable happens at home and is overseen by you and you alone. This is because the options for high-tech medical treatment of chronic kidney disease available for people, including dialysis and kidney transplants, are not available for dogs. Costs and technical difficulties preclude them. In their place, symptomatic treatment—keeping an old dog as comfortable and physiologically well-balanced as possible while she grows sicker — becomes a particularly important component of care.

The downside, in addition to having to watch your dog grow more ill over time, is that it can be rather intimidating to be thrust directly into the position of healthcare provider. The upside is that you are in a position to return to your dog the favor she has given you for so many years in the role of your most faithful, loyal companion. It is older dogs who tend to get chronic kidney failure. By one estimate, in fact, almost half of all canine kidney disease occurs in dogs older than ten.

## EARLY SIGNS AND DIAGNOSIS

The kidneys perform a variety of vital functions. For instance, they help keep the proper ratios of calcium and phosphorus — those two elements are in the blood as well as the bones, and their concentrations have to remain within tight margins for optimal health. Furthermore, the kidneys facilitate the body's maintenance of the proper electrolyte and acid-base balance; electrolytes include substances such as salt. The kidneys also eliminate from the blood a variety of toxins, allowing them to pass into the urine, where they are flushed from the body. And the kidneys help the body maintain normal water balance — excreting excess water as urine or conserving water when too little is present.

In fact, often the first thing that happens when the kidneys begin to fail is that they lose their ability to concentrate urine, resulting in a larger volume of more dilute urine. Thus, the earliest sign of kidney disease you see will probably be that your dog urinates more — and drinks more water to compensate for the increased water loss in the more dilute urine.

Of course, as we have already discussed, a number of diseases cause a dog to drink more and urinate more, including diabetes and Cushing's disease. Certain infections have the same effect. So while you should take your dog to the veterinarian if you no-

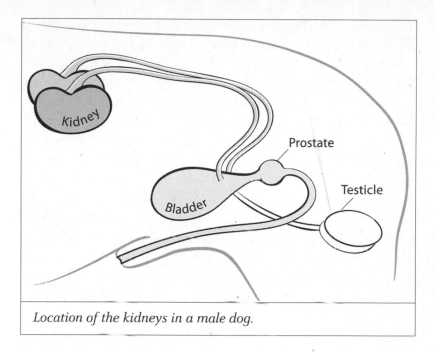

*Location of the kidneys in a male dog.*

tice her fluid intake and urine output increasing, you should not automatically assume that her kidneys have started to fail. Tests need to be conducted.

Keep in mind that in kidney disease's early stages, you might not see any signs whatsoever. The problem may very well be picked up during a routine screening or a pre-anesthetic work-up for, say, a dental procedure, to make sure the dog is healthy enough to "go under," and the veterinarian will be alerting you, rather than vice versa.

Most of the diagnosing goes on through analysis of a dog's blood and urine, both of which happen as a matter of course at your dog's annual wellness visit. One thing your veterinarian will check in your pet's blood is her blood urea nitrogen, or BUN. This is a byproduct of protein breakdown from many body tissues and also of food digestion. The vet will check your dog's blood level of creatinine, too, which is a byproduct of muscle breakdown (muscle is always being broken down and built up in the body). The levels of creatinine and blood urea nitrogen are markers of how well—or how poorly—the kidneys are functioning.

For the veterinarian to check your dog's urine, she may ask you to bring a urine sample to the office, particularly if kidney disease is suspected. Alternatively, your veterinarian can obtain a sample during the office visit, either by "free catch" or by withdrawing urine directly from the bladder, especially if a sterile sample is called for. One way to achieve the latter is to pass a catheter into your dog's bladder—more often done with males. Another way to collect a sample is via a procedure known as cystocentesis, in which the bladder is tapped with a needle. It may seem invasive to a dog owner, but for the dog, it's much quicker and less painful than dealing with a catheter.

The urinalysis will tell your vet how well the kidneys are able to concentrate urine—a marker of kidney function—and whether there are substances in the urine that shouldn't be there, such as protein, blood, or bacteria. Additional urine or blood tests may be recommended depending on urinalysis results.

All these tests taken together are very telling and can prompt the doctor to begin treating your pet for kidney disease long before she has any symptoms—an important point, because kidney failure detected in its early stages is easier to treat effectively.

Consider that a normal value for creatinine is less than 2.0. Most dogs don't feel sick, however, until the value reaches 4 or 5, a point at which the kidneys will have almost given out and your pet is vomiting, dehydrated, and feeling quite ill. If the veterinarian detects kidney disease at a value of, say, 2.5, however, she can initiate medical treatment and dietary therapy to help control symptoms and delay the inevitable, sometimes by a considerable amount of time—even years, in some cases. To give you an idea of the stakes in medical terms, by the time the value reaches 2.5, the kidneys have lost 75 percent of their ability to function properly, meaning their ability to filter waste from the body is already severely compromised.

As informative as blood and urine tests are, once they confirm that a kidney problem is present, diagnostic imaging will often be ordered. An X-ray, for instance, can show the size and shape of the kidneys, which will help determine whether the problem is indeed kidney disease or perhaps cancer that's causing the dysfunction. An X-ray can sometimes help detect kidney stones as well, which themselves can in some cases set the stage for kidney failure.

An ultrasound can provide information, too — even more than an X-ray, in fact, because it can look *inside* the kidneys. Sometimes a biopsy is recommended, but only if the results would change the course of treatment. As we said earlier, treatment is chiefly about treating symptoms, keeping the dog comfortable as the disease progresses. If kidney disease is caught early enough, treatment will help your dog live longer with a good quality of life, even though the kidney disease itself cannot be cured.

Only if the kidney failure turns out to be acute, resulting from a clearly identified problem such as an infection or the ingestion of a toxic substance such as antifreeze, can it sometimes resolve completely with the right treatment. But that tends to happen in younger dogs. Chronic kidney failure, the kind most old dogs get, is a different story. While a veterinarian can *sometimes* determine the cause of chronic kidney disease — a bacterial infection, perhaps, or congenital kidney disease, or a condition called glomerulonephritis that adversely affects the structure of the kidneys at the microscopic level — the reason behind the illness once it's diagnosed usually remains unknown. Thus, so does the cure.

That said, a dog with chronic kidney failure can live for several years if the symptoms are treated properly. And since treatment of kidney disease in a geriatric dog is very much about lifestyle, meaning that it's largely in your hands, you potentially wield a lot of power in slowing your friend's decline.

## THE KIDNEY DISEASE TREATMENT PROTOCOL

Keeping your old pal with kidney disease comfortable at home consists of a multipronged approach, all aspects of which you're capable of handling.

**Reduce Stress.** It's critical to keep the stress level of a dog with kidney disease as low as possible, because stress can impact how much she eats and drinks, which is critical to her well-being. Stress is not only psychological but physical, too. You have to take extra care, for instance, to make sure that a dog with kidney failure is not left outside on a very hot or very cold day. Her body cannot respond as well as it should to physiologic demands, and that can play out in adverse changes in her appetite and thirst level.

**Keep Water Available.** All dogs must always have a bowl of water available to quench their thirst at will, but this becomes even more important for a dog with kidney disease. More to the point, if your dog has kidney disease, you need to make a conscious effort to make sure she's drinking enough of it. Without enough water, the blood supply to her kidneys decreases, which translates to the kidneys functioning even more poorly and the dog feeling worse. In addition, water is needed to rid the body of toxic waste — the more urine produced, the "cleaner" the blood will be.

Does your dog prefer a certain water bowl? Tap water? Bottled? Does she like her water changed very frequently? How about an automatic water fountain? Do what it takes to get her to drink enough — it's not too much effort on your part for the chance to potentially extend her life by years. And make sure to be especially vigilant about water in hot weather.

**Feed a Therapeutic Diet.** Along with making sure your dog with kidney failure drinks enough water, it is crucial that she follow a reduced-protein, reduced-phosphorus diet. (Most phosphorus comes from protein-containing foods, so when you've tackled one, you've tackled the other.) A reduced-protein regimen won't necessarily slow the progression of kidney disease, but since it translates to fewer protein byproducts for the kidney to filter, it will help your dog feel better. She will have fewer kidney disease symptoms.

The reduced phosphorus in the diet *will* slow disease progres-

---

## Tricks for Getting Your Dog to Drink Enough Water

Try these tactics to get your pet with kidney disease to drink more if she's not going to her water bowl frequently enough:

- Flavor the water with just a little low-sodium bouillon.
- If you slow cook a chicken over the stove, don't salt it, and save the broth in ice cube trays. Put a cube of broth in each bowl of water.
- Try commercially flavored broth (homemade without salt is best).
- Give your dog ice cubes for treats.

If these strategies fail, your veterinarian can teach you how to administer fluid subcutaneously (under the skin) with a needle. The idea may make you uncomfortable, especially, as we mentioned earlier, because the needles are relatively large and the dog has to sit still for large amounts of fluid infusion. But most people—and their dogs—are okay with it, largely because dogs tend to have pretty loose skin. All it takes is an injection on the back of the neck (not the belly). From there, the fluid flows under the skin and gets absorbed into the body tissues—it's not like you're putting anything directly into a vein.

If even subcutaneous administration of water doesn't keep your dog from becoming dehydrated, she may have to stay in the hospital for up to a few days to be given a watery electrolyte solution intravenously.

*To make sure a dog with kidney disease is getting enough water, you may need to administer fluid from an IV drip through a needle. The process can take up to ten minutes. Some dogs sit for it better than others.*

sion. The mechanism is not completely understood, but somehow a high-phosphorus diet has an effect on parathyroid hormone that does further damage. Without that interaction, the disease doesn't worsen as quickly.

It is important to switch your dog to a therapeutic diet as soon as kidney disease is detected, even if the illness is mild at that point. Feeding an older dog less protein and phosphorus won't prevent kidney disease, but you want to ease the kidneys' load once a problem is discovered. Consider, too, that it will be easier to change your old friend's diet before she becomes very ill. Once she truly feels the effects of her disease and has less resilience, getting her to switch from food she has been eating for years is going to be particularly tough.

You can obtain a therapeutic, low-protein, reduced-phosphorus diet from your veterinarian—it is like a prescription. Some of these foods, called renal diets ("renal" and "kidney" being roughly interchangeable), contain omega-3 fatty acids. In scientific experiments, omega-3s have been shown to reduce inflammation, and it is believed that would be helpful to ailing kidneys. Some of the special diets are also formulated to help correct for the fact that a dog's body can become too acidic with renal disease.

Note that therapeutic food purchased from a veterinarian costs more than store-bought dog food. If that is a concern, discuss with your veterinarian the possibility of buying your dog's food from the supermarket or a pet food store. Some nontherapeutic diets come close in ingredients to therapeutic levels, and your vet can tell you which might be suitable for your pet.

We can't stress enough how important it is for your dog to stick to the rations prescribed. An eight-year-old beagle named Sam whom we treated for kidney disease had been doing fine on the food we told the family to feed him, when he suddenly developed life-threatening symptoms one weekend—vomiting and dehydration. It turned out that Sam developed pancreatitis. Friends of the owners' children had been feeding him potato chips and other junk food, and that only stressed his kidneys even more. The crisis had become so bad in two days' time that the owners were on the verge of putting Sam to sleep, but we were able to get his kidney function back to where it had been once we treated the pancreatitis with IV fluids.

## BEYOND LIFESTYLE CHANGES

Once you make sure your dog is not exposed to undue stress and has enough water to drink and the right food to eat, further treatment depends on the particular abnormalities and signs she is showing. For instance, the veterinarian will be monitoring the phosphorus level in her blood, and if a low-phosphorus diet isn't reducing it enough, she may be prescribed medication to bring it down further. Aluminum hydroxide, an over-the-counter preparation, is one such treatment. It binds with phosphorus in the intestinal tract and prevents it from being absorbed, decreasing the amount in the body over time.

If your dog's calcium level is low, the vet may prescribe vitamin D supplements. The vitamin D will help her absorb more calcium from her diet and keep the calcium/phosphorus ratio more normal. It may also help reduce elevated parathyroid hormone levels that can contribute to your dog's feeling poorly. (Such treatments must be coordinated. Consider that giving supplemental vitamin D to a dog with elevated blood phosphorus could result in the formation of mineral deposits in different organs — including the kidneys!)

The vet may consider omega-3 fatty acid supplements as well, in an effort to reduce kidney inflammation.

There are also histamine blockers, specifically H2 blockers. The hormone gastrin normally causes the secretion of acid by the stomach to help digest food. But the increased levels of gastrin that occur in kidney disease result in increased amounts of acid in the stomach, causing little ulcers, or erosions, in the lining of the stomach wall. H2 blockers bring down that acid-

## A Low-Sodium Diet to Reduce Blood Pressure?

Many dogs with chronic kidney disease have high blood pressure, also called hypertension. It's a result, not a cause, of the illness. It's not clear why kidney disease leads to hypertension, but it's important to treat it. High blood pressure can cause damage to various organs, harming not just the kidneys but also the heart, for instance. And it can lead to hemorrhaging in the retinas as well as detached retinas (both of these eye problems are more common in cats with kidney failure, but they also occur in dogs). Finally, dogs with high blood pressure, just like people, can have strokelike events.

Most therapeutic diets tend to be reduced in sodium, but it's not clear whether a low-sodium regimen really reduces blood pressure in a dog. That's why veterinarians prescribe blood pressure–lowering drugs for dogs with hypertension.

ity, healing or preventing ulcers, and in the process keep a dog with kidney disease more comfortable; as the stomach erosions resolve, there's a reduction in vomiting and an improvement in appetite. One H2 blocker that might be prescribed is famotidine (Pepcid), also used in people with ulcers.

Also prescribed for the reduction of vomiting—and nausea—are anti-emetics. They can be quite important when kidney disease is far along, as they help prevent dehydration that occurs when a dog is vomiting a large amount of fluid, or doesn't want to drink because she is nauseated.

If a dog becomes anemic and her red blood-cell count drops low enough to make her feel ill, she may be given the human hormone erythropoietin. That helps increase the red cell concentration. Unfortunately, up to 20 percent of dogs develop antibodies to the hormone and their systems destroy it. It's expensive, too, especially for large dogs, who need more of it, which is why it's not used unless the anemia is advanced. When it works, however, it works wonders, as the case of Petey illustrates.

A little silvery poodle, twelve-year-old Petey had been doing very well on a reduced-phosphorus diet after he had been diagnosed with kidney disease, but started acting lethargic and weak after about six months. We found that he had developed anemia, so we started him on injections of erythropoietin, and his improvement was nothing less than miraculous. The little guy was feeling great once more. He did start to falter after another six months—he developed antibodies to the treatment. But the additional half a year of happy living he enjoyed was a great boon.

## Getting Your Dog to Eat Enough

One of the vicious cycles that occurs with kidney failure is a loss of appetite and an increase in vomiting resulting from the buildup in the body of toxic substances, which only weakens a dog and diminishes kidney function even more. We treated one dog, an eleven-year-old terrier mix named Charlotte, who was so far gone from that complication that her owner was wondering whether she needed to be put to sleep. But we were able to suggest a short-term solution that he was willing to try: the insertion of a feeding tube. Charlotte had to be anesthetized so a little incision could be placed in her neck, next to the esophagus. The tube, made of rubber, was then threaded through the incision and lowered down until just before the opening where the esophagus meets the stomach, after which it was sutured into place. The owner was able to feed Charlotte by putting her food through a blender and administering it to her through the tube. The dog lived healthily and happily for another four months. The owner was in the medical field, so he was comfortable with the fix, but any dedicated, willing dog owner could be taught to perform this procedure.

## DIALYSIS AND KIDNEY TRANSPLANTS

It might seem that a kidney transplant could help a dog whose kidneys are failing. And such operations have been performed in dogs — that's how doctors learned to do kidney transplants in people. The problem for dogs is that their bodies generally reject transplanted kidneys relatively quickly; the new organs don't buy them time or health. Furthermore, the immunosuppressive drugs given to try to prevent rejection of a new kidney are expensive, and blood tests must be conducted frequently to monitor both drug levels and kidney function, adding further to the cost. All this is in addition to the price of evaluation and treatment of the dog receiving the kidney, not to mention screening the donor for compatibility and providing care for the donor dog. The price tag can reach more than $15,000 for a procedure with poor long-term results.

Another dramatic option is dialysis, a procedure that filters waste the kidney can no longer handle. Theoretically, dialysis for dogs is possible. In fact, for a dog with acute kidney failure — from an infection, for instance — dialysis is just the thing to keep her alive until her kidneys heal. But for chronic kidney failure, the logistics — and, again, the cost — usually make it prohibitive. A dog needs to be in the hospital for six to eight hours at a time, two to three days a week. And, at Tufts, at least, which is one of the first institutions to offer dialysis for dogs, the cost is a minimum of $400 per treatment session — $800 to $1,200 a week. That's not even including blood tests and the cost of treating complications that invariably arise.

The costs are similarly high for people. But older people with kidney failure are covered by Medicare, which changes the financial equation.

In other words, at some point, if kidney disease makes your dog feel ill enough, you may want to consider euthanasia. There can come a time when she is feeling constantly ill and uncomfortable, and even all the money in the world will buy her only a very short amount of very unhappy time.

Consider that as the kidneys' function worsens, one of their functions—filtering toxins from the blood—declines. The toxins, or poisons, then build up and cause general signs of illness—decreased appetite, weight loss, vomiting. Sometimes the offending substances are compounds that belong in the body at certain concentrations, but become toxic at levels to which they build when the kidneys don't dispose of them. For example, parathyroid hormone is crucial in very specific amounts to maintain proper calcium and phosphorus balance, but causes illness when there's too much of it.

In its very late stages, chronic kidney failure causes a total loss of appetite, dehydration, and mouth ulcers—erosions in the lining of the tongue, for instance. There will also be gastritis—inflammation in the stomach that leads to abdominal pain and vomiting. Bone loss in the jaw, so-called rubber jaw, is another complication.

A gradual downhill slide is also true for heart failure, and many cancers as well. There often comes a time when it could reasonably be considered kinder to let your beloved pet go. If you take the best care possible of your dog should she end up with one of these life-threatening illnesses, and you make her feel as comfortable—and loved—as possible through the process, you will be able to consider euthanasia with a clearer head should her disease become debilitating to the point that she is no longer able to experience even a moment of relief. You will know that you gave your faithful companion the good life she deserved.

# 8 | The Price of Aging Gracefully

BEA WAS A nine-year-old Dalmatian with a fractured femur, or thigh bone. Her owners told us they could afford to spend $3,500 to fix it, which was pretty much on target for what it would cost for a board-certified surgeon to reset the bone with a plate.

So we went ahead and performed the procedure, but then an infection developed around the plate. It would take a surgery to remove the plate and replace it—another $1,500. Bea's family didn't really have that kind of extra money to spare, but they said to go ahead and perform the operation anyway. Then, when Bea was coming out of anesthesia from the surgery, she aspirated some of her own stomach contents, despite having fasted since the night before, and she developed pneumonia. Dealing with that second complication, which responded poorly to treatment, added yet another $1,500, for a total of $3,000 on top of the original $3,500. Then Bea died.

Eight year old Gwen, a German shepherd cross, went through a $6,500 surgery to repair the cranial cruciate ligament in both of her hind legs. She came through the operation just fine, but then several months later developed a disease in which the immune system destroys its own blood platelets—idiopathic thrombocytopenia purpura. Gwen bled internally, because without platelets, blood can't clot. To fix the problem, her caretaker consented to a blood transfusion for her, and immunosuppressant drugs to tune down her immune system and thereby stop her platelets from being attacked by her own body. That added another $4,500 to the cost of her care; she was in the hospital for about a week for monitoring while she recovered, and a single night in the intensive care unit, with blood tests and all, comes to about $500 (a pretty typical figure for the Northeast, which would probably be lower in the Midwest and South, at least outside of large urban areas).

But that wasn't the end of Gwen's ordeal. She began to develop neurologic complications from one of the drugs she was being given, to the point where she couldn't even stand up. Blood clots then formed and traveled to her lungs—a pulmonary embolism. *Then* she developed pneumonia. When all was said and done, she had remained in the hospital for sixteen weeks. Her owner was apprised of the rising cost every single day, but wanted to keep continuing the care. In the end, she had to refinance her house to pay the $60,000 bill. Three years later, Gwen is fine, and her "mom" says she would make the same decision again in a heartbeat. She was not at all conflicted.

Neither Bea's nor Gwen's story is the norm. Typically, people bring in their dog with a condition that can be fixed for a fee under $5,000 or $10,000—a fracture, an illness, even an illness such as cancer—but have to put their canine companion to sleep because they simply can't afford the cost of treatment, not even by putting the fees on a credit card. This scenario occurs at our offices multiple times a day, every day.

Another way of putting it: chances are infinitesimally small that your pet is going to pass in his sleep or die suddenly of a heart attack. You can count not only on living longer than your dog, but also on the probability that he is going to end up with a serious illness at some point that's expensive to treat, perhaps prohibitively expensive, and involves life-and-death decisions with no guarantees, even if you can afford the bill.

As discouraging as that may sound, there *are* a couple of low-cost ways to reduce the risk for incurring large medical bills in your dog's old age, or at least push back the age at which medical care will become expensive. One way is to do every-thing in your power to keep him healthy while he's younger. For instance, it's a lot less expensive to brush your dog's teeth every single day than to take him for tooth extractions, requiring anesthesia, later on. It's also much less expensive to keep your dog trim throughout life, or slim him down, rather than allow him to remain overweight, which predisposes a dog to all kinds of joint and ligament problems, and can exacerbate every condition from arthritis to heart failure, making a bad problem more costly to treat.

Another critical component of preventive, wellness care is the annual checkup, as the veterinarian will perform a clinical exam and take blood for a lab work-up, both of which will screen for problems before they get out of hand. From a budgeting point of view, the checkup is a no-brainer. It doesn't cost much, and it's an anticipated expense—it's going to happen every year—so it doesn't throw any nasty surprises at the family ledger.

## THE ANNUAL PHYSICAL: RELATIVELY INEXPENSIVE BUT PRICELESS

Routine physical exams often run well under $200 even with blood work. But if you have an older dog, some of the most crucial, potentially lifesaving information is exchanged between you and your dog's veterinarian during the yearly checkup. A thorough history from you noting any changes since the last time your old pal went for a physical alerts the vet as to whether any tests should be ordered to diagnose or rule out a problem, as well as whether the doctor should take a particularly close look at certain areas of your pet's body. The sooner an illness is diagnosed, the better the odds are for treating it effectively and inexpensively and keeping your dog comfortable for as long as possible.

Even without your prompting, the vet should look at the following on your older dog:

**Mouth.** It is vital to check for dental disease.

**Heart.** The veterinarian will undoubtedly listen to your dog's heart with a stethoscope to see whether he can detect the slurpy sound of a murmur—or a murmur that has worsened.

**Abdomen.** The doctor will palpate (feel) your dog's abdomen to check for a mass in his liver or spleen.

**Body.** While you should always be on the lookout for new lumps and bumps, the doctor will perform his own check. Sometimes there's a bump on the inside of a leg or another hard-to-see spot that warrants consideration.

Often, the bump will not be a cancerous tumor capable of spreading but merely a lipoma—a benign fatty tumor. Lipomas require no treatment, unless they're in a spot that makes it difficult for the dog to walk or move about freely and without pain or discomfort, such as the "arm pit." They can be removed in a relatively simple surgery.

**Eyes.** The vet will look for cataracts and glaucoma, both of which impair vision and, in the case of glaucoma, can cause pain—and blindness.

If a cataract is present, it can be removed surgically. A lens can even be replaced, just as in people.

Note that a cloudy lens does not necessarily signify the presence of a cataract, or, in turn, the necessity of a surgery. A normal change of aging called lenticular sclerosis can create a cloudy lens, too. Dogs can see reasonably well with it.

Glaucoma is checked for by testing the pressure in a dog's eyes. But the pressure test is different from the one for humans, during which a short puff of air pressure is applied to the eyes in the ophthalmologist's office. In the vet's office, the doctor "deadens" a dog's eyes with a drop of anesthetic applied topically, then drops what is called a Tonopen onto the cornea. (This doesn't bother the dog at all. Dogs don't have that same reflex we do against having something put in their eyes.)

If glaucoma is detected, the dog can be given medicine to slow the course of the disease, but if your pet lives long enough,

## To Prepare for the Vet Visit

Here is a list of the what-is-my-dog-doing-differently questions you need to ask yourself in preparation for his doctor's visit:

- Is he drinking more water?
- Is he urinating more?
- Have there been changes in appetite? Has your old pal become more picky, less hungry?
- Are there changes in tolerance to exercise or physical activity in general? For instance, has it become harder for your pet to run around in warm weather? Does he appear simply less willing or able to exercise in general?
- Does he make new/different noises while breathing?
- Has the sound of his bark changed?
- Has your dog begun to have episodes of vomiting or diarrhea—even mild ones?
- Have there been unintended weight changes—gains or losses?
- Does his coat look different, perhaps thinner or dryer, or does he look different in general?
- Have you noticed changes in his desire to socialize with people or with other dogs?
- Does your pet seem disoriented? Does it appear as if he becomes lost in his own house or walks into a room and can't figure out a way to exit?
- Are there new lumps or bumps anywhere on his body?

All of these questions speak directly to the illnesses of old dogs that we've been discussing throughout this book—everything from cancer to laryngeal paralysis, tooth decay, heart disease, diabetes, Cushing's syndrome, and so on.

*Veterinarians check for glaucoma by dropping a device called a Tonopen onto a dog's cornea. This would bother a person, but the dog doesn't mind.*

he will eventually require surgery to prevent blindness. At that stage, the veterinarian will go over with you the risks of surgery in an old dog versus living with the challenges of sightlessness.

Along with the actual clinical exam, during the annual checkup the veterinarian will order some blood tests and administer vaccines.

## Blood Tests

The age at which blood tests are taken to screen for various conditions associated with aging varies from veterinary practice to practice. Our own recommendation is that blood tests should become part of the annual exam around the time your dog reaches the age of seven, eight, or nine, or somewhat earlier in very large dogs.

Yearly blood tests can be very revealing. If a dog gets sick one day, but had perfectly normal results on his blood tests at his last routine exam, the veterinarian knows that what's going on has not been gradual or chronic but, rather, is acute—occurring pretty suddenly.

One blood test your dog should be getting each year as he grows into old age is called a complete blood count, or CBC. It measures three things: white cell levels, red cell levels, and platelet levels. Decreases or increases in any of the levels can be a sign of illness and will prompt the veterinarian to do further testing.

A second blood test typically run is a serum biochemical profile, also known as a chemistry panel, or chem. (The two tests together are often noted as a CBC/chem.) The chem will measure a protein in the blood called albumin, which, if low, could be suggestive of kidney disease, GI protein loss, or liver disease. The chem will also measure liver enzymes, which, if high, can signal either liver disease or liver dysfunction resulting from Cushing's disease; blood glucose, to screen for diabetes; and electrolytes, including sodium and potassium, to see whether kidney or heart disease has taken hold.

Finally, the chem will measure creatinine and blood urea nitrogen. If these two substances are elevated, kidney disease is most likely the culprit.

## Vaccinations

Your older buddy's yearly visit to the doctor would not be complete without his annual vaccinations. Sometimes people are adverse to yearly vaccines, thinking, *We* don't get vaccinated every year—why should our dog? The reason, simply put, is that dogs are different. Their vaccines must be readministered throughout their lives, either every year or every few years, depending on the shot, to keep them protected from various illnesses.

There's another cogent way to look at it. A dog who hasn't had his rabies booster and gets bitten by a potentially rabid animal must be quarantined at a certified boarding facility for up to six months at a cost of twenty-five to thirty dollars a day, for a total of thousands of dollars. A dog who has had his rabies vaccine and ends up with unidentifiable teeth marks or an otherwise unidentified wound that might be from a rabid animal requires just a short quarantine in his own home (depending on the state you live in) for only a couple of weeks.

There are two types of necessary shots:

1. **Rabies vaccine.** How often your dog requires a rabies shot depends on where you live. Some states mandate a shot every year. But more and more states are switching to every three years — that's the recommendation from the American Animal Hospital Association. Research has shown that once every three years is enough, and scientists are even looking into whether once every five or seven years will suffice. Your veterinarian will know the schedule for your state.

2. **DHLPP.** This is shorthand for a booster recommended every three years that includes vaccination against:

*D*istemper, a viral infection of the nervous system that can cause anything from gastrointestinal upset to pneumonia to seizures or tremors.

*H*epatitis, a type of liver disease that causes acute liver failure.

*L*eptospirosis, a bacterial infection that affects the liver and kidneys and can increase the chances of death thirty- to fortyfold in severe cases. It is common in the Northeast, on the West Coast, and in the South.

*P*ara-influenza, a component of what is known as kennel cough complex, which, besides a hacking cough, can cause pneumonia.

*P*arvo virus, an ailment more common than any of the above-mentioned illnesses. This virus attacks the gastrointestinal tract and immune system and can cause symptoms ranging from severe vomiting to diarrhea. It can also cause a secondary bacterial infection that spreads from the GI tract to the rest of the body, wreaking havoc on all major systems. Parvo virus is more common in puppies, but it does occur in unvaccinated adult dogs as well.

### Discretionary Vaccines

Your veterinarian may recommend certain other vaccines, depending mainly on where you live, such as the vaccine for Lyme disease. A kennel cough vaccine may be recommended as well.

## UNANTICIPATED EXPENSES

Unfortunately, while a not-too-costly routine physical exam can do so much to catch problems early and thereby ward off or delay various huge medical expenses down the line, it cannot anticipate an accident or *unexpected* illness or disease. And it's the surprises that can throw a family budget into a tailspin.

Why is the cost of caring for a suddenly sick dog or one who has been in an accident so high? One reason is that equipment, diagnostic tests, and medicines used to treat dogs cost the same amount as those used to treat people. In addition, the amount spent training veterinarians is the same as the amount spent to train physicians who take care of humans.

Granted, a visit to a veterinarian is generally less expensive than a visit to a physician, because vets don't have to purchase expensive malpractice insurance policies. By law, if someone sues a veterinarian and wins, the judge is allowed to levy on the vet a fine only for the value of the pet, not for the emotional value (and certainly not for the dog's lost years of ability to earn a living, as with humans). Thus, unless your pet is a ten-million-dollar racehorse, a veterinarian is not going to lose his home in the settlement. The cost of veterinary care is also reined in by the fact that veterinary medicine is still very much a cottage industry, with "Mom and Pop" operations the norm. Even a large, state-of-the-art practice is often no bigger than the building it's housed in. There's no Kaiser Permanente or other large third-party involvement driving up administrative costs.

But those details aside, an operation is still an operation, regardless of the species. An echocardiogram is still an echocardiogram, and an MRI is still an MRI. In fact, the costs for veterinary care often seem steep compared to the care of people, because most people are covered by health insurance. They pay a monthly premium, or part of a premium because they are covered chiefly by their employer, and the rest is taken care of. There's just a relatively small copay even for elaborate procedures, unlike at a veterinarian's office, where full payment is generally due right at the time services are rendered (although some veterinarians will set up payment plans for people with whom they have good relationships and have achieved a high level of mutual trust).

For these reasons, we strongly suggest that you move *all* costs associated with an older dog's health, even those that can't be seen on the horizon, from the "unanticipated" to the "anticipated" column. In a way, all costs are anticipated, because a veterinarian will never perform a procedure without telling you the price up front and letting you make the decision yourself to go ahead. That's because it's the family who makes the ultimate choices on the level of medical care, and if possible, a vet will present a number of options with different price ranges and different levels of risk. Sometimes the choices change as treatment goes along, depending on the dog's condition.

But that usually means anticipated costs on a day-by-day basis once the health crisis is underway. We mean you should anticipate costs years in advance of any problem. Budget for your dog's "rainy day" so you don't have to make a decision to put him down for financial reasons. That is, budgeting to have some money on hand for when your old friend falls ill will buy you more medical options in a desperate situation. And you'll avoid the guilt that often goes with putting a dog down because of an inability to pay for treatment.

We don't think people should feel guilty. It's critical to consider cost in your thinking when it comes to your dog's health. Cold as it may sound, people have finite financial resources. And they have huge expenses: mortgages, putting children through college, having to replace a car, making do when a job is lost without warning. At the end of the day, something's got to give, and no decent veterinarian will think you're a bad dog guardian if you're focused on the money and need to ask a lot of questions on that score. Because you're not. But at least if you plan for an emergency, you'll have a better chance of being able to do for your dog what you feel he deserves when the time comes.

We want to stress that it's perfectly reasonable and acceptable for you to discontinue treatment once you've started. The way Bea's and Gwen's owners decided was not the only way to go. "Sometimes people forget that just because they committed to the initial treatment doesn't mean they can't change their minds down the road," says Tufts's Dr. Shaw, who is board-certified in emergency and critical care medicine. "Let's say a dog has a corn cob in his stomach. I would encourage anybody with the financial resources to go for the surgery to get it out, because the dog will be home fine in two or three days. But for a small percentage of dogs that have such an operation, the incision falls apart and the dog gets a bad infection in the belly. No one should feel they have to continue treatment just because they opted for the surgery in the first place. They shouldn't rethink their initial choice for the operation, either, because their initial choice was the right choice. People go on a financial roller coaster out of a guilty, misguided belief that because they started on a path, they must stick it out. It's okay to try something that doesn't work because of bad luck and then stop. As long as you love your dog till the moment you decide to put him sleep, that's okay."

## A PLAN FOR WHEN YOUR OLDER PAL DEVELOPS A SERIOUS ILLNESS

One way to prepare financially for treating your dog in the likely event of serious illness at some point is to put aside a certain amount every month as part of your household budget. It's easy to say and hard to do, but by putting away, say, fifty dollars a month every month from the time your dog turns seven, you'll have almost two thousand dollars set aside by the time he's ten. If you start when your dog is even younger, setting aside even just twenty-five a month will lead to a stash of thousands by the time your pet is well into old age.

Another option — one we think will put your money to even better work for you — is pet health insurance. About 99 percent of the dog owners who walk through our doors with their sick animals don't have it; we wish 99 percent of them did.

Like health insurance for people, it's not perfect. There are copays and deductibles and various other limitations that won't allow you to recoup every cent should your dog fall ill, including benefits schedules with a maximum on various treatments that don't match what veterinarians typically charge. But a decent policy often reduces the cost of emergency care by at least half, and sometimes significantly more than that.

Two pet health insurance companies, Veterinary Pet Insurance and PetCare Pet Insurance, comprise the lion's share of the health insurance market for dogs (and cats) in the United States, accounting for more than 80 percent of the policies people buy. Both companies are reputable, and a few other good ones exist as well, including PetPlan USA, recommended by the Humane Society, and a new plan offered by Purina that is also getting good feedback. All of these companies (see Resources) have certain things in common that are different from health insurance firms for people:

1. Policies are much less expensive than policies that cover people, ranging from roughly ten to sixty dollars a month, depending on the comprehensiveness of the plan (some cover

wellness care in addition to catastrophic events) and the dog's age and breed.

2. None works like an HMO. That is, there are no "in network" and "out of network" vets. You may bring your dog to any veterinarian you wish.

3. You have to pay the veterinarian for the dog's care and then get reimbursed, whereas often a physician treating people waits for his fees from the insurance company. Furthermore, you fill out and send in the claims form yourself, with the doctor's signature and applicable receipts; the veterinarian's administrative staff does not handle it. The forms are not onerous, tending to be only a page long. But the onus does remain on you to keep on top of the paperwork — and you have to have enough money, at least with a large enough credit limit, to pay the full bill up front.

4. Pet policies have a lower lifetime cap than policies for people, something along the lines of $150,000, as opposed to the $3 million or so allotted for human care.

The differences between policies that cover dogs come in what's covered, and to what degree. For instance, some companies won't insure a dog ten years old or older unless they have been insuring the dog since before he reached age ten. Some companies also put restrictions on certain breeds that are prone to specific conditions, either charging higher premiums or refusing to cover the dog for the illness he's most likely to get. The meaning of "preexisting condition" changes from company to company, too. With some companies, it simply means there's no coverage for a condition that the dog already has when he is signed up — the same as with health insurance policies for people. But some companies say a preexisting condition is one the dog develops after he is already on a policy, effectively turning the year in which a dog is diagnosed into the last year he will receive coverage for that condition.

When shopping around, you'll want to consider, at the very least, a policy that covers emergency care for your older dog as well as care for serious illnesses; routine care isn't what wreaks havoc on a budget.

In choosing health insurance for your pet, or even if you stuff a small amount under the mattress each month (effectively acting as your own insurer), you won't just have a better chance of staving off unnecessary premature death for your pal. You might also increase harmony between the people in your home who participate in the financial decisions. A fair number of couples end up disagreeing about when to pull the plug, so to speak, causing friction that the influx of cash from an emergency dog care fund or insurance reimbursement can defuse. The dog's well-being is the goal, of course, but it's nice if everyone benefits.

## LAST RESORTS

If you're reading this after your older dog has developed a serious condition and you have not purchased pet health insurance or added to an emergency stash over time, you may want to consider contacting CareCredit Healthcare Finance. CareCredit is a credit card just for healthcare expenses that can be used not just for human healthcare but also at many (not yet all) veterinarians' offices. CareCredit offers no-interest plans for bills that are paid in full within eighteen months, buying time for people who need to spread out their payments; and loans with interest for people who need more than eighteen months to pay off a veterinary bill, but at a lower interest rate than traditional credit cards.

For people who have fallen on hard times and can't afford to take care of their dog even if they are given the option to spread out payments, there are "angel funds." The Humane Society of the United States lists organizations that provide financial assistance to pet owners in need, including state-by-state lists, as well as organizations that provide assistance specifically to old, disabled, or ill pet owners. (See Resources.)

It also pays to contact your local shelter, which you can find in your Yellow Pages under "animal shelter," "animal control," or "humane society." (Or go to www.pets911.com and enter your Zip code to find a list of shelters and other animal care organizations in your community.) Some shelters operate or know of local subsidized veterinary clinics or veterinary assistance programs.

If you have a specific breed, you can also contact that breed's national club (the American Kennel Club has a list of the national dog clubs), which in some cases will offer veterinary financial assistance. The Humane Society has a list of breed-specific assistance groups, too.

Any and all of these are worth a try before resorting to euthanasia for a beloved old friend because of an inability to pay.

# 9 | Might the Changes You're Seeing Be Dementia?

"I DON'T KNOW what to do," the woman said. "I don't want to prolong his life for selfish reasons if he's suffering."

She had been referred to me by her dog's primary care veterinarian, having first brought her pet there because he seemed to have age-related dementia. He stared into space and at walls, and stood on the wrong side of the door to go out. He also no longer recognized familiar people and was much less interested in interacting with his owner. In addition, the fifteen-and-a-half-year-old, a Border collie named Marty, began pacing back and forth every evening as soon as it started getting dark (in people with Alzheimer's disease, this is sometimes called the sundowner's syndrome). Finally, Marty began to have house-soiling accidents, and there was no medical explanation for his incontinence. His owner had first noticed vague signs of the condition, called canine cognitive decline, when Marty was about twelve, but things had suddenly taken a turn for the worse.

After conducting a battery of tests to make sure there was no physical problem that was causing all the strange behavior, the doctor had started Marty on a drug called Anipryl, which works on the brain to increase alertness and activity. In one-third of cases, it proves positively rejuvenating, while in another third it shows useful improvement, and in the last third it doesn't lead to any improvement at all. Marty fell into the middle category: his house soiling and pacing decreased for about six weeks, but then seemed to become resistant to the drug's effects. That's when he was referred to me.

In the consulting room, his behavior was somewhat subdued, and he had a forlorn, lost look about him. He was at best only mildly interested in his new surroundings. But he did make his way across to see me and wagged his tail slowly as he lowered his head to be petted.

I told the woman that as long as Marty was not in excruciating pain (which he was not), and as long as he was eating well and paying some interest to some people some of the time (which he was), there was no reason to terminate his life prematurely. I did, however, caution that I was not sure how much better we could make him and that we would only be trying to buy more quality time for him in what was already the limited last stand.

With that we set to work. We switched Marty's diet to Hill's b/d, a ration rich in antioxidants that some experiments have suggested will help reverse various Alzheimer's-like signs in aged dogs. We also kept life interesting and novel — different routes for Marty's daily walks, new toys, and so on — as part of a strategy to "exercise" the brain, which has been shown to be useful in people as well as animals. Furthermore, I recommended that the owner give Marty supplements of coenzyme Q10 and acetyl-L-carnitine, both of which have shown promise for treating neurodegenerative disease.

A month later, Marty's owner got back in touch with the encouraging news that overall he was doing quite well on his new constellation of treatments. Reports from his daycare were that he was running around much more and paying greater interest to his surroundings. He had also begun jumping into the car when his owner picked him up, something he had not done for a long time. And he passed a whole week without urinating indoors and had only one defecation accident. He still panted and paced somewhat in the early evening, but for a shorter time and with less panic in his eyes.

That was the greatest comfort to his owner. "For the longest time," she said, "when you looked into Marty's eyes, you saw this unfocused, anxious-looking creature. But now he's back again. It's a beautiful thing. It's sort of like the lights were off. There was no one home. Now the lights are on and somebody is home."

I'm sure that Marty's improvement will eventually come to an end, as all good things do, but hopefully not for another six or twelve months. And we're not completely out of ideas if he does suffer a relapse. There are even other medications in the pipeline. In the meantime, the owner has been able to snatch Marty back from an early good-bye. It's like what you would say about anyone you don't want to lose: "If only I could spend a bit more time — give him a nice meal, or have some fun, or ask a few last questions." We bought this pair some time that until very recently was not achievable in veterinary medicine.

—*Dr. Nicholas Dodman, BVMS, DACVB*

WHEN A PERSON falls prey to dementia, either Alzheimer's or some other form, it becomes pretty clear, pretty quickly, to those around him. It's often somewhat different for a dog, Marty's case notwithstanding. A dog won't suddenly lose the car in the supermarket parking lot, keep repeating the same thing over and over, or forget how to play gin rummy even though she has been playing it for many years.

Complicating the matter is that even successful agers (and this is true for people as well as dogs) lose some of their mental agility as time passes. A gradual reduction in brain size and the loss of more neurons year by year means cognitive dexterity slows down. It becomes a little more difficult to remember things, to learn new things, and to process goings-on. Our older loved ones can do the same mental tasks, but their minds are not as nimble, so to speak; thus, it all takes a bit longer.

So how do you decide whether to suspect canine cognitive dysfunction?

One point to keep in mind is that the drop-off in expected behavior is often fairly precipitous. Within months, the dog is acting much differently than she had been over the course of many years. Marty's owner had noticed changes when he was twelve, but the shift took a rapid turn when he reached fifteen.

Sometimes the new behavior can be rather bizarre. A couple of "out there" behaviors that owners report include the dog's becoming stuck under or behind furniture when she could normally make her way out; and what we call "door issues," including refusing to walk over certain thresholds or standing at the wrong side of the door to be let out.

But even such obvious changes, which fall under the category of disorientation, are usually not enough on their own to make a presumptive diagnosis of cognitive dysfunction. There are other categories of behavior change, too, involving interactions with family members, sleep and activity, and housetraining, and we feel it is safer to begin to consider cognitive decline if at least two of these categories are affected.

Even then, you cannot make a definitive diagnosis. In fact, a diagnosis of cognitive dysfunction in a dog can never truly be definitive in a clinical sense, with lab tests and so on, but must always be a diagnosis of elimination—eliminating other possibilities for changes in a dog's behavior upon a thorough

## What Are the Chances?

As people go, so go dogs. The older a person is, the greater her risk for developing Alzheimer's disease. Nineteen percent of people seventy-five through eighty-four show signs of Alzheimer's; 43 percent of all those eighty-five and older. The trajectory with dogs is remarkably similar. In fact, the curves for dogs and people, scaled according to lifespan, are almost identical. An estimated 19 percent of dogs eleven to twelve years old (roughly seventy-seven to eighty-four in human years) have canine cognitive dysfunction; for dogs fifteen to sixteen, the proportion is 47 percent.

examination. Sometimes it takes two or three exams, perhaps with follow-ups by veterinary specialists: behaviorists, oncologists, and so on.

We treated one geriatric dog whose owners thought he had dementia because he could no longer sleep well at night and, in fact, was keeping everyone else up. It turned out the dog had a noise phobia—the boiler kept switching on and off in the silence of the wee hours, and that set the dog on edge. It's not clear why the phobia presented itself so late in the pet's life, but a lot of fears do gradually grow in a dog if not tended to, getting worse over time. Maybe the dog hit his tipping point. Or maybe the boiler had simply aged to the point that it was making more noise than it had when the dog was young. Whatever the reason, if the cause of the dog's nighttime anxiety had not been found, he might have been given a drug for dementia that wouldn't have helped, and his owners may have even relinquished him to a pound when the solution for making nighttime livable was something as simple as getting a white-noise machine.

Another dog, an eleven-year-old retriever/shepherd/husky mix named Buddy, was experiencing increasingly frequent episodes of anxious, fitful pacing and other signs of alarm such as dilated pupils. There didn't appear to be a physical cause for his agitation. When he first started having seemingly out-of-the-blue incidents of alarm two years earlier, his family took him to see their veterinarian, who diagnosed hypothyroidism and put him on thyroid medication. Buddy was also discovered to have arthritis, for which he was given a second drug. These prescriptions helped a little with his anxiety flare-ups, so it was assumed that was that. But within a year's time, he lost his appetite and twenty-two pounds, and he would no longer eat dog food.

His guardians were finally advised that because of Buddy's advancing years, his startled, worried, random outbursts might be a result of age-related dementia. The only thing that appeared to help was a prescription for a strong sedative; it made Buddy fall asleep when he began to get nervous, and he always woke fine and happy, if a little groggy, a couple of hours later. But the drug wasn't getting at the root cause of these strange incidents of anxiety.

During Buddy's first visit to Tufts, between Christmas and New Year's a few years ago, his caretakers put forth the notion that perhaps he was hearing things that they themselves were not hearing and therefore reacting in a way they couldn't understand. But they weren't holding out much hope that that's what the problem was.

## Painkillers, Not Sedatives

We see a number of older dogs at Tufts who have been put on sedatives to quiet them during outbursts of bizarre behavior presumed to be symptoms of canine dementia. But in many instances, the cause of the unusual deportment is finally found not to be dementia but a condition that causes physical pain—it can easily take more than one visit to the veterinarian to diagnose the real problem. For that reason, should your geriatric companion start acting fretful, anxious, or otherwise upset seemingly out of nowhere, we suggest not starting with a sedative—a strong drug that will only make your dog groggy and less "there." Instead, start with an analgesic, or pain reliever.

Your veterinarian might prescribe a nonsteroidal anti-inflammatory drug (NSAID), similar to aspirin, or perhaps amitriptyline (Elavil), an antidepressant that's effective for the treatment of chronic pain, or even tramadol (Ultram), an opioid. There's a good chance it will take the edge off your pet's pain until the physical cause of his anxious behavior can be found. If he does turn out to be going through cognitive decline rather than a painful disease, you won't have caused any harm. Giving sedatives, on the other hand, does not address what is truly wrong in these cases, acting neither on dementia nor a physically painful condition—and may even mask important clinical signs.

They noticed that Buddy solicited less attention from them than he used to, and was also less enthusiastic upon greeting them when they came home from work. Since seeking attention less often and showing less enthusiasm to family members are standard components of checklists for canine dementia, it seemed it was only a matter of time before Buddy would no longer be the Buddy they had grown to adore. They were hoping that perhaps he could be given a drug that would at least slow his decline to some degree. But Dr. Dodman wanted to dig a little deeper into the nature of Buddy's anxiety episodes before concluding that dementia was causing them. After all, Buddy did not seem demented. He just seemed inconsolable during his discrete episodes of anxiety, and unable, or unwilling, to eat. He still liked to play, fetching balls and refusing to give them up via fake-outs, and his basic day-to-day habits otherwise remained the same.

Upon questioning, it came out that the dog's fits of anxiety occurred mainly at night, after everyone was in bed. This discovery led to Dr. Dodman's suspicion that Buddy was suffering not from dementia but from geriatric separation anxiety, a term he coined for older dogs who have a physical problem that causes more pain or discomfort at night than during the day. It makes sense. At night, when there's nothing going on and there are no distractions, the mind focuses inward. There are no people available to provide company. So pains throb more, and there's nothing to do but be aware of the nagging discomfort. A dog may start panting, pacing, whining, even pawing at the bed. Nighttime exacerbation of pain is true for people, too. For human cancer patients, the pain can prove so sharp at night that doctors provide specific suggestions for coping.

But what could Buddy's physical problem have been? After all, he had been given the physical once-over on at least two occasions. Dr. Dodman pulled back the pet's lips, looked at his gums, listened to his chest, and then palpated his abdomen. All had been normal up to that point. Upon palpating Buddy's abdomen, however, he felt a huge solid mass—"like a rock," as he put it. He took the dog down the hall to a medical clinician, and within short order Buddy was diagnosed with a cancerous tumor of the spleen, which was probably causing him debilitating pain in sharp bursts.

No wonder Buddy had been less enthusiastic about greeting his family — and unwilling to eat! It had nothing to do with a

---

## The Cognitive Decline Checklist

The pharmaceutical firm Pfizer, which makes the canine dementia drug Anipryl, has devised a checklist to help facilitate a possible diagnosis of canine cognitive dysfunction. Obviously, the company has a vested interest in helping to identify the problem, but it is still a good list. It goes by the acronym DISH: *D* for *d*isorientation, *I* for alterations in the way your dog *i*nteracts with family members, *S* for *s*leep (and activity) disturbances, and *H* for *h*ouse soiling. These categories don't address all of the behavioral shifts that can occur as the brain ages — there's also increased anxiety, an altered response to stimuli such as noises, drop-offs in learning and memory, and sometimes increased aggression — but they cover a lot of ground.

There is a DISH version for dog owners and a somewhat more detailed one for veterinarians. We included the veterinarian's version on page 186, only slightly modified, because it's easy enough to be understood by laypeople and will allow for a little more thoughtful evaluation of your dog's behavior.

If you suspect your dog is beginning to experience cognitive decline, go through this checklist once a month for a few months. (And complete it annually once your dog turns ten, even if you're not particularly noticing cognitive changes.) Checks in any one area are not especially telling, but if you are putting checks in more than one area, and particularly if you are seeing an increasing number of checks over time, take your pet to the veterinarian for a thorough physical and perhaps a neurological exam as well.

*checklist appears on page 186*

## Senior Dog Behavior History Form

Date _____

**Disorientation**

____ Wanders aimlessly

____ Appears lost or confused in house or yard

____ Gets "stuck" in corners, or under/behind furniture

____ Stares into space or at walls

____ Has difficulty finding door; stands at hinge side of
door; stands at wrong side of door to go outside

____ Does not recognize familiar people

____ Does not respond to verbal cues or name

____ Appears to forget reason for going outdoors

**Interaction with Family Members**

____ Solicits attention less often

____ Is less likely to stand/lie for petting (walks away)

____ Is less enthusiastic upon greeting

____ No longer greets owners (once dog is aware owners
have arrived)

**Sleep and Activity**

____ Sleeps more (overall) in a twenty-four-hour day

____ Sleeps less during the night

____ Shows decrease in purposeful activity in a
twenty-four-hour day

____ Shows increase in aimless activity (wanders, paces)
in a twenty-four-hour day

**Housetraining**

____ Urinates indoors (# incidents per week)

____ Defecates indoors (# incidents per week)

____ Urinates or defecates indoors in view of owners

____ Urinates or defecates indoors soon after being outside

____ Signals less often to go outside

waning desire to engage in life's pleasures. He simply felt awful and presumably was dealing with periodic spikes in pain.

He was admitted for surgery just after New Year's, whereupon the tumor was removed. Two days later, Buddy was discharged from the hospital and was eating and drinking comfortably upon his arrival home.

Why the tumor had been missed in earlier examinations is not clear. Perhaps it had not yet grown large enough to detect. The point is that while a lot of older dogs do develop canine cognitive decline (also referred to as cognitive dysfunction syndrome), what often seems like a cognitive deficit is sometimes another age-related condition entirely, and you have to be certain you're diagnosing and treating the right problem. Correct diagnosis can truly be a matter of life and death, and not just because an untreated cancer will kill. Many dogs end up at shelters and pounds for what's perceived to be cognitive dysfunction when, in fact, they have a fixable condition — and an old, sick dog is not going to be adopted but, rather, put down. Indeed, as we said earlier, an estimated 20 percent of dogs are brought to shelters and pounds to meet certain death because they are "too old," and by "too old" what is often meant is seemingly demented.

We cannot stress enough that because the signs of dementia overlap with those of other conditions, your veterinarian must *always* be the one to make the diagnosis. Only a medical professional can take the necessary steps to tell whether a dog is sleeping more as the result of a decline in brain function or because of energy loss due to, say, anemia.

Keep in mind, too, that your dog's not seeming to recognize familiar people or not responding to well-known verbal cues, including her own name, might be attributable to vision or hearing loss. In a similar vein, going to the bathroom indoors might simply be a sign of a bladder infection — cystitis.

The problem could be behavioral as well as physical. Some dogs, even at older ages, experience a breakdown in housetraining. If the human caretaker is gone for many, many hours, even once, and the dog finally urinates indoors, she realizes she *can* urinate indoors and continues to do so. The house is no longer a sacrosanct den, the spell is broken, and the dog must be redirected to her outdoor toilet habits with renewed training.

Long story short: the reasons a dog may engage in any one behavior are many, and a veterinarian has to rule out all the medical causes, and perhaps refer you to a behaviorist, before concluding that cognitive decline is the cause of the unwelcome behavior.

## ONCE THE DIAGNOSIS HAS BEEN MADE

The vet has conducted a battery of tests—there's no cancer, nighttime phobias, pain, infection, or other medical problem. You've paid extra money to see a behavioral specialist, too, who has told you it's not a training issue and that canine cognitive dysfunction is the likely diagnosis. Your dog's mind is fading. Now what?

Sometimes you don't have to do much of anything. A number of dogs decline fairly rapidly to a certain point, but don't really get significantly worse after that. We knew of one "old lady," a thirteen-year-old Portuguese water dog, who could no longer romp by herself in the woods because she would get lost. And she sometimes stood at door thresholds barking at nothing and needing to be pushed over them when it was time to go for a walk. But she was still sweet and loving and was able to appreciate her family's affection as well as show affection of her own, so she lived peacefully, if somewhat less actively, at home for two more years, until she died of cancer at age fifteen.

But the decline doesn't always progress so gently, and in those cases, steps need to be taken to try to slow it. Most of those steps involve things the dog takes—drugs, foods, or supplements.

### The Pharmaceutical Route

One avenue is to try the drug deprenyl (Anipryl), which must be prescribed by your veterinarian. The only drug approved for dogs with cognitive decline, deprenyl prevents the breakdown in the brain of a neurotransmitter called dopamine, which facili-

---

## Don't Try Deprenyl If . . .

If your dog wears a tick collar containing amitraz (Mitaban), do not give her deprenyl. Because the two drugs work similarly, there's a risk for additive effects and unsafe fluctuations in blood pressure. Similarly, deprenyl, an MAO inhibitor, may have untoward additive effects with other MAO inhibitors (although these are used rarely to never in veterinary medicine). It is also advised that deprenyl not be given to a dog taking fluoxetine (Prozac) or any other selective serotonin reuptake inhibitors (SSRIs) because of the possibility of adverse drug interactions. Opioids such as morphine and meperidine should not be used in conjunction with deprenyl, either; there have been reports of negative interactions between those two medications in humans, resulting in rigidity, delirium, hyperthermia, convulsions, and death. Finally, if your dog is receiving PPA (phenylpropanolamine) for urinary incontinence, deprenyl is not recommended, because the two together can result in hypertension.

---

tates the connection between thought and action. It does that by inhibiting a substance known as MAO-B, an enzyme that breaks down dopamine. Unfortunately, results with deprenyl are quite variable, ranging from remarkable turnarounds to no improvement whatsoever.

In one well-controlled trial conducted with this drug, 69 percent of demented dogs who took one tablet daily did show improvement in at least one clinical sign after a month. But so did 52 percent of dogs on a placebo, making the difference a relatively small one. Still, the possibility of some improvement is better than none.

### A Therapeutic Diet

A brand of food you can get only from your veterinarian, Hill's b/d (the b/d presumably stands for "brain diet"), contains a number of substances that have been studied for their effect on brain function and are hypothesized to play a positive role. Among them are antioxidants. Researchers believe oxidative damage to brain cells may have a significant negative impact on advancing canine cognitive disorder, and antioxidants inhibit the detrimental oxidative action of compounds known as free radicals. Hill's b/d also contains omega-3 fatty acids, which preliminary research suggests might change the nature of cell membranes in such a way that makes it easier for messages to get from one brain cell to another.

In addition, this food formulation contains an antioxidant in fats called lipoic acid, along with L-carnitine, a vitaminlike compound. These substances assist in the function of mitochondria—the energy centers of every cell in the body. It is theorized that consuming extra amounts of lipoic acid and L-carnitine might provide more "octane" to the brain cells, in a manner of speaking, increasing their ability to heal and restore themselves.

Note that evidence for the efficacy of Hill's b/d is weak. However, we believe it's reasonable to talk with your vet about giving your dog this food should it be established that canine cognitive decline is underway. It's a "can't hurt/might help" approach.

### A Role for Supplements?

A wide variety of dietary supplements is marketed to people as aids to slowing, or even preventing, cognitive decline, and some dog owners want to try them out on their pets. The supplements include everything from ginkgo biloba to coenzyme Q10, ginseng, various B vitamins, and certain fruit extracts. The scientific evidence for these substances helping to slow the course of canine cognitive dysfunction is scant to nil. On the other hand, so is the evidence for their causing new problems. If your dog is far down the road of cognitive decline—seriously disoriented, with a loss of house training and other problems that are significantly interfering with her quality of life—it is not unreasonable to speak to your veterinarian about giving one or more of these products a try if you've hit a wall with other options for treating her.

Do consult with your vet first. Dietary supplements currently do not require proof of safety or efficacy to be marketed. Therefore, veterinarians should consider recommending specific brands of dietary supplements that bear the logo of the United States Pharmacopeia Dietary Supplement Verification Program (DSVP), which at least tests human dietary supplements for ingredients, concentrations, dissolvability, and contaminants. Another good resource is Consumerlab.com, which performs independent testing of dietary supplements (primarily human supplements, but also some pet products). To just go to the store and choose something without professional input is akin to practicing veterinary medicine without a license. You certainly want more for your dog than that.

## Why Treatment Options Often Yield Less-Than-Spectacular Results

No one drug, food, or supplement has been hailed as a wonder substance for stalling canine cognitive decline. Results are often equivocal at best, partly because, just as with people, it's not yet clear how age-related dementia begins in the first place, leaving scientists uncertain about which disease processes to target. For instance, on post mortem, research veterinarians have found a protein called beta amyloid in the brains of dogs with canine cognitive decline (it coalesces into plaques, just like in people), and the quantities they discovered are thought by some to correlate well with the degree of behavior changes before death.

That makes targeting beta amyloid a promising therapeutic strategy. This strategy is currently being tested in human trials, and perhaps in the future a treatment may be found that will be appropriate for dogs.

However, a number of other changes have also been identified in the brains of older dogs. They include reduced brain mass; calcium deposits in the layers of membranes surrounding the brain (meningeal calcification); demyelination, which is a loss of protective, fatty sheaths around nerve fibers; neuroaxonal degeneration, or degeneration of "wires" that connect nerve cell bodies to nerve endings; increased lipofuscin, a wear-and-tear pigment found in aging nerve cells; and increased apoptotic bodies, which result from cells dying off.

Which one may be at the root cause of canine cognitive decline remains anybody's guess. In the meantime, all that currently available treatments can do is address the *symptoms* of canine dementia — which may be why none of them is universally (or completely) effective.

Note that there's a fair amount of anecdotal evidence involved in making current recommendations, based on just a single dog here or there. That's largely because while no treatment has been found that works across the board, when a particular treatment hits the right target in a particular dog, results can be dramatic. The substance employed in that case may be acting on the very deficiency that is causing the drop in that one dog's cognitive ability.

We heard of such a case in one of the earlier trials of dogs placed on deprenyl. The subject was an eleven-year-old Afghan showing marked signs of dementia. He had already lost control of his bladder, in addition to having undergone other cognitive changes. But by the end of the study, he was acting as though he were two years old again.

Marty, too, achieved a rather dramatic upswing, although it's hard to know which one of the therapies we employed did the trick, or even whether he needed the full arsenal.

Nobody knows why the treatments that worked in those particular dogs worked so successfully. Presumably, the drug (in the first case) and one or more agents (in the second case) specifically targeted some physiologic or biochemical abnormality that was causing the bulk of the dog's symptoms. Unfortunately, until the research community — for humans as well as for dogs — better understands the physiologic mechanisms underlying age-related dementia, the hit-and-miss approach is going to have to suffice.

The good news is that scientists are making inroads all the time. And what's available now is certainly better than nothing — which would have been the treatment option only a decade ago. Better still, even without drugs and dietary options, there are lifestyle steps you can take to slow a dog's descent into canine cognitive dysfunction — and perhaps even keep it from taking hold in the first place.

## THE POWER OF ENVIRONMENTAL ENRICHMENT

As a dog reaches her golden years, she may slow down considerably, becoming less active and also seeking less attention from her human family. And that makes it all too easy for many busy dog guardians to spend less time keeping their loved charges engaged. If you're exhausted after a long day at work, and your dog now seems content just to get a pat on the head and be let out in the yard rather than go for a walk or join in a game of fetch, why go out of your way to tire either one of you?

The reason to do so is that dog brains, like human brains, operate according to the use-it-or-lose-it axiom. Indeed, a dog's cognitive decline will hasten if she's left more on her own rather than paid lots of attention   *and* given new challenges. It has been proven empirically that teaching an old dog new tricks — and yes, they can learn them, just more slowly than when they were younger — helps them retain their cognitive abilities.

In a study conducted by researchers at the University of Toronto and the Institute for Brain Aging and Dementia at the University of California, beagles nine to twelve years old were put on a program of enhanced cognitive enrichment. Specifically, they were given specialized memory training, being taught to distinguish between various objects, with a morsel of tasty food as a reward. A year later, those dogs subjected to the training did much better telling the difference between closely related objects than dogs not given the special lessons. This finding is not surprising, given that previous research on people had indicated specialized memory training improved the level of cognitive function in those who already had dementia.

The dogs who underwent memory training also received more exercise than the other dogs and more social stimulation, both with people and with other dogs. Furthermore, they were given sets of toys that were rotated on a weekly basis. All of these strategies were thought to play a part—as they do across species.

Research has shown that older people who participate in a social network, participate in regular exercise, and continue to challenge their brains with learning are less likely to end up with dementia than others. And if they do become senile, it often happens later in life and more gradually than for those lacking social, physical, and mental stimulation. That's what you want for your dog. Indeed, pushing back cognitive decline, or at least severe cognitive decline, for a year or two could mean that rather than stumbling through mental deterioration as she becomes a shadow of her former self, your dog enjoys a happy, successful end of life in which death comes quickly after a short illness unrelated to a cognitive deficit.

With that in mind, here are some strategies you can employ that might very well stem any cognitive decline you suspect may be occurring in your dog. The earlier you start, the more impact these strategies are likely to have. If you have been arranging your dog's lifestyle along these lines throughout her life, so much the better. You may have kept at bay the advent of cognitive decline by some 15 percent of your pal's life. But even instituting these changes for a newly geriatric dog—for instance, one who is eight years old—could make a significant impact on her cognitive stability down the line.

Note that these steps are easy to implement; you just have to make the time.

• **Older dog, newer tricks.** Throughout your dog's life, long after she has learned "sit," "stay," "down," and "wait," you should be training her on a daily or near-daily basis. In sessions that last just five to ten minutes each day, she can be taught to roll over, fetch something from another room or another floor in the house, distinguish between two similar-looking objects for the prize of a tasty food reward, and the list goes on. You want to keep her neurons firing signals to each other, and she'll enjoy the attention along with the mental stimulation.

• **Shuffle your pet's geography.** We hope it's obvious that letting your dog in the backyard two or three times a day to "do her business" will never be enough to satisfy her natural curiosity—her instinct to sniff and explore. But when you do walk her, don't always take the same route or let her off-leash in the same park. Mix it up a little. Smelling the same hydrants and other landmarks day in and day out will not give her brain an opportunity to process new discoveries.

• **Allow opportunities for your dog to act on her predatory instinct.** Almost every breed group of dog—from sporting to herding to terrier—has a built-in desire to seek out prey, at least to some degree. Deny a dog the opportunity to chase things, and you are denying her the expression of a big part of what her brain tells her to do. There are several ways to allow your pet prey-seeking outlets. One is simply to use food toys—kongs, food balls, and the like—which are available at virtually all pet supply stores. They will get your dog to use mental as well as physical energy trying to extract the prize, whether it's a little peanut butter, frozen yogurt, or some other treat. You can also enroll your dog, even your older dog (provided she doesn't have advanced dementia), in courses specifically designed to have her act on her prey drive. There are courses in which she can follow a scent, herd sheep, and chase objects in games such as flyball. These courses are offered all over the country. Google your options, check your Yellow Pages, or ask your vet where there are opportunities near you. Finally, your canine companion can satisfy her urge to chase by having some time off-leash in a safe setting, whether in a park that allows dogs to romp freely or a wooded area with trails for you to hike while she roams. A dog's brain really thrives on some freeform sniffing, looking, listening, and darting off after her intended target.

• **Get a second dog.** Of course, this is not possible for everyone, and not desired by all dogs, whether or not they have a degree of dementia. A very old dog, who probably has sundry aches and pains, has every reason not to want to start sharing her territory, and if that's the case (you'll know, or can certainly find out in short order by bringing in a second dog on a trial basis), her preference should be respected. But there are few things better for brain health than companionship, particularly the companionship of one who is more or less like-minded. Dogs love being together in packs, even a pack of two, and will keep each other company — and keep each other's mind busy — not only when you're away from home but also when you're around. Thus, early in life and even a little past middle age, a canine companion of her own might be just the thing to keep your dog mentally engaged. If you don't want or can't deal with a second dog, consider enrolling your pet in doggie daycare a few times a week to keep her socializing. Just make sure the place you choose is well-run and uses only positive techniques, with no hitting or other kinds of punishment to adjust a dog's behavior.

## IF YOU HIT A WALL

There may come a point at which no matter what lengths you've gone to for the sake of warding off or stemming your pet's deep descent into dementia, she loses all quality of life. Despite the medicine, the modified diet, the supplements, the physical activity, the new toys, and all your other efforts to bring mental stimulation and points of excitement into her life, she can no longer participate in day-to-day living and derive pleasure. She staggers around, no longer responds to her own name, isn't able to enjoy your attention, stares at walls, doesn't want to budge over the threshold to go out, urinates inside, won't eat, can't perk up, and can't calm down if agitated. Perhaps she even reaches a point that she's living in a vegetative state.

If that becomes the case, heartbreaking as it may be, it might be time to have a discussion with your pet's veterinarian about whether to release her from life. It's a miserable decision to have to make, and miserable even to think about. But if your dog is suffering, isolated in her dementia, you might come to the decision that it's in her best interest to let her go, rather than see her through to an end that's increasingly mentally uncomfortable and disorienting. Only you can decide, but the option is there. Your vet will not think you're a bad caretaker for bringing it up—and will be able to help you determine whether you're contemplating the decision at the right juncture in your dog's illness.

Whatever choice you make, take heart that cognitive canine dysfunction, like Alzheimer's disease, is going to see progressively more effective treatments and techniques that lead to better and earlier detection. No one is sure when, but age-related mental decline is a research priority in esteemed scientific institutions worldwide and is sure to bear fruit over time.

# 10 | Changing the Environment to Suit the Dog

WE ONCE HAD a case of an old dog hemorrhaging so much blood that he came out of surgery doing very poorly. It would have been unfair to keep him alive, not to mention terribly costly. Euthanizing him wasn't our decision to make by ourselves, however. It was chiefly the owners'. The degree to which a veterinarian treats depends in good measure on the owners' wishes.

Problem was, the owners were in Africa at the time and impossible to find. The dog was at our hospital only because the pet sitter brought him in when it became irrefutably clear that something was wrong. Getting a decision made about what to do became a costly and logistical nightmare, and in the end it was the dog who suffered most.

We tell you this story to illustrate that a dog's environment doesn't consist of just the stairs in your home or your slippery floor—settings that might be hard for an old dog to manage. The environment also consists of the people in his life. And when you're not there, who those people are, and the instructions given to them on how to act in an emergency, become all the more important—because an emergency is more likely to occur in an older dog, especially one with some preexisting health issues.

Even today, in the age of cell phones, your availability to make crucial decisions for your dog while away might not be constant.

You could be in flight on the way to Australia, or camping in the mountains, where cell phone reception is iffy at best, or in a series of back-to-back overseas business meetings that can't be interrupted.

## THE PEOPLE IN YOUR DOG'S ENVIRONMENT

Let's say you're going to be traveling and will be leaving your dog at a boarding facility. Or perhaps someone's going to stay at your home to pet-sit in your absence, or simply come by a few times a day to walk him, feed him, and pay him some attention. No matter what the situation, it's imperative that you leave good contact information so the dog sitter has the best chance of reaching you should an emergency arise. Equally important is leaving information and instructions should you *not* be found.

Apprise the people taking care of your dog in your absence of any medical conditions he has and what to watch out for. In addition, leave instructions for what to do in the event of the unexpected. It's extremely difficult for someone else to make the decision to put your dog to sleep.

Perhaps you want to put a dollar amount on it. If the bill reaches $X, they have your permission to let the dog go. Or maybe you want the caretaker to make the decision after receiving input from a veterinarian you know and trust. Maybe it's about hospitalization. Your dog has kidney disease but has been able to remain at home, yet when the only way to keep him alive is at the clinic, it's time to put him down. The more specific you can be, the better the chance your dog has of being treated according to your wishes should you be unavailable to make decisions yourself. "Here's his food; I'll see you a week from Thursday" is not enough for a dog getting on in years.

The people who care for your older dog in your absence are not the only ones in his environment warranting special consideration. Newcomers to your household will affect your friend as well.

## If There's a Baby in the House . . .

Maybe the newcomer is a newborn. Is certain ways, a geriatric dog will be easier with a new baby than a younger dog. Inquisitiveness tends to lessen in a dog's older years, so he won't be as likely to get in your way as you tend to the little one. That said, *never* leave the baby and the dog alone together, in case the dog's predatory instinct gets the better of him (it has happened in extremely rare cases), or he tries to nuzzle the infant in a well-meaning gesture but is too rough in his affection.

Keep in mind that an older dog is going to be relatively set in his ways, and it will be harder to maintain his routine when you feel exhausted from the 2:00 A.M. feedings. Try as hard as you can to make sure he's walked and fed according to his usual schedule, so he does not see the addition to the family as an unwelcome intruder. A comforting routine will make him less inclined to mind the baby's touching his toys and clumsy attempts at petting once crawling and toddling get underway.

Also make a special effort to continue to treat your dog well in other ways. Let him sniff the baby, because it's a dog's way of identifying the infant as a member of "the pack." In addition, pet the dog in front of the baby, speaking gently to your canine companion as you do so and maybe even offering him a treat. Any warm treatment you offer that the dog associates with the child will only make your canine pal more inclined to feel good about the child's being in the home. Saving up kindness for when the baby is in the crib only sets the stage for "sibling" rivalry, giving the dog the message that when the infant is around, he doesn't rate.

## If an Elderly Person Comes to Live with You and Your Dog . . .

Introducing an older person into your household presents a different set of considerations. Say your aging parent or grandparent comes to live with you and your wire-haired terrier, Huck. You need to explain to the person how Huck "works." For instance, maybe your relative would be inclined to just let Huck

*Getting to know you . . .*

out when he indicates that he needs to "go," but Huck is accustomed to being taken out on a leash. That would need to be explained, along with the fact that Huck is better off waiting for you to come home than to be let out by someone who isn't up to walking him, or perhaps not physically capable.

The elderly person might also enjoy Huck's pleasure from being given delectable food treats without limits, but you notice that Huck is getting too heavy for his own good—which could only predispose him to a joint problem or exacerbate one that already exists. Similarly, someone new to the household—especially someone who has never owned a dog—might not understand that an old dog, in particular, cannot be left outside for hours on end. Each of these points is significant even individually. Put them together and they add up to an overall quality-of-life issue that could affect not only your pet's comfort in a number of ways but also his safety. That's why those new to your household need to be instructed about how to do best by your dog; his good care can't be taken for granted.

## If You're Considering Getting a Second Dog . . .

Be as mindful introducing new dogs into the household as new people. An eight-year-old dog with a lot of pep might really enjoy the canine companionship a second dog would bring, even a puppy with frenetic energy. But a slow and perhaps crotchety twelve- or fourteen-year-old dog might not appreciate a jumpy pal who wants to roughhouse—when he's not eating out of the older dog's food bowl.

If you do take in a second dog, remember that the dog who was there first *always* has the pole position. He should be fed first, be able to have his favorite toy all to himself if he wants to, receive the first pat when you come home from work, and so on. It is only fair that the original dog remains top dog.

Tip: Choose a second dog of the opposite sex from the first. That cuts down on aggression from both sides.

*This older gal and the new addition to her home happily share a chew toy.*

## STAIRCASES AND SLIPPERY FLOORS

The people and other dogs in your old pal's life are only one aspect of his environment that may need adjusting, or at least special consideration. There's also the lay of the land. Can the dog who has slept in your bed every night for a decade still climb the stairs to make it to your bedroom? If he can, is the mattress too high for him to jump on once he gets there? What about your highly polished wood floors, with four coats of polyurethane making them even shinier? Is the dog still steady enough on his feet to be able to make it from one end of such a slick surface to another?

### Stair Cares

The biggest physical obstacle in the house for many older dogs is the staircase. If your dog is a toy poodle or dachshund, it's a nonissue. You just swoop him up and take him where he wants to go. But a lot of dogs, particularly large dogs that are difficult if not impossible to carry, are prone to arthritis born of hip dysplasia, elbow problems, and other orthopedic afflictions, and simply can no longer get up the stairs on their own when they are older. What do you do?

We know one owner of a sixty-five-pound dog who carried his pal up to bed every night and back down again every morning for the last two years of the dog's sixteen-year life. Skittish and somewhat mournful, the dog had never slept outside of her owners' bedroom before, and fortunately, the husband had enough strength to do what it took to get her there.

If carrying the dog is out of the question, you can try using a sling underneath his belly and back legs as an extra support while he climbs up or down. A towel will work as a sling, or you can buy a dog sling. Admittedly, this works better for the two or three stairs leading from the deck to the backyard than for the staircase leading from the first floor to the second. For a dog who's game, however, it's worth a try.

Keep in mind that a sling will work only if the dog still has

*A ramp can make car travel smooth and easy.*

some strength and ability. If he can barely use his legs at all and he's too big too carry, you may need a ramp to get him outside from the kitchen or front door (there's usually at least one step). It doesn't have to be fancy. A couple of two-by-fours and some plywood should do it.

For getting in and out of the car, you can buy a car ramp rather than fashion one. That might come in especially handy if you have an SUV or some other vehicle with doors higher off the ground than those of a standard sedan. Little ramps or small sets of movable stairs will also help a smaller dog make his way up to your bed from the floor.

At night, an essentially immobile dog who's too heavy to carry will have to stay downstairs. Make sure he has a soft, comfy dog bed to cushion his aching joints.

### Keeping Your Dog on Sure Footing and Other Considerations

Tile and wood floors, which many households have, are slippery even for young dogs who generally don't have trouble getting around. For an older dog, gaining traction on a smooth surface becomes even more of an issue, especially after he has been lying down and wants to get up.

Undesirable as it may be for your décor, put down runners, even cheap rubber runners that go under rugs. One family we know went so far as to carpet a hallway that had shiny linoleum. A little rug right next to the bed or couch your dog normally rests on is a good idea, too, so he has a good, solid place to plant his feet when he jumps off. Remember, you're not going to have your older pal forever. Interfering with the look of your home to keep him comfortable is a small sacrifice. You'll keep him safe, too. A dog who falls from lack of traction is more prone to injuring, or reinjuring, himself.

Other simple fixes can also help keep your dog safe and comfortable in old age:

• Put extra padding where he lies or sits in the car, and consider

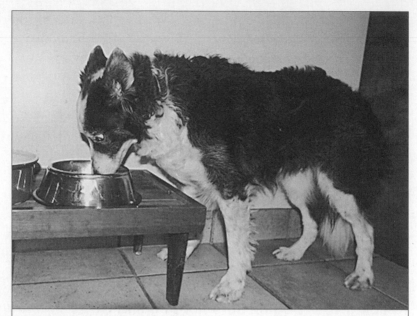

*Putting the food bowl on a low table allows this arthritic dog not to bend too far when he eats.*

buying (and using) a harness that attaches to the seat belt. If you make a short stop or sharp turn and there's nothing to hold him in place or cushion the impact, he's more likely to pitch forward and fall off the seat as the car rocks and rolls—and more likely to feel pain in creaky joints and bones.

• If your dog has trouble bending his head down between his paws, consider buying an elevated dog bowl. It will make eating and drinking more comfortable.

• When boarding your dog, bring his nice, soft, thick-cushioned bed to the kennel. Otherwise, he might have to lie on the floor with nothing but a sheet or towel.

• Some older dogs are stubborn and keep trying to climb stairs at their peril, sliding down as they go and really hurting themselves. If that describes your dog, put a baby gate at the bottom of the staircase (and also at the top, if you carry him upstairs).

• Make life easier, if necessary, by buying doggie diapers. Leaking at night rather than during the day is generally more of an issue if your dog develops incontinence, so you may not have to keep a diaper on him all day. You can also buy diaper pads—flat sheets filled with diaper material—to put on your old friend's bed. The leaking, especially among females, tends to occur when

## Some Dogs Have Wheels!

A canine wheelchair won't help your pet get up and down the stairs, but it might very well allow him to walk around outside—and do his "business" without your help.

It's most useful if your pet has lost function in his hind legs. The wheelchair—a cart, really—hooks onto him, and the wheels do the work that those legs no longer can. The contraption is not cheap, running anywhere from $500 to $2,000. But especially for a dog who's otherwise incontinent because he can't make his way about the lawn, they can be a godsend.

*Life is good.*

the dog has been lying in one spot for a while. Of course, before you go the diaper route, have your leaking dog checked out by the veterinarian to make sure there isn't a problem with his urinary tract. (In many cases, the problem is poor sphincter tone that can be corrected with medication.)

As to whether your dog will resist the diapers, it's impossible to say beforehand. Some dogs don't even notice they have them on. Others spend every moment trying to rip them off. Stay calm — it takes a lot of patience to cope with an incontinent dog, even one that you love very much.

## A CHECK ON THE WEATHER

You've heard it before, but it bears repeating — and heeding. Your dog's body, as he ages, is not going to be as tolerant of weather extremes as when he was young. He can become overheated in hot weather and hypothermic in cold much more easily. Thus, if your old friend likes to sit out in the sun in summertime, make sure he has a fresh bowl of cold water right next to him, and don't let him sit out for very long. Perhaps shift his spot to a shady place under a tree.

Likewise, make sure your dog is sheltered from wind and bitter cold during the winter. A short-haired dog like a Weimaraner will definitely benefit from a coat, as will many toy dogs who just don't have the resilience to withstand frigid temperatures. Whoever the dog, he'll probably like cozying up with you once he's back inside, especially if you wipe his paws free of snow and ice. An old dog has been through a lot of winters; he deserves that consideration.

# 11 | Emergency, Rather Urgent, or Non-Emergency?

WHEN AVA, a delightful beagle, was a puppy, she was brought to the emergency room twice: once because she ate some raisins, which (along with grapes) have been associated with kidney failure in dogs, even in small quantities; and once because she got into a fight with another dog who bit off part of her ear. We then didn't see her for years—until she was nine. She was brought in because, in addition to drinking and urinating like crazy, she suddenly had become very weak. We diagnosed her with diabetes and taught her family how to administer insulin injections, and even today she is living out a happy old age in a house on four acres, with plenty of room to romp.

In terms of emergency room visits, she is as typical as a dog gets. The emergency service at Tufts sees approximately twelve thousand dogs a year, many of them older than seven. And what we have found is this: emergencies for puppies and other very young dogs often come in the form of poisonings from ingestion of toxic substances and injuries resulting from getting hit by a car or ending up in a brawl with another dog. But as a dog ages, she becomes much less curious about the taste of antifreeze or the might of a rival, and there's also a good chance she will have learned to distinguish the sidewalk from the roadway. Thus, medical emergencies for older dogs tend less to be the result of accidents with the outside world and more a matter of organ failure, a metabolic derangement, or some other breakdown in the workings of the body.

The question for you is how can you tell if it is, indeed, an emergency? Should you take your older dog in today, Sunday afternoon, for a $200 fee, or wait till Monday and get a $50 appointment during regular office hours? Here are some common clinical signs that, at the very least, should prompt a phone call to the vet's office—and will often involve an unplanned trip there as well.

If there's doubt, which there often is because it can be difficult to impossible to diagnose over the phone even with the clearest description of symptoms, you'll be advised to make the trip in. Go. It's always better to be safe than sorry.

## LOSS OF ABILITY TO MOVE AROUND

If your old friend was able to "do her business" and have a little something to eat in the morning, or follow through on whatever her usual routine is upon waking, and now can't get up, you need to bring her in; chances are the problem isn't going to go away on its own. Very often, the reason for a sudden inability to stand and walk is either cardiovascular or neurologic in nature, and either way requires immediate attention. Perhaps there's a bulging disk that reached a tipping point or a tumor in the dog's back that has finally grown big enough to impinge on a nerve (or set of nerves) and cause acute paralysis. Emergency surgery may be required.

## VOMITING

One or two episodes of retching are no reason to run to the emergency room. But if your pet vomits four or five times, take her in. What we worry about most in such situations is something getting stuck in the gastrointestinal tract—perhaps in the stomach or small intestine. Repeated vomiting, particularly in an older dog, can also be a symptom of kidney or liver failure.

## If You're on the Fence, Test Your Dog's Vital Signs

Belle (or Bridget, or Mimi) doesn't seem like herself, but you're not sure that whatever ails her is enough to warrant a trip to the emergency room. Why not check her vital signs? If something's amiss, you'll at least know to call the doctor's office to get professional advice about whether to make the trip.

Checking vital signs is *not* about feeling a dog's nose. Contrary to popular belief, that will not tell you anything about her health. Cool or warm, wet or dry, or somewhere in between, are all normal. Instead, look at:

1. **The gums.** The gums inside your dog's lip should be bright pink. Even breeds like chows or Akitas, with a lot of black pigment, should have at least some pink. If the inside gums are pale or muddy in color, it could be a sign of shock. (Take a couple of minutes now to learn your dog's normal gum color so you can figure out whether it has changed in the event you suspect something is amiss.)

2. **The temperature.** "Normal" is not a single number. It's a range from approximately 100 to 102.5 degrees Fahrenheit. The way to take your dog's temperature is with a rectal thermometer that you keep on hand only for use with your canine family member.

3. **The pulse.** You'll generally be able to feel the beat on the inside of your dog's thigh. Cup your hands around one of her rear legs and gently press your fingers into the depression in the center of her groin. The resting heart rate for most dogs falls between 80 and 120 beats per minute. If your dog's pulse is above 140 even when she is in a calm, resting state, it's cause for concern.

4. **The breathing.** Panting is normal. But struggling to breathe (dyspnea)—or making a lot of noise to take in and breathe out air—is an indication that something is very wrong.

## DIARRHEA

*Any* diarrhea is severe when it occurs on your white sofa. But as with vomiting, we're not talking about one or two episodes. That's just the sign of a short-lived problem that may well resolve on its own. It's four or five episodes of diarrhea that warrant a trip to the emergency room. Watery stools can dehydrate

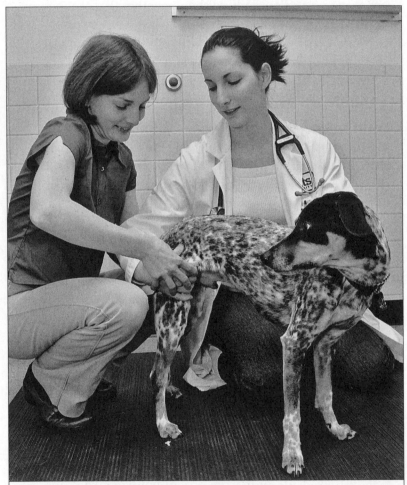

*The pulse of a healthy dog in a resting state falls between 80 and 120 beats per minute.*

a dog pretty quickly, particularly an older dog, and no matter what the cause might be, it's important to see whether your pet needs to have lost fluid replaced with an injection of saline just under the skin or perhaps even an intravenous drip. In some cases, the doctor may give you medication to administer in order to help control the diarrhea—but you should never give antidiarrheal drugs on your own, since they can actually make things worse rather than better.

## LIMPING

Sprains and strains are relatively common in older dogs. Their muscles, joints, and tendons don't have the resilience that a younger dog's have. But sprains and strains don't necessarily require a trip to the emergency room. If your dog is stiff or sore—especially the day after a particularly active outing—but is otherwise acting okay, with a good appetite and a happy disposition, chances are she will start to feel better on her own. Perhaps the veterinarian has already prescribed medication that you can administer for routine soreness or achiness, the way people sometimes take arthritis medicine after they've overdone it.

However, if your dog is limping severely and you've sat tight for a few hours and there hasn't been any improvement—perhaps she's continuing to make sure she doesn't bear any weight on a particular leg—it's a good idea to take her in. She may have a soft tissue injury or another problem that needs professional tending.

## OBVIOUS EMERGENCIES

Vomiting, diarrhea, limping—these are symptoms about which it might be hard to make a judgment call, at least initially. But there are some circumstances that call for getting in the car and driving to the emergency room without any hesitation.

## Trauma

Even if your dog is only bumped by a car backing out of a drive-way, rather than hit by one careening down the street, and even if she seems perfectly fine, take her in. Let's say she has a wound that seems slight, perhaps only slightly more than ¼ inch deep. It will probably still need to be stitched. Your dog may also need to be prescribed antibiotics to prevent infection from taking hold.

Then, too, there can be *hidden* injuries from a bump or other physical trauma. Consider that there might be a ruptured blad-der that won't be identified without an X-ray and a thorough physical. Sometimes, even *then* the problem won't be clear. It can take two to three days, or in some cases as many as five to seven, for the complication to become evident even to a trained veterinarian. But at least if you take the dog in, you and the vet can be on the watch together for any delayed reactions. For in-stance, the vet may send your pet home after she has been hit and subsequently examined, but tell you to watch her carefully for forty-eight to seventy-two hours for any signs of problems and to bring her back in for a second evaluation. At that point, a complication resulting from the accident could reveal itself to a medical professional's eye, or at least to the eye of diagnostic technology. And if the dog starts to falter before the second ap-pointment and you rush her back in, the veterinarian will have a better sense of what to check for. She won't be diagnosing in the dark, so to speak.

Other times, the veterinarian may recommend that the dog stay overnight for observation. We had one dog, a Jack Russell terrier, who seemed absolutely fine after having been bumped by a car—no apparent wound, normal pulse rate, good blood pressure, gums of good color, even no fluid in his abdomen as seen on an X-ray. But after several hours, he started to have trou-ble breathing. The reason, not caught at first, was that there had been a very small tear in his diaphragm that led to a herniation of his intestine into his chest, making it difficult for his lungs to expand for proper breathing.

Of course, if your dog has an obvious accident with blunt force, such as a speeding car or some other object, it's clear that you have to take her to the vet's office. But it may not be obvious how to do that safely. Some dogs who love their owners as much as a pet could end up biting them in an act of pain-induced aggression when the owners run over to help—the dog is simply too traumatized to be able to react the way she usually would. If you think that could never happen between you and your dog, consider that it's not at all unusual for us to send dog owners to the human emergency room when they bring in a pet who has been injured in a car accident.

One of our worst cases occurred when a Lab mix was hit by a car. As her owner went to pick her up, she bit him on the hand. He dropped off the dog (who was fine after a few days in the hospital) and then went off to a local hospital for people. It turned out that the dog bit through three tendons in the man's hand, and he required a couple of surgeries to get it repaired. The Lab was a total love who never would have bitten anyone under normal circumstances.

Some dogs become so upset, or disoriented, upon being hit by a car that they don't even let their owners near them. The moral here: approach a physically traumatized dog carefully, even your very own beloved one who has slept in your bed for ten years and who "would never hurt a fly."

If the dog is the size of, say, a cocker spaniel, throw a blanket over her before picking her up. She'll generally calm down that way.

For a bigger dog, you may need to use a belt or necktie as an improvised muzzle. It's often a good idea to get such a dog onto a heavy blanket or sheet, which can then be used as a kind of sling to get her out of the road and transport her to the hospital. A board or piece of plywood will work, too, but the problem with them is that they often won't fit into the car.

On the emergency room side, it's easier to move the dog into triage on a big blanket—there's more flexibility for those moving

## Keep Your Medicine Chest Properly Stocked

Having the proper first-aid materials in your home can help stem damage should a medical emergency arise. You will have started treatment even before getting to the doctor's office and thereby have warded off, or at least mitigated, complications. Sometimes a well-stocked first-aid kit can keep a problem from turning into an emergency altogether. All dog owners should have on hand the following:

**Gauze, sterile pads, and vet wrap**—a self-clinging elastic wrap. Each of these can be used to wrap a wound before driving over to the vet's office.

**Scissors**

**Styptic pencil or powder,** which can stop a nail from bleeding if it has been cut too close. This is a problem more for dogs with black nails than pink ones, because the color makes it harder, if not impossible, for the nail trimmer to see the sensitive quick.

**Tweezers or forceps** to remove foreign objects such as splinters and ticks

**Triple antibiotic ointment,** which will inhibit bacterial growth and infection when applied to a wound. But apply only upon direction by a vet, because she may want to examine some wounds before they are treated.

**Antiseptic,** good for preventing infection in minor cuts and for disinfecting minor wounds

**Hydrocortisone cream** to reduce itching caused by insect bites and allergies

**Diphenhydramine,** an antihistamine for allergic reactions

**Cold pack** to reduce swelling

**Eyewash** to rinse foreign objects or dust from your dog's eyes

**Hydrogen peroxide** (10 percent strength, available over

*continued on page 217*

her, which translates to more comfort for the dog as well. (Using a blanket is a good way to move any large dog who can't stand on her own.)

If there's a lot of bleeding or a big wound on a dog who has suffered a significant blunt trauma, apply pressure with a clean towel right over the spot that's bleeding as soon as you can. But don't use a tourniquet—that can cut off *too much* circulation.

## Bloat

If it suddenly looks like someone inflated a giant balloon inside your dog's abdomen, get her to the emergency room without a moment's delay. Chances are she has gastric dilatation volvulus, a life-threatening condition known in lay terms as "bloat and

---

### Keep Your Medicine Chest Properly Stocked,
*continued from page 216*

the counter) to induce vomiting in case of poisoning. Admittedly, this tends to be more a problem with puppies, but you never know. Your veterinarian or poison control center will be able to tell you the proper dose. (They should also be able to tell you whether induction of vomiting is appropriate in the first place; sometimes it can worsen the poisoning, depending on the toxin.)

**Antiseptic wipes** for cleaning your own hands as well as a cut on the dog

**Alcohol prep pads** to clean scissors and tweezers before using. (These pads should not be used directly on a wound because alcohol is toxic to the tissues, and it also stings.)

**Muzzle,** because a scared or shocked dog in pain may bite even a loved one

**Latex gloves**

**A ready, updated list of emergency healthcare provider phone numbers**

twist." The stomach fills with air and flips over, literally twisting upon itself and knotting up important blood vessels in the process, blocking off the esophagus on the top end of the stomach and the small intestine on the bottom end.

The problem tends to occur in large-breed dogs with deep chests, including Great Danes, Irish setters, Greater Swiss mountain dogs, Akitas, and German shepherds. You can't miss the inflated look, but the dog may also be anxious, uncomfortable, unable to settle down, and vomiting white foam. The sooner you recognize the signs of bloat and bring your dog to the veterinarian's office for emergency surgery, the better her odds for recovery. During the operation, the doctor will flip her stomach back over and permanently secure it to the inner wall of the abdominal cavity in a procedure known as a gastropexy. Once the stomach is firmly attached to the abdominal wall, it will not flip again.

Be aware that gastric dilatation volvulus is not a rare phenomenon. At our hospital, we perform some sixty-five emergency gastropexies each year to correct it — more than one a week.

**Fine-tuning the bloat prognosis.** It has been known for some time that the higher the lactic acid level when a dog is brought in for gastric dilatation volvulus, the worse her prognosis. But what if, after administering intravenous fluids to correct the shock of a dog affected by bloat, you measure the lactic acid again? Does that second measurement improve the prediction of how well the dog will do?

In a 2010 study, Dr. Berg and Tufts colleagues found that the answer is yes. The initial lactic acid reading is not nearly as telling as the second one. If it remains high despite treatment for shock, the dog is more likely to have complications and die. High lactic acid concentrations signify a greater risk for dead stomach tissue, as well as heart arrhythmias.

Fully 85 percent of dogs do make it through surgery for bloat just fine, with lactic acid concentrations where they should be,

## When Cancer Requires Emergency Treatment

While cancer is often dire, it's not necessarily thought of as something that requires on-the-spot medical care in order to avoid immediate death. People often perceive it as something slow growing, with crises anticipated over time. But dogs (as well as people) with cancer often feel perfectly fine and exhibit no symptoms that would lead to a work-up and diagnosis—until a catastrophe occurs.

Sometimes the first sign that a dog has cancer is difficulty breathing. For instance, lymphoma can cause fluid to build up in what is called the pleural space around the lungs, making it harder for them to expand and contract properly. Or the lymph nodes in front of the heart are affected by the disease, which means fluid builds up in the chest, because those nodes can no longer do their job of draining fluid. The excess fluid causes the breathing to become labored.

A cancer of any sort can also cause hard breathing if it metastasizes to the lungs. If cancer cell clusters obliterate enough lung tissue, the lungs simply can't work the way they're supposed to. In general, a cancer that has spread to the lungs and is causing difficulty breathing means a dog is reaching the end of the line. A veterinarian may be able to introduce some short-term palliative care, but not do much more.

Another way cancer becomes an immediate life-and-death situation is for a malignant tumor to enlarge silently over a long period of time in a noncritical spot, and then finally press on critical tissue that suddenly causes the dog's life to hang in the balance.

A tumor might begin to hemorrhage copious amounts

*continued on page 221*

so it's only a small proportion of dogs for whom this is an issue. But for that small proportion, the second lactic acid reading helps the veterinarian convey to the owners the likelihood of complications, which can be weighed against the costs of the surgery.

### Labored Breathing

If your older pal has been running around on a hot day and pants heavily before lapping up some water and resting in a shady spot, that's no cause for alarm. But other than that, hard or labored breathing should *always* be considered an emergency for a geriatric dog and requires a trip straight to the emergency room. It doesn't take much for an old dog to go from mild to moderate trouble breathing to dying from respiratory distress. (Young and middle-aged dogs rarely breathe hard other than as a result of exercising vigorously.)

Possible causes of hard breathing in an older dog:

**Laryngeal paralysis.** The most common reason a dog with this condition ends up with an emergency appointment is that she becomes overheated or overexcited. Often the first hot day of summer triggers the breathing crisis. The dog has been cool and comfortable indoors and cannot adjust to the warmer environment. The doctor will ameliorate the problem by sedating your dog and providing supplemental oxygen.

**Congestive heart failure.** You don't always see it coming, especially in small-breed dogs like Cavalier King Charles spaniels. They can even be diagnosed with a murmur but show no signs of congestive heart failure until they struggle to breathe one day.

**Pneumonia.** This, too, tends to be an older dog problem. Dogs with laryngeal paralysis are particularly susceptible, as we discussed in Chapter 3. Normally, when a dog swallows, her epiglottis

## When Cancer Requires Emergency Treatment,
*continued from page 219*

of blood, too. In a dog with hemangiosarcoma, for instance, a tumor growing on the spleen can grow as large as a baseball, or even bigger, without causing any outward symptoms, and then suddenly rupture. The dog loses so much blood by bleeding internally that all of a sudden she becomes too weak to stand, even though just a day earlier she was out playing Frisbee. Another scenario is blood from a ruptured cancerous tumor getting into the sac around the heart, the pericardium, effectively squeezing the heart so that it is unable to pump blood to the rest of the body. This condition is called hemopericardium.

Labradors, shepherds, and other large breeds are more prone to this type of cancer complication; it is common enough that if a large-breed dog comes into our emergency service collapsed, we check for a ruptured splenic tumor and a hemopericardium. The cancer in such cases can't be cured, but emergency surgery to remove the ruptured spleen or draw excess fluid from around the heart can keep the dog comfortable and perhaps give her several more months of life.

Yet another type of cancer that can creep up seemingly out of nowhere is a brain tumor. An older dog seems fine one day, and then will start having seizures out of the blue (seizures in a younger dog tend to be a sign of epilepsy). Once a stroke is ruled out and the tumor is deemed reachable by surgery, the prognosis is often good, affording the dog two to three more years of high-quality life. Treatment is expensive—up to $10,000 between the surgery and the attendant radiation—but if you have health insurance for your dog, costs come down considerably.

closes, so food and water don't go down her windpipe and into her lungs. But in a dog with laryngeal paralysis, the nerves and muscles over the airway at the back of the throat don't work properly, so food and water can get into the lungs and lead to an infection. Sometimes the pneumonia is mild—your dog may be coughing, but not at death's door. Even so, get her to the veterinarian's office right away. A dog with pneumonia can go from seeming "not quite right" to extremely sick very quickly.

Often, the doctor will take a chest X-ray to see whether there's fluid in the lungs. If it's not a severe case, your dog may simply be prescribed antibiotics and sent on her way. In advanced situations, though, she may require oxygen supplementation in order to breathe, along with IV fluids and IV antibiotics that require a hospital stay of five to seven days.

*Note:* Dogs who get pneumonia are at increased risk of getting it again; the vulnerability that allowed it to take hold doesn't go away. The good news is that owners become much more attuned to the symptoms, so they tend to bring in their dogs much sooner the second time around—before the illness becomes more difficult and more expensive to treat.

### Seizures

If your dog does not have epilepsy and unexpectedly has a seizure, or a series of seizures, get her to the veterinarian's office immediately. In a phenomenon called kindling, seizures left un-

---

## To the Front or the Back of the Line?

Emergency room doctors tend to think: heart, brain, or lungs. Severe, life-threatening illnesses almost always cause derangements in one of those three organs, and the initial assessment—the triage out in the waiting room—often focuses on them. If any one of these organs appears compromised, the dog goes to the front of the line. Otherwise, she waits her turn.

treated cause more seizures, which can lead to brain damage. The doctor will administer medications to stop the seizing as quickly as possible, and then try to determine the cause.

Seizures in an older dog commonly result from a brain tumor, but a stroke or brain inflammation can also be the culprit. No matter the cause, a seizure leads to the creation of a great deal of body heat; a seizure lasting longer than three to four minutes can give your dog heat stroke, adding a complication to an already serious situation.

### Abrupt Change in State of Mind

Gradual lapses in memory or a dog's ability to make her way around a well-known park can be signs of senility. But if such changes come quickly, they could mean the growth of a brain tumor that has finally reached a critical point. Examples include a dog walking into a corner and not being able to figure her way out or an inability to stop circling. (These can be signs of senility, too, even if they come on rather suddenly, so nothing can be ruled out without a professional diagnosis.)

Sometimes behavior change comes suddenly in the form of a dog's head tilting to one side accompanied by nystagmus—a very rapid back-and-forth movement of the eyes. Most likely it's a condition called old dog vestibular syndrome. The problem doesn't usually get much worse than that (although there can be a bit of stumbling), and it often resolves on its own. But you still need to take the dog in to the vet's office to rule out a more serious condition.

### BEHAVIOR CHANGE

This is different from a change in cognitive ability and can be rather vague, which makes it tough to assess, both at home and at the doctor's office. Perhaps your dog doesn't want to eat, doesn't feel like drinking any water, or doesn't want to play the way she normally would. How can you tell whether it's an emergency?

Here's a test. It's not foolproof, but it's a start. Does your dog want to do her favorite thing: go for a car ride, perhaps, or roll over on her back for a belly rub during a cuddle? If not, take her in. If so, wait and see how she feels tomorrow. An old dog, like a young one, can feel under par some days, then bounce back once whatever has been ailing her makes its way through her system.

That doesn't mean, of course, that there won't be a trip to the emergency room another day. It's the rare dog who lives till old age and doesn't make any unanticipated visits to the doctor. But at least now you have the basics for knowing when to put emergency treatment into motion.

# 12 | End-of-Life Decisions

WE KNEW Francie wasn't well. Although she still seemed to love to sit with us, it didn't appear to matter to her whether we petted her, and she didn't get excited to be offered a lick of ice cream anymore or to be handed a new toy. Her arthritis was pretty bad, too. For the last four months she had to be carried to the backyard to go to the bathroom. She could stand and bend as needed once we got her out there, but it was hard for her to go from a resting position to standing by herself, and she couldn't walk the thirty-five to forty steps to her spot once we had her on the patio. It wasn't easy, because she weighed more than fifty pounds. But as long as she could hold out, we could hold out. We figured we had another six months to a year left. She was already fifteen.

But then one Sunday afternoon when company was over, she kept struggling to get up from her doggie bed, which we now kept in the family room, but to no avail. We carried her outside, but she kept collapsing. She could not stand even to relieve herself.

Thinking it was her arthritis getting the better of her, we took her to the emergency room. It wasn't her arthritis. They ran some blood tests and found that her blood platelet count was less than half what it should have been. She was apparently bleeding internally and had no energy. They told us they could go in and see for sure what was wrong, but that she might not survive the surgery, and that even if she did, she probably had only a couple of months left no matter what the treatment available.

Francie wasn't even looking at us nervously or expectantly, the way she always did at the vet's office. She was just lying there. The vet on call that Sunday said they would do what we chose, but that if we wanted to end her suffering, they would support our decision.

We got Patrick as a young puppy six months after Francie died, and he's just now calming down to the point where we can start bonding with him. He's a crazy little fireball, wearing us out daily, and despite that and maybe even a little because of it, we're sure we'll grow to bond with him over time. But even today, two years later, we ache for Francie: for the way she would open her mouth in a smile if we surprised her with a treat; for the way she covered our son with his blanket when he was a baby by carefully nudging it onto him with her snout; for the way she decided she was the horizontal line in the middle of a capital "H" every night, pushing us to the edges of the bed. It was very, very hard to let her go, but at that point, it would have been cruel to make her stay.

—*A communication from Francie's family*

IT'S ALWAYS TOUCHING for any of us when we walk over to the clinic from our offices and see two people sitting outside on a seat, crying—or just one person, or a whole family. We know, even though we don't know the particular dog, what has happened.

Of course, the best way for an old dog to die would be the same as the best way for a person—peacefully, in his sleep, or suddenly, because of a heart attack or stroke that takes his life in a single moment. Unfortunately, as we said earlier, it rarely happens that way. There's more than an even chance that euthanasia is in your older friend's future.

When we bring up the choice to people, we do it in a spot that's like a grief counseling room, a quiet space with large chairs. We take a lot of time to explain everything involved and try to gently counsel dog owners through the steps of what, despite being very sad, is a peaceful demise process—infinitely more peaceful, in fact, than many natural deaths.

Even though the whole point of this book is to help you give your dog a happy, healthy, *longer* old age, it's probably best to keep that notion in the back of your mind—that you're most likely going to outlive him, and therefore going to be given a suggestion by his vet that you need to make an awful but responsible decision about letting him go when he tells you he has had enough. If you are cognizant of that beforehand, it will allow you to act rationally about something that, of course, is heavily weighted with emotion.

"But how will I know for sure that it's time?" you may ask yourself. Oftentimes, you won't, at least not up front. Many conditions of older dogs that look like "this is the end" are actually very treatable. For that reason, you should never make a choice to euthanize your dog without first taking him to your veterinarian for a definitive diagnosis. You might be surprised—and relieved—to find that his time has not yet come. We've delivered that good news to many greatly relieved owners.

On the other hand, when a definitive diagnosis of an ultimately terminal disease *has* been made, or the illness isn't identified with certainty, but it's clear that it's terminal and painful, as in Francie's case, it's important to be able to recognize the point at which, for all intents and purposes, the dog's life is over. Dogs often do not vocalize their suffering by crying out, moaning in pain, or changing their facial expressions, like people do. But with your veterinarian's help, you can identify the crossover from living to merely existing in pain, with no quality of life. Depending on the illness, it could be anything from the inability to rise or walk to an unrelenting cough.

Sometimes, a dog will show that he has reached the end of the line rather subtly, simply by not acting like himself. He may stop exhibiting interest in playing; he may stop eating; he may stop showing any enthusiasm for family members. What's important to know is that a dog who feels sick enough not to eat or play is in about as much physical distress as a dog can be. Thus, such changes in your dog's quality of life will be your tip-off that he has unbearable physical suffering. By that stage, you shouldn't have to go through much agonizing about the decision to put him down.

There's agony all the time about whether to treat an illness, and to what degree. But whether or not to authorize euthanasia once a grim diagnosis has been made and the dog exhibits telltale signs of extreme distress generally does not require a lot of weighing of circumstances.

That said, some people do struggle with the decision to euthanize when a dog indicates that he is done wanting to live, and it is perfectly normal. It takes some pet owners two to three weeks to come to terms with the decision after seeing their dog not wanting to engage in life anymore. The owners of a black Lab named Valentino that we treated were adamant that they would not put him down, despite a cancer that clearly left him wanting "out." They, too, however, were finally able to separate what they *wanted* from what was *good* for their pet. They accepted that even though they didn't want to lose the dog, the dog was suffering continuously, and the misery would not stop.

The more difficult part of euthanasia tends not to be whether it's the right decision for a pet who doesn't want to go on, but the guilt engendered by making the decision to end the life of a loved one. Because it's legal with animals and not with humans, a certain uncertainty about whether it's okay is bound to tug at some dog owners.

We believe the option for euthanasia when it comes to a pet is a good thing. If a dog is so done with living, so miserable, and perhaps in so much pain that he doesn't even want to greet you when you come through the door, putting him down instead of making him wait to die naturally is a way of sparing him the agony of death. It's a tool to end suffering.

Most people, once they've made the choice, feel that way, too, including the family of Valentino, or Tino, as they called him. They don't wonder whether they did the right thing, even if they struggled with the decision initially. They simply feel bad for

*Children often deal with the decision to put down a dog better than parents expect.*

their dog and, like anyone who loses a beloved family member, aggrieved. As all dog lovers can attest, it can be quite difficult to get over the loss.

Being familiar with the process, though, and deciding how to handle certain aspects beforehand will at least allow you to grieve without having to think through mundane details at the time your emotional pain is most raw.

## CHOOSING THE MOMENT

Francie's owners were not lucky. Their dog became unable to stand seemingly out of the blue, and they had to rush her to the emergency room on a Sunday, when their regular vet wasn't available, to find that her life was essentially over. It was only logical for euthanasia to be performed during the same office visit. But oftentimes, you can pick your moment, say, if your dog has heart failure, cancer, or kidney disease, and finally reaches the tipping point, no longer wishing to eat or exhibiting any emotion.

If that's the case, pick a time after which you'll be able to go home and tend to your feelings for a few days. You're going to feel pretty drained at first, so why choose a Monday morning when you'll have to rush off to work rather than a Friday afternoon, after which you'll have a chance to be by yourself or with loved ones, and perhaps cry with abandon or reflect privately in whatever way you need?

Decide beforehand, too, what you're going to have done with the body. The vet will ask, and it will be easier for you not to have to make the decision on the spot. The choices are as follows:

1. You can take the body home and dig a grave in the backyard. (Be aware that states have laws about the required depth of the hole, and it may have to be quite big for a large dog.)

2. You can opt for cremation, after which you'll get the ashes back in a box. (It typically takes a week or more for the ashes to be returned, with the cost ranging from $150 to $350, depending on the dog's body size and the area of the country in which you live.)

3. You can opt for a mass cremation, in which your dog's body is burned with those of other dogs, so the ashes are not returned. (This is a less expensive option, with a price of roughly $50 to $150.)

4. You can inter your dog in a pet cemetery. People have been burying pets in ritual fashion since the time of ancient Egypt, and there are currently more than six hundred pet cemeteries in the United States, according to the International Association of Pet Cemeteries. Most operate in conjunction with other pet-related businesses, including boarding kennels and groom-

ing centers. In some cases, there's a chapel on the cemetery grounds. Prices for burial in a pet cemetery vary widely depending on location and such variables as the make of the casket. See Resources.

When you do bring your dog in, we strongly suggest you pay for the euthanasia beforehand; it will cost somewhere between $50 and $250. The reason it's a good idea to pay up front is that afterward, you're just going to want to get in your car and leave. The last thing you'll feel like doing is talking to strangers at the front desk, filling out paperwork, being nice with small talk, and making others in the waiting room feel okay by exhibiting a "stiff upper lip."

## DELAYING THE MOMENT?

Some dog owners prepare for the pending death of their pet by partnering with their veterinarian's office to provide hospice care at home beforehand. That buys them some time, if necessary, to make a decision about euthanasia, and also allows them to gear up for grieving in the aftermath.

Not all dogs would do well to have hospice care. Those who are telling you with complete apathy and lack of interest in living that they don't want to be here anymore would not appreciate having their lives prolonged. On the other hand, dogs with a terminal illness who are getting sicker and sicker but still relish life and show and return affection can benefit from the pain control and palliative care that hospice provides. (Palliative care isn't directed at the disease itself; it's intended to relieve symptoms.)

Most veterinary practices participate in hospice care by teaching the dog's family members to administer pain medications — analgesics — at home, as well as how to tend to other necessary routine care — perhaps giving fluids and so on. Family caretakers may also be instructed in the assessment of their dog's pain levels and stages of organ system failure. In large, urban areas, periodic visits to the home by the veterinarian and trained staff may be part of hospice care, too, if you are willing to pay for the house calls.

The family may also learn how to keep their dog clean and how to manage a dog who is unable to walk and therefore has specialized needs for toilet care. Such pets are called "down dogs." Of course, a dog's inability to walk is often a tipping point in favor of euthanasia. An immobile, dying dog is often suffering with no relief from pain—not a good situation to maintain. But if a dog can't get up because of severe arthritis or is paralyzed with a neurological problem such as a spinal cord disease, care can reasonably include helping with his bathroom needs and other issues relating to lack of movement.

It's extremely difficult, though. You have to turn, or rotate, the dog every few hours—even during the night—so he doesn't get bedsores, which are extremely difficult to heal. Such sores develop on pressure points of the body where skin directly overlies the bone: the ankle joint, elbows, hip region, and sometimes near the shoulders. If those become dirty, particularly with urine, they're even more prone to sores. Urine is very irritating to skin tissue and causes it to weaken. For that reason, a dog who can't get up needs to be cleaned with aloe baby wipes and towels as soon as he pees on himself, which he invariably will, every time he goes to the bathroom. Stools also need to be cleaned away when the dog defecates, which is going to happen wherever he's lying, whenever the need arises.

Whether or not the dog is a down one, he remains at home during hospice care until death occurs or the desire for euthanasia is made clear.

We should point out that veterinary hospice care, even though it lasts only weeks to months, is sometimes expensive, because it can take a lot of time for the veterinary staff. Teaching people how to take care of a dying dog is labor intensive. Still, some dog owners appreciate the opportunity because it allows for a "good" death and for "good" grieving, according to a group called the Nikki Hospice Foundation for Pets. See Resources for more information.

## THE PROCEDURE ITSELF

Euthanasia is performed by the veterinarian with an injection—a combination of pentobarbital and phenytoin. Pentobarbital is a barbiturate that formerly was used as an anesthetic induction agent. In this case it is given in an overdose. The phenytoin adds to the nervous system depression and stops the heart.

The whole procedure is a completely painless process. The barbiturate literally causes your dog to fall asleep. Then, because it severely depresses the respiratory system at the brain level, it causes respiratory and cardiac arrest—without the dog being aware.

Unconsciousness occurs in about thirty seconds, at most, and death ensues in short order. The vet puts a little intravenous catheter into a vein in one of the dog's front limbs, then injects the drug—a liquid—through the catheter. Within fifteen seconds, the dog is asleep and within a minute, he's gone. Some vets even give a tranquilizer first to calm the dog for the procedure, although by that point in the dog's life, it's not usually necessary. Afterward, the doctor will check for a heartbeat with a stethoscope, feel for the lack of a pulse by one of the back legs, and tap the dog's eyes to make sure there's no blink response.

Should you be in the room during the euthanasia? We recommend it, if you can. Owners who are present are rarely sorry about it afterward. You're there for the dog in his last moments, and also, it provides closure. But it's a very individual decision. If you can't watch, you can't. You are still doing right by your dog if he no longer has a quality of life worth preserving.

Be aware that if you decide to stay, the dog may lose bladder control at the very end, which some people find distressing. In addition, the dog often looks dead, not asleep, with his eyes open. Finally, some dogs take what are known as agonal breaths as the body systems shut down. These are deep, almost sighing, breaths, and it looks like the dog is trying to live. But they are simply an unconsciously generated respiratory pattern often associated with death. Agonal breaths are not driven by the experience of what is happening.

## AFTER THE FACT

It is perfectly normal to feel inconsolable afterward. You get a dog in the first place because you want to have a close bond with one. Why wouldn't the break of that bond hurt?

The grieving process is different for different people. Some want to be alone. Others prefer to rely on a support system of loved ones, particularly fellow animal lovers. Whichever feels right to you is the right way to go about it.

In some cases, a person has to go beyond his or her own support network. For that, Tufts has a grief counseling service, available to anyone, anywhere in the country. Called the Pet Loss Hotline, it is run by veterinary students who receive training from a psychologist. See Resources at the back of the book for details.

## TALKING WITH CHILDREN

Parents may worry about how their children will react to their decision to choose euthanasia. In our experience, children often deal with the death better than adults.

Little children tend to live in the moment, so they do not carry the dog's death around with them. In addition, if your child is still very young, chances are that she or he has not had as many years with the dog as you have—the bond simply is not as strong. The child in Francie's house, age six when she died, felt sad, but more because his parents felt sad than because he felt devastated about the dog. Within two weeks, he was asking about getting another dog. Then, too, small children, and even children ten to twelve years of age and up to middle school, accept as a matter of course that such decisions are out of their hands. Finally, children are naturally resilient. Chances are they will bounce back more easily than you do.

If the children in the home are in high school or college-aged, yes, they will be more affected. But they will also have the emotional and intellectual maturity to grieve and cope; they will have more of the tools necessary for dealing with death.

Note that for a child of almost any age, learning about death and euthanasia is a valuable part of having a pet. In age-appropriate language, you can talk to your children about the life cycle and about choices that get made for animals in unrelenting pain.

## A NEXT DOG?

Some people wonder whether to get a new dog when it seems clear that the dog they have is dying. They feel it might be easier if there's no gap between pets. We recommend against it; it's not fair to the old dog in your care. He needs your undivided affection and attention at that point, and nothing will draw away attention like a new dog, especially if you get a puppy, who needs to bond with you and get used to your household. Furthermore, your dog may not *like* the new dog, so you risk subjecting him to unhappy social interactions in his last days. Even if he does like the new pet, he won't be up to the second dog's energy and desire to play. Toward the end of life, old dogs often don't want to be bothered.

As for taking in a dog after you lose one, most people don't want to until they're done grieving, and their instincts are right. It doesn't feel good to try to bond with a new pet while the loss of the one you have loved for a decade or more remains raw. It's not fair to the new dog, either. A dog's entry into your family should be a really happy time, with the pet getting lots of attention. He, as well as you, deserves to feel good about it.

Thus, do not try to "replace" the pet you miss as soon as

possible, in the mistaken belief that it will help you get over the loss faster. Give it the time it needs. For some people, that's weeks. For others, it's months — or longer.

Sometimes, someone who loses a beloved dog feels, "I'm not sure I can go through this again." That's perfectly understandable, and if the feeling lasts, you should respect it. Keep in mind, too, that no dog can truly replace another. They all have wonderful attributes that make you fall in love with them, and those attributes may overlap, but the package as a whole is going to be different from one dog to another.

That said, be aware that dogs' lifespans are lengthening all the time. The dog you just lost probably lived longer than he would have ten or twenty years ago, and the dog you may consider bringing into your home now may very well live longer than the one you're missing.

It is our goal to make that happen, and to enrich all the time you have with your pet by shoring up his health, even as he reaches the upper limits of his lifespan. We fully expect it will come to pass. Medical advances are occurring continuously, many right here on our own campus. Repairing a dog's heart valve rather than just treating a faulty one may very well come within our grasp. In addition, older dogs' nutrition requirements will be better understood as distinct from those of middle-aged dogs, allowing for health-enhancing tweaks to geriatric dogs' diets. Orthopedic treatments to keep arthritic dogs mobile will keep improving, too. And further headway will be made on brain research and the stemming of cognitive decline.

All of which is to say that if you do decide to get another dog, the sadness of loss will likely be further off, while the joy of his companionship will lengthen.

# Resources

THE FOLLOWING RESOURCES should by no means be considered an exhaustive list of where to find further information about caring for an older dog. But they will help you get started as you go forward.

Note that any mentions of product manufacturers should be thought of as guides to get you on your way; they should not be construed as endorsements of one brand over another. Note, too, that websites for various organizations and companies change over time. If we've listed one that no longer exists when you try to find it, you may be able to locate it at another site with your search engine.

### 1. "OLD" IS NOT A DISEASE
For transporting dogs safely and comfortably in extreme weather conditions, **Komfort Pets, www.KomfortPets.com,** makes climate-controlled pet carriers. A conduction plate on the floor of each crate warms or cools as necessary, depending on ambient temperature.

### 2. HOW TO MAKE SURE YOU'RE CHOOSING THE RIGHT DIET
The **American College of Veterinary Nutrition, www.acvn.org,** offers links to websites for pet owners interested in learning more about their dog's nutrition from veterinary nutritionists and from experienced veterinarians who specialize in pet nutrition. The **American Academy of Veterinary Nutrition, www.aavn.org,** lists veterinary schools and other respected organizations that offer phone consultations for pet owners with specific concerns. (Click on "Nutrition Resources.") And articles on the site address such topics as managing your pet's weight.

### 3. FIVE COMMON MEDICAL CONDITIONS OF THE OLDER DOG

The Veterinary Oral Health Council, www.vohc.org, lists dog (and cat) foods awarded the organization's seal of approval for helping in plaque and tartar control. And the American Veterinary Dental College, www.avdc.org, lists board-certified veterinary dentists by state, along with providing information on everything from dental X-rays to oral cancers.

Three companies that make beds for dogs with urinary incontinence are Handicapped Pets, www.handicappedpets.com; Kuranda Dog Beds, www.kuranda.com; and the Pet Cot Company, www.petcot.com.

### 4. PROTECTING JOINTS STOPS PAIN

For detailed information on how to recognize pain in your pet as well as the specifics of various pain treatments and finding a veterinarian in your area who specializes in pain management, go to the website of the International Veterinary Academy of Pain Management, www.ivapm.org. The Canine Rehabilitation Institute in Wellington, Florida, can help you locate a veterinarian certified in canine rehabilitation, as well as a veterinary technician, who goes through a different certification course. See www.caninerehab institute.com.

### 8. THE PRICE OF AGING GRACEFULLY

Two of the largest companies that sell healthcare insurance policies for pets are Veterinary Pet Insurance, www.petinsurance .com, and PetCare Pet Insurance, www.petcareinsurance.com, but they are not the only ones. For instance, there's also PetPlan USA, www.gopetplan.com, recommended by the Humane Society of the United States, and Purina Care, www.purinacare.com. People who don't have health insurance for their dog but whose canine friend has developed an illness that's very expensive to treat might want to consider CareCredit Healthcare Finance, www.carecredit.com, which allows payments to be spread over eighteen months with no interest. And the Humane Society, www.humanesociety.org, lists organizations that provide "angel funds"—money to treat sick dogs for pet owners who don't have the resources to spread out payments.

As far as routine care, the **American Veterinary Medical Association,** while mostly an organization for veterinarians, also offers information for pet owners on everything from disaster preparedness to pet food recalls to microchipping. Go to **www.avma.org.**

### 9. MIGHT THE CHANGES YOU'RE SEEING BE DEMENTIA?

Just as engaging in new and exciting activities helps keep an aging human mind nimble, so it goes for dogs. If your older pal is still in good physical shape, you might want to consider signing him or her up for courses ranging from agility to herding, flyball, tracking (good for scent hounds), luring (good for sight hounds), therapy giving (excellent for gentle dogs who enjoy being around people), and the list goes on. The **American Kennel Club, www.akc.org,** lists such courses. Just type in the kind of environmental enrichment you seek for your canine friend, and see what comes up.

### 10. CHANGING THE ENVIRONMENT TO SUIT THE DOG

HandicappedPets.com is one of several sites that sells everything from dog wheelchairs to ramps, slings, seat belts, and other equipment to make life easier for physically compromised dogs. Typing in the kind of product you want in an Internet search might also identify companies that sell the item you're looking for, which would allow you to comparison shop.

### 11. EMERGENCY, RATHER URGENT, OR NON-EMERGENCY?

It's usually puppies who end up ingesting something poisonous, but if by some chance you think your older buddy might have gotten into the antifreeze or swallowed something off the Christmas tree, the **Animal Control Poison Center** of the American Society for the Prevention of Cruelty to Animals, **www.aspca.org,** has a twenty-four-hour hotline, 365 days a year, to help you through. Call 1-888-426-4435. (You may be charged a sixty-dollar consultation fee.)

## 12. END-OF-LIFE DECISIONS

If your dog's illness can't be cured but you want to provide your friend with palliative care until the end, the **Nikki Hospice Foundation, www.pethospice.org,** lists resources for finding hospice veterinarians and veterinary hospice care products. The **American Veterinary Medical Association, www.avma.org,** offers a good, free brochure with guidelines for hospice care.

The **International Association of Pet Cemeteries, www.iaopc .com,** lists contact information for a number of pet cemeteries throughout the United States.

And the **Cummings School of Veterinary Medicine at Tufts University** offers a **Pet Loss Support Hotline** at 508-839-7966. The hotline is staffed by veterinary students who have gone through training with a licensed psychologist. Its goal is to support callers with the knowledge that they are not alone and that they are not silly or ridiculous for having strong feelings about the loss of their pet. To learn more about the hotline, where phone callers may speak as long as they wish, visit **www.tufts.edu/vet/petloss.**

# Tufts Faculty Contributors

BY VIRTUE OF their ongoing clinical and research work with older dogs and the information they help us to accumulate on the best options for geriatric canine care, *all* the faculty at the Cummings Schools of Veterinary Medicine at Tufts University are contributors to *Good Old Dog*. Certain faculty members, however, are direct contributors, having overseen the writing of whole chapters or large segments of information presented in this book:

*Dr. Berg and Keyser.*

**John Berg, DVM,** chair of the Department of Clinical Sciences at Tufts Cummings School of Veterinary Medicine, is a board-certified surgeon specializing in small animal soft tissue who has taught and practiced for more than twenty years. Dr. Berg's special interest is surgical oncology — the application of surgery to the treatment of cancer. His research has been published in the prestigious *Journal of the American Veterinary Medical Association, Journal of Veterinary Surgery, Journal of Veterinary Internal Medicine,* and *Cancer* (the journal of the American Cancer Society). He lives in Westborough, Massachusetts, with his wife and two daughters.

**Suzanne Cunningham, DVM,** board-certified by the American College of Veterinary Internal Medicine in Cardiology, originally debated going into law or politics, but her love of animals won out, fueled by the fact that her first boxer dog died of heart disease when she was nine. "I know how difficult it is to lose an animal as a result of heart disease and have particular interest in investigating new therapies for

*Dr. Cunningham with Roxie (left) and Tyler.*

treatment of heart disease in dogs," she says. Dr. Cunningham's research interests include the use of blood-based markers to diagnose and guide therapy of heart disease, and, specifically, the investigation and treatment of blood vessel dysfunction that may accompany the condition. She has published papers in the *Journal of Veterinary Internal Medicine, Journal of the American Veterinary Medical Association,* and *Journal of Veterinary Cardiology* and

*Dr. Freeman and Hazel.*

has also written book chapters on cardiology. She lives near the Cummings School campus with her thirteen-year-old boxer, Roxie (whose photo appears on page iv), and her boxer puppy, Tyler.

**Lisa M. Freeman, DVM, PhD,** is a professor in the Department of Clinical Sciences at Tufts Cummings School of Veterinary Medicine. As a board-certified veterinary nutritionist, she has a special interest in nutritional modulation of heart disease and critical care nutrition. Dr. Freeman lectures both nationally and internationally on clinical nutrition and has published numerous articles and book chapters on her work.

The daughter of a veterinarian father and a dentist mother, **Jean Joo, DVM,** is a veterinary dentist who completed a residency in dentistry and oral surgery after graduating from veterinary school. She is particularly fascinated by oral oncology and endodontics. Dr.

*Dr. Joo and Logan.*

Joo (pictured in scrubs, extracting a diseased tooth on page 65) is owned by three cats and a pointer puppy that she hopes will one day be a good old dog.

*Dr. Kowaleski with his human "pups," Nick (left) and Alex.*

**Michael P. Kowaleski, DVM,** is an associate professor of small animal orthopedic surgery at Tufts Cummings School of Veterinary Medicine. His areas of clinical and research interest include arthroscopy, fracture repair and orthopedic implants, total joint replacement, clinical and radiological assessment of limb alignment, osteoarthritis, and management of chronic pain. He lives in Grafton, Massachusetts, with his wife and two sons.

Growing up in the suburbs of Chicago, **Linda Ross, DVM, MS,** a board-certified specialist in small animal internal medicine, would make family visits to her grandfather's dairy farm in Wisconsin. Those visits fostered an ambition to own a farm, which she later channeled into becoming a veterinarian. Today, Dr. Ross has a special interest in diseases related to the workings of the kidney and urinary tract, as well as hormone-mediated conditions, including diabetes. She has published numerous articles and book chapters on urinary tract disorders and lectures both

*Dr. Ross and Velvet.*

nationally and internationally. In handling dialysis for dogs with acute kidney failure, she says that "it is very gratifying to be able to provide this sophisticated treatment and help animals survive that would otherwise likely die." Dr. Ross, who lives in Massachusetts, has achieved the rare honor of being elected to the Cummings School Faculty Hall of Fame.

*Dr. Shaw with (from left) Lilly, Emily, and Toby. (Violet, a chocolate Lab, was camera-shy.)*

**Scott Shaw, DVM,** an assistant professor in the Department of Clinical Sciences at Tufts Cummings School of Veterinary Medicine, is board-certified in emergency and critical care medicine. He is a frequent lecturer at veterinary meetings across the country, including the annual Veterinary Emergency and Critical Care Symposium and the American College of Veterinary Internal Medicine Forum. Dr. Shaw's research interests include the treatment of life-threatening infections and the blood coagulation system. Along with his wife, he is a breeder of Labrador retrievers. They live in Oxford, Massachusetts, with one son, four dogs, and two cats.

*Dr. Dodman and Rusty.*

## About the Editor

**Nicholas Dodman, BVMS, DACVB,** is one of the world's most noted and celebrated veterinary behaviorists. Born in England and trained as a veterinarian in Scotland, he joined the faculty of the Glasgow Veterinary School at age twenty-six, making him the youngest veterinary faculty member in Great Britain. Dr. Dodman emigrated to the United States in 1981, when he became a faculty member at the Cummings School of Veterinary Medicine at Tufts. Originally specializing in surgery and anesthesiology and then in behavioral pharmacology, he founded the Animal Behavior Clinic at Tufts in 1986.

Dr. Dodman has written five acclaimed best-selling books: *The Dog Who Loved Too Much, The Cat Who Cried for Help, Dogs Behaving Badly, If Only They Could Speak,* and *The Well-Adjusted Dog.* He also edited *Puppy's First Steps* (the first of Tufts's Cummings School's books for the lay public), coauthored two textbooks, and has written more than one hundred peer-reviewed articles that have appeared in scientific books and journals.

A columnist for Martha Stewart's *Body and Soul* magazine and former columnist for *Life* magazine and *Family Dog* (a quarterly publication of the American Kennel Club), Dr. Dodman has appeared on many television and radio shows, including *20/20, Oprah, Today, Good Morning America, Dateline, World News Tonight,* the Discovery Channel, *NOVA, Animal Planet, Inside Edition, CNN'S Headline News,* and the BBC and CBC. He has been interviewed for NPR's *Fresh Air, Talk of the Nation,* and *The Connection* and has had a regular segment on WBUR's *Here & Now.*

Dr. Dodman is a member of the American Veterinary Medical Association and the Humane Society Veterinary Medical Association. In addition, he is board-certified by the American College of Veterinary Anesthesiologists and the American College of Veterinary Behaviorists. A father of four, he lives near Tufts University with his wife, Linda Breitman-Dodman, DVM.

*Larry Lindner and Franklin.*

## About the Writer

**Lawrence Lindner** is a *New York Times* best-selling coauthor and collaborating writer on a wide variety of books ranging from health topics to memoirs. In addition, he penned a nationally syndicated biweekly column in the *Washington Post* for several years and wrote a monthly column for the *Boston Globe.* His freelance work has appeared in many publications, including the *Los Angeles Times, Condé Nast Traveler,* the *International Herald Tribune,* and *Reader's Digest.* He lives with his wife, son, and nephew in Hingham, Massachusetts.

# Acknowledgments

EVERYONE WHO WORKED on this book would like to thank our editor at Houghton Mifflin Harcourt, Susan Canavan, for giving us the opportunity to help people take care of their older canine friends. Thanks, too, to our agent and fellow dog lover, Wendy Weil, for getting this project into the right hands in the first place. Much appreciation also goes to the Cummings School Media Services director Andy Cunningham for his pictures, each worth a thousand words and then some.

Contributor John Berg, DVM, DACVS, would like to thank and express his love for his wife, Gail, and his daughters, Cara and Sidney, whose love of animals — including but not limited to dogs, cats, horses, hamsters, goats, baby opossums, foxes, mice, frogs, toads, hermit crabs, and fish — is truly boundless. He would also like to acknowledge Keyser, the family's German shepherd dog, who is getting older but certainly not acting like it.

Contributor Suzanne Cunningham, DVM, expresses gratitude to her parents for their unwavering love and support; to her own good old dog, Roxie, who has been with her through college and vet school, internship, and residency, "and will always have a special place in my heart"; and to all the patients and clients "who have inspired me over the years and made me realize what a great job this is!"

Contributor Jean Joo, DVM, gives thanks to her mentors, Dr. Frank Verstraete, Dr. Helena Kuntsi-Vaattovaara, Dr. Milinda Lommer, and Dr. Jamie Anderson, for sharing their knowledge and experience; her parents, Drs. Gregory and Seok Hie Joo, for their love and guidance; and Richard Fox, for his seemingly endless supply of tolerance for tooth-related puns (and love and support).

Contributor Michael Kowaleski, DVM, is grateful to his wife, Lisa, his sons, Alex and Nick, and his parents, Paul and Carolyn, for their unwavering support and encouragement.

Contributor Linda Ross, DVM, MS, would like to thank those veterinarians, too numerous to name, who served as role models during her training and the early years of her career. She would especially like to acknowledge her own pets over the years, both dogs and cats, including the current crew: Velvet, her yellow Labrador retriever, and cats Mindy, Caylie, and Monty. "I believe it is only by having our own pets—dealing with their personalities, problems, illnesses, and ultimately their passing—that gives us, as veterinarians, a true understanding of people's relationships with their pets," she says.

Contributor Scott Shaw, DVM, thanks his wife, Pam, and his son, Otto, "who put up with my long work days and a pager that goes off every hour of the day or night."

Editor Nicholas Dodman, BVMS, DACVB, expresses love and appreciation to his wife, Linda, and his four children: Stevie, Vicky, Keisha, and Danny.

Writing collaborator Larry Lindner thanks all the Tufts veterinarians who worked on this book for their time, patience in explaining the finer points (again and again), and putting up with his constant nagging to meet deadlines; Drs. Berg and Dodman, in particular, for their steadfast confidence in his ability to translate the science for the lay public; his nephew, Quinlen Anderson, for the joy he brings as he enriches the hearts of those lucky enough to hold him close; his son, John, fellow dog lover extraordinaire and the greatest gift of his life; and his wife, Constance, bearer of that gift and so many others.

# Illustration Credits

# Index

*Page numbers in italics refer to photographs and illustrations.*